D0864724

ADVANCE PRAISE FOR

Public Policy Argumentation and Debate, Second Edition

"The second edition of *Public Policy Argumentation and Debate* adds to and amplifies all that made the original necessary reading for any student interested in public argument. With an updated framework, examples, and critical questions that speak to our current civic context, the book prepares readers to be effective public advocates. Even more, it provides students a window through which to observe, engage, reflect on and critique the state-of-the-art practices demonstrated by some of today's most effective professional and lay public policy advocates. Perhaps more importantly, this edition accomplishes something even more powerful and necessary. It helps to demonstrate to, and persuade, students that public advocacy is something for them, something they can do, something they should participate in even if they think they don't have the power, the pedigree, the access or position to advocate for themselves or the society they believe should be made a reality. *Public Policy Argumentation and Debate* helps to motivate all of us to see ourselves as change agents, and arms us with the tools to act accordingly."

> —**Charlton McIlwain**, Vice Provost of Faculty Engagement & Development;
> Professor of Media, Culture and Communication at New York University;
> author of *Black Software: The Internet and Racial Justice*
> *From the AfroNet to Black Lives Matter* (2019)

"The second edition of this book *Public Policy Argumentation and Debate* successfully continues a tradition of learning argumentation and debate as part of making public proposals for change. Rather than cordoning off argumentation as abstract academic contemplation, the text encourages students to understand it as essential to practical social change. This focus makes argumentation the source of empowerment that it should be and gives students a concrete structure for action. Updated examples and activities make the new edition especially relevant at a time when public advocacy is more important than ever."

> —**David Worth**, Director of the George R. Brown Forensics Society;
> Senior Lecturer in the School of Humanities at Rice University

"Dalton and Butler offer a thoughtful, contemporary approach to argument that extends beyond theory and functions in everyday lived experiences. The updates to this edition artfully address so many of the current forces that shape public opinion and offer the learner tools to find their way through to effective argument."

—**Archana Pathak**, Director of the Q Collective, an LGBTQIA+ research and advocacy center; Associate Professor of Gender, Sexuality, and Women's Studies at Virginia Commonwealth University

"As a scientist that engages the public in socially-controversial areas, it is imperative to understand the formal nuances of argument and advocacy. Dalton and Butler accessibly illuminate key aspects of rhetorical communication that will help novice and expert alike tailor their content, presentation and targeting for maximum influence. A must read for those creating change."

—**Kevin Folta**, Professor of Horticultural Sciences at the University of Florida; public science advocate; host of the podcast *Talking Biotech*

"I was thrown into the student loan debate with nothing more than my wits to guide me. In an era where so much bad public policy is allowed to persist based upon poor arguments, dubious data, big money and brute force, this book is a breath of fresh air. It provides all the tools for even the least well-resourced advocate to win the day armed with nothing more than a strong argument, and wise planning. I wish I had read it years ago. Just mapping my own experience into it is fascinating!"

—**Alan Collinge**, founder of StudentLoanJustice.org; author of *The Student Loan Scam* (2009); selected as one of seven "Financial Heroes" by CNN/*Money Magazine* in December 2008

Public Policy Argumentation and Debate

This book is part of the Peter Lang Media and Communication list.
Every volume is peer reviewed and meets
the highest quality standards for content and production.

PETER LANG
New York • Bern • Berlin
Brussels • Vienna • Oxford • Warsaw

Philip Dalton and John R. Butler

Public Policy Argumentation and Debate

A Practical Guide for Advocacy

Second Edition

PETER LANG
New York • Bern • Berlin
Brussels • Vienna • Oxford • Warsaw

Library of Congress Cataloging-in-Publication Data

Names: Dalton, Philip, author. | Butler, John R., author.
Title: Public policy argumentation and debate: a practical guide for
advocacy / Philip Dalton, John R. Butler.
Description: [Second edition] | New York: Peter Lang, 2021
Includes bibliographical references and index.
Identifiers: LCCN 2020054240 (print) | LCCN 2020054241 (ebook)
ISBN 978-1-4331-7469-8 (paperback) | ISBN 978-1-4331-7470-4 (ebook pdf)
ISBN 978-1-4331-7471-1 (epub) | ISBN 978-1-4331-7472-8 (mobi)
Subjects: LCSH: Debates and debating. | Rhetoric. | Policy sciences. |
Communication—Political aspects.
Classification: LCC PN4181 .D25 2021 (print) | LCC PN4181 (ebook) |
DDC 808.53—dc23
LC record available at https://lccn.loc.gov/2020054240
LC ebook record available at https://lccn.loc.gov/2020054241
DOI 10.3726/b16217

Bibliographic information published by **Die Deutsche Nationalbibliothek**.
Die Deutsche Nationalbibliothek lists this publication in the "Deutsche
Nationalbibliografie"; detailed bibliographic data are available
on the Internet at http://dnb.d-nb.de/.

Cover design by Gregg Rojewski; background image from a protest organized by the Illinois
AFL-CIO at the Illinois Capitol, Springfield, Illinois, May 18, 2016.

© 2021 Peter Lang Publishing, Inc., New York
80 Broad Street, 5th floor, New York, NY 10004
www.peterlang.com

All rights reserved.
Reprint or reproduction, even partially, in all forms such as microfilm,
xerography, microfiche, microcard, and offset strictly prohibited.

To . . .
M. Jack Parker, Dorothy Bishop, Martha Cooper,
and Robert P. Newman.
The teachers and coaches who taught us how to argue.

CONTENTS

ACKNOWLEDGMENTS

After we decided to write a book about public policy advocacy, our minds returned to when we initially encountered the various concepts that make up our understanding of argumentation and debate. All of that happened while we were undergraduate students at Northern Illinois University and members of NIU Forensics. There we worked with the people who generously devoted their careers to teaching us, and countless others, how to argue. Every memory we have of these extraordinary mentors—M. Jack Parker, Dorothy Bishop, and Martha Cooper—is cherished. While they are no longer with us, we hope the lessons and guidance we have assembled here is a clear indication of the significance of their influence on us and the discipline of Communication Studies. John had the added good fortune to work for a time with the legendary Robert P. Newman, who taught him and many others that advocacy is at its best when it is aimed in the direction of justice. This book is dedicated to these four teachers, coaches, scholars, and advocates.

NIU Forensics and the other programs with which we have had the pleasure of working—including the William Pitt Debate Union at the University of Pittsburgh and Hofstra University's Speech and Debate program—provide transformative experiences to aspiring advocates. These programs benefit from the steadfast passion of forensics educators like Judy Santacaterina at

NIU, and many other coaches and mentors who continue long-established traditions and invite innovations in forensics pedagogy and programming.

We are each fortunate to share our lives with people whose generosity and encouragement were critical to the publication of the first and second editions of this book. Phil is grateful to his wife Lisa Dalton for absorbing an unfair share of the child rearing duties for their boys—Eli and Parker—while he undertook the task of co-authoring and revising this book. John wishes to acknowledge the patience and support of Sharon Butler, Jane McCarthy, and Ricardo Gomez Renteria, who saw much less of him than usual because of this project and listened to his lengthy explanations of concepts and ideas while they were being developed. We are also blessed to have employers and colleagues who support our work. Phil wishes to recognize the Department of Writing Studies and Rhetoric, and the Center for Civic Engagement, at Hofstra University for the resources they provided, in terms of both the teaching releases and funding that were crucial to the completion of this project. John is thrilled to work with the leaders of the Painters District Council No. 30, the International Union of Painters and Allied Trades, and others associated with the labor movement in Illinois and the United States, with whom he regularly addresses practical advocacy challenges of great consequence. John also wishes to acknowledge lessons he has learned about advocacy as a member of the Board of Trustees at Northern Illinois University and to thank his board colleagues and the many talented leaders at NIU for their role in forming his perspectives and approaches to public policy advocacy.

Both of us are grateful to Dave Naze who read and commented on the proposal for our second edition, and Sharon Butler who read the draft chapters as we completed them and provided us with valuable feedback. We are especially thankful for the time and attention of Marisa Richards, who sagaciously copyedited the manuscript as we developed it, as well as the editors at Peter Lang Press and a discerning anonymous reviewer who offered valuable guidance.

Finally, we wish to extend our highest regards to each other. Throughout this and other scholarly projects, and over the course of a lengthy friendship, we have developed mutual respect and admiration for each other as scholars, teachers, and advocates and the trust required to blend our voices in the hopes of making a difference.

Philip Dalton and John R. Butler, October 2020

PREFACE

The two of us entered the world of argumentation and debate at just about the same time, both as undergraduates at Northern Illinois University (Dekalb, Illinois) studying political science in the early 1990s. We came to NIU's debate team from similar backgrounds: both from working-class suburbs west and south of Chicago, both from families who valued education as a route to political and economic empowerment, and both interested and involved in political issues. We were very ambitious, full of outrage and discontent, and never short of opinions; but, like many undergraduate students, our elementary and secondary education experiences did not leave us with a comprehensive understanding of history, politics, and science upon which to draw conclusions with any certainty, or the research, writing, and analytical skills required to piece together alternatives to policy directions we did not support. Religion, while present in our family systems to varying degrees, was not a sensemaking force for either of us when it came to societal problems. It is not surprising to us today that our search for a system through which we could filter what we learned and enable us to determine how to solve problems would lead us to the study of argumentation and debate.

Traditions and Innovations

While we did not know it at the time, joining the debate team at NIU was tantamount to being brought on board a particularly styled vessel, piloted by a captain and first officer. We would learn later that the coaching team of M. Jack Parker and Dorothy Bishop, both faculty members in NIU's Department of Communication, had invited many other students to become part of their teaching and learning community. Once we found ourselves safely inside the unfamiliar vessel, we marveled at its gears and levers and were quick to agree to stay on board.

When students are first introduced to the academic field of argumentation and debate, typically unknown to them at the time, they find themselves in vessels that are designed to function in particular ways. Only if they continue to study argumentation might they learn some of the mechanics behind the façades of gears and levers, or anything about the engineers who built them. These metaphorical vessels might be called intellectual traditions, hereditary lines of thinking and teaching that formed communities across generations that have passed on knowledge and skills in particular ways. In the study of argumentation, many of these communities have read the same foundational texts—Aristotle's *On Rhetoric*, Cicero's *De Inventione*, and other works commonly encountered in the academic field of argumentation—but each creates, presents, and engages in advocacy within unique frameworks and formats found in textbooks and passed on through coaching protocols.

Our intellectual tradition can be found most vividly described in the 1963 work of Robert B. Huber, *Influencing through Argument*.[1] *Influencing through Argument* was the culmination of several years of learning and teaching argumentation by Huber, then a faculty member in the Department of Speech at the University of Vermont, and a community of colleagues and graduate students who worked with him, including the person who would become our debate coach, M. Jack Parker (the textbook was reissued in 2006 by Huber's student, Alfred Snider[2]). Huber forms an inventory of objections that incorporates many of the complex rules of logic, and formal and informal fallacies, that take students years to master. His self-titled "lines of argument" approach to explaining argumentation is an "attempt," he explains, "to translate the tests of evidence, the tests of reasoning, and the methods by which fallacies can be revealed into language readily available to the student speaker."[3] Moreover, unlike the logicians of his time, Huber is aware he is helping students *both* analyze proposals *and* speak about them.[4] Huber's focus on a set of common objections in the teaching of argumentation and debate, and his particular interest in the role of argument in policymaking, offered us a framework for engaging the world of public policy, a world in which people use argument to influence others to alter the status quo—to alleviate what Huber called "evils"[5]—or maintain the status quo.

One exceptional work that we place within the legacy of Huber's approach is Martha Cooper's *Analyzing Public Discourse*.[6] Cooper was once a graduate assistant working for Parker and Bishop and eventually joined them on the faculty at NIU. She taught both authors and became the master's degree advisor to Phil Dalton; and, for a brief time before her death, John Butler was her departmental colleague. In *Analyzing Public Discourse*, Cooper seeks to identify practical lessons from public controversies, where argumentation and debate leads to real consequences for real people, as opposed to focusing on lessons that might come from the increasingly technical practice and study of argumentation occurring in the intercollegiate competitive debate community. Consistent with Huber's lines of argument, her text places an emphasis on the "critical tools for analyzing messages."[7] Huber, Cooper, and many others appreciate the challenges of teaching students to apply formal logic and logical fallacies to "everyday argument," and seek to develop "objections that are fairly typical in the course of discussions regarding public issues" that are easy to recall and deploy.[8]

The motivation behind Cooper's text is the same impulse that drove us to write the first, and now drives us to write the second, edition of this book: a desire to teach aspiring advocates to marshal their capacity to analyze and engage in public policy advocacy. Gordon Mitchell uses the term "argumentative agency" to describe the impulse to resist the status quo or challenges to the status quo and a willingness to act on that impulse.[9] Mitchell was a championship intercollegiate debater who became a scholar of public argument and frequent contributor to efforts to break down boundaries between the academic/competitive debate activity and realms of actual public policymaking. In the following words, he describes his concerns about competitive debate training:

> To the extent that the academic space begins to take on characteristics of a laboratory, the barriers demarcating such a space from other spheres of deliberation beyond the school grow taller and less permeable. When such barriers reach insurmountable dimensions, argumentation in the academic setting unfolds on a purely simulated plane, with students practicing critical thinking and advocacy skills in strictly hypothetical thought-spaces. Although they may research and track public argument as it

unfolds outside the confines of the laboratory for research purposes, in this approach, students witness argumentation beyond the walls of the academy as spectators, with little or no apparent recourse to directly participate or alter the course of events.[10]

We believe this book offers one approach to bridge the gap between the lessons and concepts used in the "laboratory" of the classroom and the practical impact students of debate may have on public controversies.

We also strongly support the mission of so many of our contemporaries in the speech and debate community who ask, "How can we, as educators, help revitalize our nation's civic health?"[11] The challenge, in our view, is how to develop an *instructional* environment that encourages people to engage in the controversies of their time and place. Too often, argumentation and debate teachers and coaches limit their role to what Mitchell refers to as "preparatory pedagogy," which, as the term suggests, focuses on *future* advocacy. It is also a practice steeped in assumptions and conventional wisdom about the sheer power and emancipatory potential of learning how to argue, the belief that students—"hooked" the moment they experience an actual formal debate round—will continue from that point into a life characterized by high levels of argumentative agency. Seldom have we found the allure of the debate round to be as formative for aspiring advocates. In our experience, for every student who is captivated by academic debate, several quietly never return for subsequent instruction. It is impossible to know with certainty why or what becomes of them, but we have a sinking suspicion they leave feeling like the world of public policy advocacy is not for them, that it is a world made up of culturally powerful, naturally intelligent, and articulate individuals. We suspect the disenfranchised have an idealistic notion of competency in advocacy, likely fueled by images in the news and entertainment media that mostly feature white males in the exercise of social and political power in formal deliberative spaces.[12]

Something must be done to convince more people that they can lead, or contribute productively to, an effort to change the status quo or defend it against changes that will produce disadvantages. You may be ready for a full court press or you may need to develop argumentative agency more incrementally. Your entry into public policy controversies may require you to address some of the damage done to your spirit through interactions with parents, school officials, law enforcement (police, judges, etc.), politicians, employers and supervisors, the media, and other authorities you've encountered thus far in your life. If you are less argumentative, simply becoming aware of activity or behavior with which you disagree may be the first step. You should know it is ok to disagree and that doing so is essential to the development of good public policy and the overall health of democratic systems.

Our Framework

We intend *Public Policy Argumentation and Debate* to provide aspiring advocates a system for engaging in advocacy. We accomplish this objective in three parts.

First, we seek to motivate and empower you to argue. We view this as a process that begins with you appreciating your existing knowledge of, and experience with, advocacy in everyday encounters and interactions, and continues with you building on that experience to learn about the unique characteristics, burdens, and complexities of public controversies. We encourage you to choose to act as advocates; and, this choice, we suspect, will likely amount to exciting, although sometimes disappointing, experiences. Our system is built on a foundation that borrows from many firmly established conventions, or settled distinctions, that make up the "rules" of argumentation and debate. Our goal is to contend with what otherwise might be mysterious about the interplay of claims and counterclaims within public controversies, and encourage you to apply a limited number of principles and techniques to clarify what is occurring and develop your advocacy. You will learn how to discern the contours of a public issue, or controversy, and determine which "side" you are on. This analysis is an essential first step in developing messages, what you plan to argue specifically (or, more simply, *what to say*). We advise you to identify the unique burdens you have when you seek to change the status quo, or if you seek instead to defend the status quo.

Second, we seek to equip you to develop public policy advocacy—the content that makes up your advocacy. Our process begins with the introduction of *stock issues*, or matters of potential dispute, those advocating for reforms typically address—that there is a problem, a cause of that problem, a possible solution, and advantages that accompany the solution—and related burdens that serve as starting points in the practical planning advocates must do to craft messages. Once you understand your burdens, you can construct appealing messages, which can take on many characteristics. Based on our personal experiences as advocates and scholarly considerations of public controversies, we focus on limited and particular ways in which advocates typically reason when they are attempting to address problems and proposals for reform. Rather than attempting an exhaustive discussion about the available forms of reasoning, we observe what people do in practice, and initially limit our coverage to claims of causality you will encounter within public policy controversies. In the context of a controversy or disagreement, advocates are typically quarreling over what does (or does not), or might (or might not), *cause* something to happen. We advise you to pose *critical questions* when you construct or encounter these causal claims so you can build thoughtful and effective advocacy. We also expose you to the main reasoning infrastructures that support causal and other rational claims, which will help you more thoughtfully assess problems and proposed solutions (or defend against advocacy meant to distract you from, or cloud, what could otherwise be a thoughtful debate).

Belonging also to the category of firmly established conventions of argumentation are settled ideas about the appropriate use of evidence. Our system takes into consideration evidence as a distinct topic because we wish to encourage you to reflect on the quality of evidence offered in support of highly consequential claims. Moreover, like our focus on causality and other specific forms of reasoning, we hope to highlight unique occasions within public policy advocacy that generate certain uses of evidence, and disagreements over the way claims are supported with evidence. Guiding aspiring advocates in the selection, use, and proper consideration of evidence has risen in importance in the present era, a time in which evidence-based conclusions and guidance is sometimes inexplicably attacked; as such, the critical questions concerning the use of evidence commonly used in public policy advocacy are essential elements of our system.

Third, after we set you on a course for practical engagement, we consider more complex subjects related to public policy advocacy that are essential to the goal of creating good public policy. This information will allow you to reflect on how advocates define their target audience, set their advocacy goals, explore ethical dilemmas that inevitably emerge when advocates want to "win," and dynamically consider the manner in which the setting, or environment, affects the range of available advocacy strategies. Your choice to enter a controversy is situated in the context of a controversy that involves an audience and a set of expectations particular to an advocacy setting. You choose—more or less—to accommodate these dynamics. To rely on a metaphor to illustrate this point, developing advocacy is much like making a meal for your family. You encounter family members demanding specific things and refusing to accept other options. The resulting meal is limited considerably by your available supplies and perhaps financial resources, and there are relationship issues with which you must contend, such as whose preferences should be given the most weight in the decision, how to divide the preparation responsibilities, and so forth. Like the meal, your advocacy is often a product of your thoughtful use of available resources guided by a carefully nuanced effort to address the needs of your target audience within the constraints of a particular setting.

The resulting text is ideal for both students of argumentation and debate, and professionals who work within environments that involve public policy advocacy. Teachers of argumentation and debate will find that the concepts in this text, while not intended to train students to navigate academic and intercollegiate competitive debate contests, align with common protocols for teaching and coaching debate. Initially and throughout, we also draw on a variety of examples of controversies with which readers may easily identify.

Throughout this book, you will find that we believe the process of developing compelling messages is aided by certain assumptions you can make as advocates. One is that *you* can assess what you need to do in an advocacy situation and craft appealing messages based on that assessment. Another is that commonalities you share with others in your community also include a *common rationality* that you can rely on for the practical purpose of developing messages. Another way of making this point: once you have learned some basic rules about rational argumentation, it might be helpful to assume others will reason about problems and proposed solutions in the same way you do. This is what we mean by a "common rationality." While not always practical or noticeable in operation, assuming this permits you to expect advocacy to conform to general structural norms and to pose several basic questions that help steer your advocacy in a rational direction. We understand that well-funded advocacy campaigns may benefit from more precise audience analysis protocols, both qualitative and quantitative, and that advocacy directed at larger audiences, or audiences outside of your community, may require a more culturally-focused assessment of history, relationships, needs, demands, grievances, and more. Nevertheless, we view these assumptions as critical to the practical challenges you will face when seeking to develop compelling messages. Our objective is to give you a starting point, a foundation on which you may build an ever-improving capacity to engage the important issues in your worlds.

The Second Edition

The Second Edition is divided into three parts: Part I: Emergence; Part II: Arguing; and Part III: Reasonable Goals. By "Emergence," we refer to your entry into controversies, your determination of which "side" you are on, the formation of any policy goals you have, and how to begin thinking about the issues within controversies. By "Arguing," we refer to the process of building thoughtful and effective messages by identifying and addressing the burdens that accompany your advocacy, and considering reasoning infrastructures and evidence—particularly reasoning and evidence that support causal predictions. By "Reasonable Goals," we refer to two aspects of a controversy over which you can have more control if you choose to consciously consider them: your target audience and the varied and complex goals and norms tied to your advocacy settings.

In the Second Edition, we also bring the content up to date since the First Edition was published in 2015. This leads to some shifts in focus that align with what we judge to be particular about the political dilemmas of our historical time, examples of which we will briefly mention here. We draw attention to the way policy communication originating from government agents and political candidates often overtakes the airways or emerges as a dominant voice crowding out citizen-driven public policy advocacy. We include new material on how analyzing public discourse as an intellectual activity, alongside or instead of direct participation, might offer a rewarding means of civic engagement. We focus more in this edition on how public policy disputes might deviate from expectations you might have for a "fair fight." We place more emphasis, for instance, in the reasoning chapters on how elements of context and subject matter provide opportunities to exploit public inclinations to reason poorly. And, we supplement our consideration of evidence with considerations that are timely, including discussions of the diminishing level of public confidence in authorities. Throughout, we construct several new case studies and interviews that illustrate the relevancy of concepts discussed in the chapters to recent controversies. Within each chapter, we continue to provide a list of "takeaways" and an exercise designed to guide your personal engagement with public policy advocacy. We conclude the text with a summary, or matrix, of critical questions that have been introduced throughout the book, which underscores the intent of the project to serve as a practical guide for advocacy.

Chapters 1 and 2 consider subjects we judge to be related to your emergence as an advocate, the organizing principle behind Part I (Emergence).
In Chapter 1, we encourage you to view advocacy as essential to a healthy
democracy and necessary to effectively address a range of societal problems.
We situate such advocacy in the larger realm of political communication
and draw attention to the critical importance of citizen-driven public policy
advocacy. You will learn that public controversies center on particular issues
about which there is typically disagreement (whether there is a problem that
warrants a solution, what causes the problem, and so forth). And, we outline
several tenets of "good" public policy advocacy that help frame what you will
learn throughout the text. In Chapter 2, we discuss how to determine the
public issue at the center of a controversy and establish a clear sense of what
positions you wish to take in relation to the issue and/or any existing policy proposals. We focus intensely on deciphering the *policy proposition* under
which advocacy is occurring as a necessary first step in determining what is,
and what is not, germane to a public policy controversy. We begin our discussion of stock issues, matters of potential dispute (problem, cause, solution,
and advantages). We also introduce you to the usefulness and practical merits of understanding and critically engaging controversies as an intellectual
activity.

Chapter 3 kicks off Part II (Arguing), which runs through Chapter 7. In
Chapter 3 you learn that advocates are either calling for a change in the status
quo or defending the status quo, and we provide a comprehensive review of
stock issues and related burdens. Chapters 4 and 5 consider reasoning—how
advocates link ideas and evidence they believe their audience will accept to
conclusions they hope their audience will draw. We initially focus on causal
claims, drawing attention to the role of prediction in public policy advocacy.
In Chapter 5 we expand our focus to cover deductive reasoning, inductive
reasoning, and reasoning through analogy. You will learn from these chapters
that we favor an approach that poses a limited set of *critical questions* designed
to assist your own critical thinking and discover flaws in the reasoning of
others. Chapters 6 and 7 expose you to settled ideas about the appropriate use
and role of evidence in public policy advocacy. By refreshing the relevance
and efficacy of foundational work in the theory and uses of evidence, our goal
is to encourage deep reflection among advocates on the quality of evidence
offered in support of what are often highly consequential claims. Similar to
our approach to causality and other specific forms of reasoning, we provide

critical questions to guide advocates in the selection, use, and proper consideration of evidence from authorities and statistics. In our consideration of evidence from authorities, we also offer "source-specific considerations" that focus on the news media and scholarship, including some consideration of the concern over "fake news."

Chapters 8 and 9 are collected under Part III (Reasonable Goals). In these chapters, we discuss how to conceive of a target audience and consider the dynamics of the advocacy setting. In Chapter 8, we encourage you to set goals for what you might reasonably achieve with your advocacy based on an analysis of who is likely to care about the issue, how much they know about it, what opinions they might have formed about it already, and how close they are to agreeing with your objectives. In Chapter 9, we consider the way the advocacy setting affects the range of available advocacy strategies. We discuss how advocates carefully adapt their messages to the nature of the situation, navigate the norms of the advocacy setting, and choose a medium (or media) to convey their messages. In addition to traditional public address settings, we address mediated advocacy, signaling that we view media platforms (from letters, to PowerPoint, to email, to social media, to television) to be matters of setting.

If you have significant experience in the worlds of academic and intercollegiate competitive debate, you may find throughout this book that we make several statements with a degree of confidence and certainty that may not ring true to the way you were introduced to policy debate. We do not contend that the system we assembled will apply perfectly to all public advocacy situations. Our goal is to inspire your thoughtful and ethical entry into the public policy world, where many new lessons will be learned. The sooner you reach beyond the ideas in this book to develop more complex understandings of argumentation, and attendant aspirations for what public policy advocacy can achieve, the better, as far as we are concerned.

Notes

1 Robert B. Huber, *Influencing through Argument* (New York: David McKay Company, 1963).
2 Robert B. Huber and Alfred C. Snider, *Influencing through Argument* (Updated Edition) (New York: International Debate Education Association, 2006).
3 Huber, v.
4 Ibid., v.
5 Ibid., 236.
6 Martha Cooper, *Analyzing Public Discourse* (Long Grove, IL: Waveland Press, Inc., 1989).

7 Ibid., x.

8 Ibid., 119.

9 Gordon Mitchell, "Pedagogical Possibilities for Argumentative Agency in Academic Debate," *Argumentation and Advocacy* 35, no. 2 (1998), 41–60.

10 Ibid., 43.

11 J. Michael Hogan and Jessica A. Kurr, "Introduction: Speech and Debate as Civic Education," in *Speech and Debate as Civic Education*, eds. J. Michael Hogan, Jessica A. Kurr, Michael J. Bergmaier, and Jeremy D. Johnson (University Park: The Pennsylvania State University Press, 2017), 5.

12 Significant resistance to the traditional norms of competitive policy debate may be altering this dynamic. See Sarah Stone Watt, "Debaters as Citizens: Rethinking Debate Frameworks to Address the Policy/Performance Divide," in Hogan et al., *Speech and Debate*, 163-173. Listen also to "Debatable," *Radiolab* (podcast), WNYC Studios, March 11, 2016, produced by Matt Kielty; reported by Abigail Keel, https://www.wnycstudios.org/podcasts/radiolab/articles/debatable.

Part I
EMERGENCE

1

ORIENTATION

Takeaways

(1) Public policy advocacy is essential for the proper function of a democratic governing system.

(2) Citizen-driven public policy advocacy is a type of political communication that faces many challenges when compared to the public policy advocacy of candidates and government officials.

(3) Public policy advocacy consists of reasons for changing or maintaining the status quo. Those reasons typically support thoughtful predictions of what may happen in the future, are offered within a public space where ordinary people can assess validity and value, and appeal directly to existing or new audiences.

(4) Good public policy advocacy *emerges* when you engage the public with your advocacy; accept that "victory" is often achieved over a sustained advocacy effort; and identify the general controversy, the "side" you are on, and your policy goal.

(5) Good public policy advocacy *occurs by means of messages* that adhere to the unique burdens of your position; recognize that the

disagreement is mainly over what might (or might not) cause something to happen; protect your advocacy against the onslaught of fallacious reasoning; and control for how evidence is practically used, misused, or underused, and what it can reveal about the intentions of an advocate.

(6) Good public policy advocacy is *based on reasonable goals* that understand and respect the concerns of a target audience, and practices that effectively navigate the situational norms and constraints of the advocacy setting.

Black Lives Matter activist Sharhonda Bossier was born in 1984 and grew up in the care of her grandparents, who had both moved to Los Angeles from Louisiana during the "Great Migration." Her "journey to the front lines, and the lessons she's learned about the pace of change," is superbly documented in the August 5, 2020 episode of the *New York Times* podcast, *The Daily*.[1] Bossier grew up in the Watts neighborhood in southern Los Angeles, and was 7 years old when a store owner in her community suspected that 15-year-old Latasha Harlins was going to steal some orange juice. A confrontation led the store owner to shoot Harlins in the back of the head after she had put the juice bottle on the counter and attempted to leave (the event was captured on store video). The store owner would only receive a sentence of five years probation. Shortly after, video footage of Los Angeles police officers beating Rodney King was discovered, leading to charges against the police. As is well-known today, the officers were acquitted, leading to the 1991 Los Angeles Riots.

Following the riots, Bossier recalls that her family settled back into its routines—"we just didn't talk about it"—until their world was upended by her grandmother's heart attack and unnecessary death at a local hospital known for not providing good care. At 13, Bossier became known among her teachers as an angry young woman, prompting one of her teachers to tell her one day, "you know, you could really do something with all this anger that you're feeling ... you can protest. You can try to change these things that you don't think are fair. You can become an activist." Bossier did just that. Beginning with a school walkout organized to protest the fact that their school was named after a slave owner (George Washington High), Bossier recalls the moment when she paused before she reached the doors of the school: "And I remember security guards standing at the gates and saying, if you walk out, we're going to report your name to the front office." She recounts taking a deep breath and thinking, "am I doing this?"

> I think I was setting out to prove to myself and to others that, as the kids say now, I was about this life. That I could work up the courage to stand up to authority in a way that could result in real consequences for me. It's my life. And I get to do with it what I want.

Bossier continued speaking out, joining protests in her community, and eventually becoming a teacher. She was excited to be one of many young Black professionals who joined the campaign of presidential candidate Barack Obama. And then, in 2012, Trayvon Martin was killed in Sanford, Florida, by George Zimmerman.[2]

> And so we begin to show up to marches, and we begin to show up to protest. And I think one of the things that is beautiful about this particular moment is that there is this sense that any one of us can put out a call to action and someone will show up.

Then followed the 2014 police shooting of Michael Brown in Ferguson, Missouri. "So she just gets on that train, and starts to become a part of the movement," recounts the *Times*. "We were a grassroots, pretty leaderless, dispersed network of people, all guided by a sort of North star, which was #BlackLivesMatter," recounts Bossier.[3]

Bossier's journey is a captivating depiction of *emergence*, the phenomenon of discovering one's argumentative agency. We hope you are encountering this book somewhere along your own journey to take those important first steps, or to continue to seek solutions to problems within your community; and, we hope part of that journey involves learning to skillfully argue. We wrote this book suspecting you have already learned how to argue to some degree. By formally studying argumentation and debate, you indicate your desire to expand your repertoire and enhance your skills. In this text, we instruct you to apply what you have learned, along with some concepts that are perhaps new, to real-world public policy controversies.

At the core of public policy controversies are *issues*. An issue is a matter of public concern about which interested parties disagree. Disputing parties typically disagree about the following:

(a) whether there is a problem that warrants a solution
(b) what causes the problem
(c) whether a proposed solution will alleviate the problem
(d) whether the advantages of a proposal are greater than the disadvantages

As you can discern from the above, a defining characteristic of public policymaking is that the outcomes of decisions cannot be determined until after society executes plans. *Will this tax cut help the economy? Do charter schools improve education outcomes? Will a border wall improve the quality of life for U.S. citizens?* Humans can be very intelligent, but they cannot precisely predict the future. For the above questions, advocates can only make predictions that are supported by evidence and are well-reasoned, and base their decisions on those predictions.

In this chapter, we ask you to spend some time orienting yourself to the context in which debate over these predictions occurs—the context of a democratic political system and your contemplation of your role in that system. Orientation involves both positioning yourself in relation to something else—in this case, a democratic political system—and considering your basic attitude, beliefs, or feelings in relation to a particular subject or issue—in this case, public policy argumentation and debate.[4] We situate public policy advocacy as a form of political communication and make clear how important public voices are in a system that can easily tilt in favor of the most powerful in society. We consider some common attitudes, beliefs, or feelings that you and others may have about argumentation and debate that may interrupt or frustrate your participation in the important controversies of the day. We distinguish public policy advocacy from other forms of communication that you may encounter within the various spheres of your life, and close the chapter with several tenets of good public policy advocacy that follow the contours of the lessons we set forth in the chapters of this book.

Public Policy Advocacy and the Democratic Political System

That a society is a democracy (a federal democracy in the case of the United States) means much more than people voting for individuals to represent them in legislative and executive offices. The central reason that democratic practice emerged out of the monarchies of Western Europe is because the assumption that reasonable people could evaluate ideas and make decisions *as well as, if not better than,* monarchs gained credence among the property-owning class. John Milton, in his *Areopagitica,* written in 1644, asserts that truth prevails in a "free and open encounter."[5] John Stuart Mill writes similarly in 1859, in *On Liberty,* that, "Wrong opinions and practices gradually yield to fact and argument: but facts and arguments, to produce any effect on the mind, must be brought before it."[6] This attitude is evident in the Supreme

Court's free speech ruling in the 1919 case, *Abrams v. United States*. In that ruling, Justice Oliver Wendell Holmes writes:

> ... the best test of truth is the power of the thought to get itself accepted in the competition of the market, and that truth is the only ground upon which their wishes safely can be carried out. That at any rate is the theory of our Constitution.[7]

This "marketplace of ideas" metaphor draws on the ideas undergirding free market economics, Adam Smith's writings about capitalism's ability to reward the best products through mass consumer consumption. By applying this notion to ideas, or public policy, many scholars and thinkers, and generations of students of argumentation, accept the idea that policy proposals that survive or prevail in a debate are the "best" proposals. While surviving public scrutiny may not necessarily ensure that a policy is good, public debate is still, according to many, the best mechanism for vetting public policy proposals.

The alternative to public scrutiny is silence, and the consequences of silence on issues of public importance are almost always less desirable than the outcomes of healthy public policy debate. "The squeaky wheel gets the grease" is a commonly used idiom that captures an important political reality: opinions must be voiced in order to be given public consideration. Those who hold an opinion but fail to express it (silence) may find it much more difficult to express later. Elisabeth Noelle-Neumann warns of the public communication phenomenon she terms the "spiral of silence"—when silence begets silence because the impression that one's opinion is a minority position discourages the minority from voicing it.[8] This process, she explains, continues (spirals) until the position is rarely heard at all. And when it *is* expressed at a much later point in time, its novelty renders it more readily dismissed by the public as a fringe argument. This phenomenon often occurs in the case of newer opinions that emerge out of changing social consciousness, positions advocates assume are unpopular and/or lack widespread support.

Democracy assumes that disputing parties will disagree about issues in a shared pursuit of good public policy. For the sake of clarity and simplicity, we will define "good public policy" as *policy that solves a problem without causing other new problems that are more troubling than the original problem*. For residents of democratic societies, the pursuit of good public policy occurs in a governmental system within which people have the capacity to shape the character of their communities by enlisting the support of others for their ideas. The champions of democracy wrested authority from outmoded governing systems and replaced them with democratic systems that assume participants will develop good policy by relying on valid evidence and sound reasoning. As a result, the legitimacy of policies relies not only on gaining support within a democratic system but also on the level of public participation leading up to the adoption of policies.

Public Policy Argumentation and Debate as a Type of Political Communication

Advocates are drawn into public policy advocacy for a variety of reasons and from a wide range of starting points. As advocacy educators who tend to work most closely with aspiring advocates (for whom advocacy is a relatively new endeavor), we find ourselves often clarifying that citizen-driven public policy advocacy is essential to the success of a democratic political system. We believe, therefore, it is helpful to orient the type of communication we are addressing in this book as a form of political communication. In his book *Political Communication in Action*, David Helfert identifies three kinds of political communication: election campaigns, policy communication, and advocacy communication.[9] Whereas election campaign communication is performed to get candidates elected, the distinction between policy communication and advocacy communication is more nuanced. Policy communication is messaging that governments and elected officials, along with their staffs and strong supporters, communicate about public policy. As public officials, they get to select and promote issues, shape how they are discussed, and target their messages to constituents. Put simply, policy communication is top-down. Advocacy communication, by comparison, is initiated from the bottom-up; it often begins at the "grass roots" level. Helfert explains that advocates may begin with an issue of which the public is barely aware, and work to publicize it. While the categories of policy communication and advocacy communication are not mutually exclusive, and we do not intend to suggest that the lessons of this book are exclusively fashioned for bottom-up advocacy, Helfert's categories provide helpful language for identifying advantages and limitations faced by different kinds of public policy advocates (and their messages).

These distinctions are also useful in casting a sharper and more distinct purpose for aspiring advocates and aligning the teachings of this text with what we judge to be particular about the political dilemmas of the historical time in which we write. Policy communication has several advantages over advocacy communication. We observe first that advocates with no established institutional power are seldom able to rely on built-in audiences or possess the means of publicity or tools to disseminate their messages in the same manner public officials do. Among other things, public officials can access news media attention with relative ease and may themselves possess the resources to skillfully craft and distribute messages. Advocates, by contrast, are quite often up against considerable odds. Imagine being a member of a marginalized community that is trying to draw public attention to a specific injustice. The barriers to success may seem insurmountable. Consider, for instance, taking up the argument for bail reform (often phrased as a call for "no cash bond"), laws to remove bail requirements for those accused of nonviolent offenses. If such reform were adopted, someone found in possession of a small amount of an illegal substance would not be required to post bail to leave jail as they await trial. At the core of the advocacy for bail reform are statistics showing that poor people cannot afford bail, and therefore suffer considerably due to loss of jobs and income. Moreover, advocates of bail reform argue, posting bail makes almost no difference in the number of people who show up for trial. While reforming bail appears to make good sense based on the claimed harms of the existing system, taking up the cause of bail reform can be challenging. Less established advocates need to craft a compelling rationale for changing the system, communicate that rationale effectively, and build a supportive audience that eventually accepts the advocates' assessment of the status quo and the need to reform the system. Fearing political consequences, public officials may be reluctant to support policy proposals that do not have strong public support, leaving advocates in the difficult position of needing to develop and manage publicity, audience response, and the complexities of a lawmaking process that relies on the support and willingness of public officials to author and introduce policy proposals.

Second, we share a widely discussed concern that the deliberative system in the United States has grown increasingly top-down. In other words, government and other powerful actors use policy communication to legitimize existing policies or the policies they wish to enact. James Bohman argues that public deliberation between free and equal people "is necessary if decisions are not to be merely imposed upon them," to ensure that laws have the consent of the governed, that their legitimacy is a product of their development by and for the public, and that the public is provided reasons to comply that are presented by their peers, or equals.[10] But, Bohman warns, for deliberation to be effective in producing legitimate public policy, it must affect "uptake," or "promote deliberation on reasons addressed to others, who are expected to respond to them in dialogue."[11] A healthy deliberative system must ensure that the side with the most support, or the "plurality," can emerge, so that not only the current ruling regime holds sway over all policies. Otherwise, argues Bohman, those in power *perform* deliberation while tailoring public discussions to already existing opinions.[12] Public officials and institutions, according to this perspective, have become more effective at controlling the public policy agenda, and the public has become more complacent and compliant. More generally, political philosopher Jurgen Habermas warns against something similar with his concept, "refeudalization," a process of surrendering hard-fought privileges of public participation in the development of policy to those who already steer the ship of state.[13]

It can often be difficult to notice this shift in power—from the public to the powerful—operating in real time. For instance, many may have felt like President Barack Obama was being anti-establishment when he promoted insurance enrollment under the Affordable Care Act (ACA, or "Obamacare") on Zach Galifianakis' comical web series *Between Two Ferns*. This episode was widely viewed as a watershed moment in the drive to sign up millions of young people under the plans offered through the ACA's healthcare exchanges. Watching that program, it is clear Galifianakis endeavors to mimic cheaply-produced cable access programs, giving the viewer the impression the host and his guests are local, ordinary people, not the international power brokers and superstars they actually are. Lost also in the mix of appeals and personalities is the fact that the program that became the ACA was originally drafted by a conservative think tank (The Heritage Foundation) with the intention of expanding health coverage while protecting the profit-oriented insurance industry. Those in need of healthcare might not have imagined the solution to their plight was supported by the very business interests that had made affordable healthcare such a challenging prospect in the first place.

That society should hear from and incorporate the ideas and concerns of multiple voices is essential to the legitimacy of a democratic political system. Nancy Fraser uses the term "counterpublics" to describe groups and identities often excluded from participation in the public sphere by various means.[14] Counterpublics can often be highly effective in advancing grass roots arguments and movement building; their advocacy can contest and alter the norms of public engagement, opening new forms of protest and demanding the attention of public officials. They are forced, at times by necessity, to communicate in ways that shock and disrupt the norms of public propriety. Consequently, "good" public policy advocacy may not always look like the type of "model" civil discourse and deliberation imagined by those who crafted the founding documents and institutions of U.S. government.[15] Without breaking from the model, however, some advocates might never be heard.

Third, we developed this book in part to address another dynamic of government and candidate communication, and what we have learned from this dynamic: that some introduce distractions and obstructions that stand in the way of effective citizen-driven advocacy and adoption of good public policy. Benefiting from enhanced access and substantial resources, government actors and candidates can overtake the airways and emerge as dominant voices crowding out grass roots advocacy, or even the most determined opposition. Paradoxically, such imbalances within the democratic system can sometimes generate more-determined resistance. Most often, those with more formal power and plentiful resources take full advantage of their access, communication infrastructures, and relationships with public audiences to introduce claims that make it especially challenging to focus on the most substantive question: whether a proposed policy solves a problem without causing other new problems that are more troubling than the original problem. Well-capitalized leaders and candidates pivot and shift public attention away from the policy goals to which they are opposed, and the attendant policy issues that should be central to how a policy proposal is evaluated. Instead, advocacy is bent toward ad hominem attacks, the introduction of "red herrings," conflation and equivocation, unrelated scandal, guilt by association, dismissal of entire professions as inherently untrustworthy, and more. These non-substantive inputs break the focus of advocates away from their policy goals. Much attention of late has focused on the accusation that some analyses of policy proposals constitute "fake news" without interrogating the claims at the center of the information, or news.

Silence = Death

An excellent illustration of the challenges faced within the realm of advocacy communication is provided by the activist group ACT UP. Formed in 1987, ACT UP engaged in direct political action aimed at bringing an end to the AIDS pandemic. In the 1980s, gay men were predominantly the victims of HIV/AIDS. Because the pandemic was publicly associated with sex among men who had sex with men, and the culture of the time was such that it was difficult for people to come out as gay, those most harshly affected by HIV/AIDS were people on the margins of mainstream society. By 1987, already six years had passed and over 20,000 people had died from AIDS. The U.S. president at the time, Ronald Reagan, would not actually say the word "AIDS" until 1987, six years after the disease first began taking the lives of Americans (Pat Buchanan, who become Reagan's communications director, infamously wrote in 1983 that homosexuals "declared war upon nature, and now nature is exacting an awful retribution").[16]

ACT UP's policy goal was nevertheless logical and understandable. They wished to expedite the delivery of drug therapies that were proving effective against HIV/AIDS, and for a more coordinated national policy to fight the disease. Facing an obstinate U.S. Food and Drug Administration (FDA), ACT UP adopted the slogan, "Silence = Death," and initiated a multifaceted campaign to bring national attention to their cause. This included demonstrations that caused major disruptions, such as in downtown New York City, where they disrupted the stock exchange, or when they led hundreds of people to lie down in the middle of the Wall Street and Broadway intersection to draw attention to the high price of antiretroviral drugs like AZT and the FDA's slow progress in approving such drugs. In addition to demonstrations, ACT UP also produced data to inform both public and formal discussion on the HIV/AIDS crisis. Members of the organization became among the top worldwide experts on the pandemic and treatment protocols. The first item addressed at a 1989 activism teach-in, provided by ACT UP's Treatment and Data committee, was:

> Know your shit. Knowledge is power. Every significant gain won by ACT UP has flowed from our unassailable command of the issues.[17]

Peter Staley, an early member of ACT UP, explains this strategy of combining an outside (demonstrations) and inside (rational advocacy) approach:

> [W]e had to tell her [Burroughs Wellcome CEO Dr. Ellen Cooper] what we wanted in very clear terms and then apply the external pressure to make her do what we wanted. But you weren't going to get her to do exactly what we wanted unless you did both things—the external pressure and sitting down and talking it out with her, explaining exactly what you needed, exactly what you wanted, and also making her realize that she was dealing with highly motivated, highly rational and intelligent people who had something to say, and not just some screaming raving idiots who were calling her a murderer and marching outside her front door. It was that combination that I thought was our power, the entire time.[18]

Calls for "expanded access" and "compassionate use" of experimental drugs is much more common today than it was in the late 1980s, early 1990s. Indeed, in just a few short months following the outbreak of COVID-19 in the United States—in late April, 2020—the FDA Commissioner announced that agency's plan to approve expanded access to promising treatments for patients severely ill with COVID-19 disease (compare that rapid response to the *decade* of advocacy it took for ACT UP and others to affect the same policy).[19]

To Those Less Inclined to Engage in Public Policy Advocacy

The causes that motivate you to engage in public policy advocacy may not always involve life or death urgency. By becoming familiar with the conventions of public policy advocacy, we hope you will be better equipped to bring your voice to a controversy that matters to you. So, democracy depends on you. But you knew that already, right? The squeaky wheel gets the grease? A lack of familiarity with the foundational principles of democracy (or with old idioms) is seldom the reason people fail to engage in public policy advocacy. There are other reasons that might contribute to such reticence.

First, some people do not like to argue because they feel doing so might harm their relationships. When you disagree with others, you may fear that they will view your words as signs of disapproval, not merely of their position on an issue, but of them more narrowly. You may fear they are ego-involved or will feel face-threatened (diminished in the eyes of others) when you disagree with them or reveal a flaw in their reasoning or use of evidence. Because it is only natural to want people to like and agree with you, you may avoid initiating disagreements altogether.

Another reason some may have adopted a negative disposition toward public policy advocacy is that they perceive argumentation to be a highly technical and mysterious skill, requiring a mastery of technique. Many competitive college debaters experience moments when friends refuse to argue with them, reporting that their friends fear an engagement with someone who has an unfair advantage, as though debate experience can make arguments appear better than they are. And sometimes, skilled arguers *do* bully opponents with forceful language and confrontational tactics, which, of course, does nothing to advance the pursuit of good policy.

Still another reason people avoid arguments is because of negative associations with the activity of arguing. Those who devote a significant amount of their lives studying and teaching others how to argue are constantly encountering the bad rap that argument, as an activity and term, has within certain sectors of society. We have each experienced multiple occasions when we have used the term "argue" in settings where argument is common, only to be corrected by someone who responds with, "I don't think 'argue' is the right word," or something similar. Preferring terms such as "discussion," "dialogue," or "advise," these people clearly associate argument with negative speech acts like verbal aggression and combativeness. Others may confuse verbal aggression and argument because they can both *feel* combative. Negative perceptions of argument may cause some to believe that something constructive can be achieved by avoiding it. You may believe the harmony of relationships will be better served by avoiding disagreements. In the public sphere, people often express a desire to see less conflict over public policy. Many claim to want "bipartisanship" and "compromise," conceiving these as accomplishments in and of themselves. The goal of compromise can be troubling if viewed this way because, in matters of public policy, the stakes can be enormous. Inadequate criticism of policy ideas in favor of harmony can have harmful consequences that are often avoidable.

An important by-product of argumentation and debate training is the awareness that the constructive outcomes of argument, particularly when done well, outweigh the elements of argument that turn people off. After all, your decision *not to argue* may be considered a policy decision, as disengagement can be perceived as an endorsement of the status quo. Also, debate introduces you to different ways of seeing the world. Such openness can expose you to superior policy alternatives and constructive criticism that may not have occurred to you. A satisfying advocacy experience, whether through formal instruction or actual practice, will help thaw your resistance to argument in ways that cause you to perceive it for the positive and constructive activity that it can be and often is, and thus prepare you to participate in public policymaking.

What Is Public Policy Advocacy?

You have engaged in many forms of argument at various points in your life; thus you already generally know what argument *is*. It might then be more helpful to consider what comprises argument in the realm of public policy when advocates are doing it well. To that end, we will focus on four key elements of public policy advocacy before offering several brief tenets of good public policy argument.

First, at its most basic, public policy advocacy is the assertion of reasons for changing or maintaining the status quo. Martha Cooper defines argument for the ordinary person as "reasons," writing, "when advocates present arguments, they present reasons that justify their positions."[20] Public policy advocacy, in this regard, is comprised of reasons that support proposals in opposition to, or in defense of, the status quo.

Second, those reasons typically support thoughtful predictions of what may happen in the future. This book is about one type of argument often referred to as "deliberative" argument. Deliberative argument deals with matters of the future—*what will be done?* or *what should be done?* This differs from two other types of argument commonly referred to as "forensic" and "epideictic" argument. Forensic argument is about matters of the past—*What happened?*—and thus is commonly associated with legal argument, such as that practiced in a courtroom. Others may relate the term "forensic" to forensic science, because that too concerns itself with argument about the past (some of the most popular television series chronicle the lives of forensics scientists who attempt to establish how someone died by weaving pieces of evidence into a likely scenario). Forensic argument might focus on whether something did or did not happen, or whether someone did or did not do something. Epideictic argument, on the other hand, seeks to engender appreciation of values or knowledge—or people, organizations, or institutions that uphold those values and embody such knowledge—at a particular moment in time. That is, epideictic argument is about matters of the present—*What is happening now, and what do we, or don't we, appreciate about it?* Epideictic speech might praise or blame as it seeks an audience's commitment to a set of values or body of knowledge. Eulogies are commonly cited examples of epideictic argument, as speakers seek to move the audience to extol the admirable qualities of the deceased and call on the audience to adopt the same qualities as they live out the rest of their lives. Often epideictic argument is mistaken for substantive policy advocacy, even though it is, more generally, commentary about the present situation. Public university administrators blaming their state legislature for failing to properly support higher education is epidictic argument that blames. They are commenting on something occurring in the present, without expressly calling for a policy action.

Future action gives policy advocacy its defining characteristic—that it is concerned with predictions. *Will natural gas fracking in New York's upstate watershed pollute the state's freshwater supply? Will income tax increases slow or reduce job creation? Will a border wall reduce opioid overdoses in the United States?*

Because you cannot know the future with certainty, on matters of public policy you will most likely put forward predictions, which are probable outcomes based on reasoning and evidence. Such uncertainty is a general characteristic of the democratic decision-making culture in which public policy advocacy occurs. Reflecting on his own emerging consciousness as a competitive academic debater, distinguished communication scholar David Zarefsky describes this dynamic of "public life" this way:

> Debating both sides of the question, making opposing arguments in successive hours, was a powerful teacher. It did not induce vicious relativism—even my emerging convictions were stronger than that—but it did induce some sense of humility rooted in the recognition that we might be wrong. It helped teach me that there is very little we know *for sure*. When it works well, public life is the province of restrained partisans, people who are committed to their viewpoint yet respectful of and willing to engage alternative views. When it malfunctions, public life is under the sway of those who apply the certainty of their unshakeable convictions to matters about which certainty is not given to us.[21]

When you engage in public policy advocacy, you assert *probable* future outcomes of a proposed policy, relying on evidence and reasoning to determine the best courses of action. Instead of limiting your public pronouncements to condemnations of police departments whose excessive force resulted in the unnecessary death of a person within your community, for instance (remarking on the present state of affairs), you could also propose a funding agenda that shifts city resources from police departments to social services, and articulate advantages you believe would come from that proposal, including fewer life-threatening confrontations between residents and police (predicting a better future).

Third, the reasons advocates assert for which course of action is best are offered within a *public* space where ordinary people can assess the validity and value of such reasons in relation to contemporary problems. In the field of Communication Studies, which includes the study of argumentation, much is written about public advocacy. According to rhetorical scholar Thomas Goodnight, the capacity of this type of "public argument" to yield "a probable answer to questions of preferable conduct" is a desirable "alternative to decisions based on authority or blind chance."[22] Goodnight provides further insight as to what comprises public policy advocacy. One central facet of argument in the "public sphere" is that its consequences extend beyond "personal" and "technical" spheres—other settings in which advocacy occurs. Argument in the public sphere is also situated between the formal standards for evidence and reasoning of technical settings and the informal demands of private settings. In other words, what is accepted as legitimate argument in the astrophysicist's lab differs remarkably from what is accepted at the Thanksgiving table; how someone argues in a public forum lies somewhere in between. As such, students of public argument may also find it useful to delve more deeply into knowledge about argumentation within particular technical spheres.

Fourth, reasons offered by advocates can appeal directly to existing audiences or new collectives of concerned people for whom the consequences of a public debate become especially important. When developing advocacy, you must consider more than merely what *you* find persuasive, as what is persuasive to you may be less convincing to your audience. Identifying a target audience and choosing the proper places to start your advocacy require knowledge, strategy, skill, and resources. Further complicating the notion of "audience" is the idea that the audience may be constituted (called into existence) *by* argument. Your advocacy can make individuals aware of an issue and activate their concern about it. A person in Redwood City, California, may have no knowledge of the existence of like-minded individuals in Fort Wayne, Indiana, or Valdosta, Georgia; but public policy advocacy can bring such people together and transform them into a defined target audience. Public policy advocates generate awareness of shared needs among people, and such people may form a "public"—a phenomenon that is a testament to the power of advocacy to generate shared concern.

Those who study public argumentation have introduced many ways to think about how audiences, publics, or "the people," are constituted. We will detail some of this work in our chapter devoted to audience. A body of people is at once real and also the product of an advocate's imagination, when advocacy is directed to issue-aligned communities that coalesce because of, and around, public policy advocacy. We will use terms like "demographic" and "psychographic" to distinguish ways in which you might view groups of people that make up a target audience. There may be no material ties between people who are connected by the shared interests brought to their attention by advocacy, but they nevertheless exist as an entity that can be addressed. Aspiring advocates may find it challenging to derive a detailed profile of their target audience; but, we are optimistic about the potential of ordinary people to perform issues analyses that are more complex than general assumptions advocates might otherwise make about the people living in their communities.

"Good" Public Policy Advocacy

Good public policy advocacy is not measured by persuasiveness alone. We maintain that the factual veracity, soundness, and contributions to civic participation, community, and public policymaking produced by such advocacy make it essential to our political system. After all, little good may come from a persuasive but poorly developed policy proposal.

Quite often, college debate students perform debate in the classroom, and these debates are shaped by various rules and expectations that offer aspiring advocates a rubric for "good" advocacy that is not easily aligned with the advocacy environment they will encounter outside the classroom. When arguing is an academic event, there are precise timelines, rules for turn-taking, and final voting decisions. Participants are taught to use high quality evidence, good reasoning, and thoughtful organization to refute and withstand their opponent's likely arguments. Real public issue debates almost never operate like this. However, we observe substantive public policy advocacy occurring throughout these real encounters. Various foundational elements of debate can be found in debates that do not resemble classroom debates and in forums that are nothing like classroom debates. A single letter to the editor may be part of a larger exchange of positions, even if it is only one person's perspective. A statement by the president of a city's teachers union on the evening news may constitute a position in a public policy dispute. A comment made by the White House Press Secretary during a press conference is almost always a fragment of a larger public policy debate.

We are not arguing there are no significant differences between academic debate and public policy advocacy; of course there are. We are arguing for a different standard for what constitutes "good" public policy advocacy, because the standards applied to classroom or tournament debate are insufficient to account for the wisdom and skills derived through practical engagement with public issues and controversies. For this reason, we advance the following principles to help aspiring advocates navigate the lessons of this book, and the advocacy they invent and encounter in the realm of public policy.

(1) Good public policy advocacy involves making arguments in public.
It may seem obvious, but the first condition of good public policy advocacy is that it involves making arguments in public. Countless people refuse to participate in public controversies, failing to share their personal experiences, knowledge, reasoning, and preferences when matters of significant

consequence to them are being debated. Beginning with our Preface, we make clear our goal to motivate and empower individuals to become public advocates. We view this as a process that begins with an appreciation for your existing knowledge of, and experience with, advocacy in everyday encounters and interactions, and builds on that experience to acclimate you to the unique characteristics, burdens, and complexities of argument in the context of public controversies. We encourage you to choose to act as a public advocate, cultivating your "argumentative agency," like when young Sharhonda Bossier chose to participate in a school walkout and later become part of the Black Lives Matter movement; and, this choice, we suspect, will likely amount to an exciting and formative experience, even if sometimes you are disappointed with the results.

(2) Good public policy advocacy is sustained.
Many advocates are frustrated when they find themselves up against entrenched opposition and wonder if they will ever achieve their policy goal. Often any sort of "victory" is achieved over a sustained advocacy effort; therefore, it is far more helpful to think of such advocacy instances as part of a larger *social controversy*. Kathryn Olson and Thomas Goodnight describe a social controversy's tendency to be "an *extended* rhetorical engagement."[23] Good public policy advocacy often requires you to be committed to a long view.

When you and a friend take up an argument about healthcare, for instance, consider the fact that you are entering a controversy that has been enduring for years. Calls for major reform of the U.S. healthcare system did not begin with Obamacare or Bernie Sanders. Progressives in the United States have advocated for some sort of national healthcare system since the early 20th century. Even still, when the Affordable Care Act of 2010 was signed into law, it was indeed a huge reform effort. However, few of its proponents would have claimed their policy goal had been completely achieved. Accepting that some policy goals will only be achieved incrementally is an important principle, because sustained public policy advocacy is often required before significant policy change is realized.

(3) Good public policy advocacy articulates a clear endpoint, a policy goal, that either changes the status quo or maintains it.
A proposed policy solution is the endpoint of public policy advocacy, the destination at which the advocate hopes to arrive. This means it is wise to identify the objective of your or another's advocacy (a policy goal) that exists under a more general position you take *for* or *against* reform of the status

quo. Once identified, this endpoint will have implications for every element of your advocacy. As an advocate, you seek to "take" your audience from its current position to a new "destination" by way of your skillful selection, arrangement, and delivery of arguments supported by thoughtful reasoning and high quality evidence. Importantly, identifying a policy goal begins with developing an understanding of the general controversy and its "sides," and which side you are on. Students of argumentation and debate are trained to develop a fairly worded and balanced *proposition* which one side affirms and the other side negates. In real public policy advocacy, rarely does anyone bother to clarify what the larger disagreement is about, preferring instead to advance only their preferences. Good public policy advocacy, however, derives from a single proposition with each side articulating their general position (for or against policy reform) and a more-specific policy goal as an endpoint of their advocacy (either a proposed solution or the maintenance of the status quo).

Because what two sides are arguing about is often unclear, good public policy advocacy clarifies what is unstated, allowing advocates on both sides of the debate to clearly articulate their policy goals and be held accountable for them. At first, you may not have the particulars of your advocacy determined, but it is clear there is a difference of opinion, or dispute, between you and another; and, this disagreement follows a basic formula: *someone wants a change, and someone doesn't.* People criticizing a current law may argue it is unfair for particular reasons. They may blog about how harmful it is and the advantages that would come from repealing it. Those defending the law might point to good things that have happened since the law went into effect. None of these arguments paint a clear picture of the proposition, but a general idea can be discerned with care. Proponents of repeal will likely have an additional specific policy goal that introduces another reform agenda they support, and they might outline the advantages of that policy goal. Opponents negating the proposition will likely defend the status quo and do so by outlining the disadvantages of repealing the law. Good public policy advocacy will clarify the fundamentally different policy goals of each side.

(4) Good public policy advocacy consists of, and demands, messages that fulfill argumentative burdens associated with an advocate's position.

Once you discern the contours of a public issue, or controversy, and determine which side you are on, you should identify the unique burdens you have when you seek to change the status quo with a proposal, or seek instead to defend the status quo. Good public policy advocacy understands these burdens as guidelines for developing messages, or the content that makes up your advocacy. These guidelines begin with *stock issues*, or standard matters of potential dispute, that advocates need to address—such as substantiating that there is a problem, a cause of that problem, a possible solution, and that advantages will accompany that solution (and related burdens for those defending the status quo)—as starting points in the practical planning advocates must do to craft their messages. Once you understand your burdens, you can construct appealing messages that can take on many characteristics.

(5) Good public policy advocacy consists of, and demands, well-reasoned messages.
After you have considered the stock issues related to your advocacy, we advise you to focus on limited and particular ways in which advocates reason when they are attempting to address societal problems and proposals for reform. In the context of a controversy or disagreement, good public policy advocacy typically involves quarreling over what does (or does not), or might (or might not), *cause* something to happen. We advise you to pose *critical questions* when you construct and encounter these claims of causality so you can build thoughtful and potent advocacy. We also expose you to other forms of reasoning you will encounter which may generate more thoughtful assessments of the problems advocates are attempting to solve. Like reasoning about cause, these forms of reasoning can be addressed through sets of simple critical questions, which we provide.

Good public policy advocacy also recognizes how some reasoning challenges might serve to distract advocates from, or cloud, what could otherwise be a thoughtful debate. Students of argumentation and debate are often taught to identify argumentative fallacies—instances where language, reasoning, or evidence attempt to misleadingly influence the conclusions advocates and their audiences draw. While you might do the same in public policy advocacy, it will only seldom help you. That is because public policy argument is awash in fallacies, whether arguers are attacking the source (calling Joe Biden a "socialist," for instance), or insisting public policy should not change because of tradition (arguing, "Our country never does that," for instance). If there were debate judges overseeing public policy controversies, fallacious appeals would be out of order, and only the most logical and sensible appeals would stand. Rather than count on the identification and correction of fallacies to function as some magical corrective, we advise you to focus your attention on whether an advocate's policy goal will actually improve conditions or prevent disadvantages not already occurring.

(6) Good public policy advocacy is supported by, and demands, high quality evidence.
Good public policy advocacy involves deep reflection on the quality of evidence offered in support of highly consequential claims. Similar to our advice to focus on causality and other ways of reasoning, we observe many occasions within public policy controversies that generate certain uses of, and disagreements over, the manner in which claims are supported with evidence. Evidence standing on its own can often point to the existence of a larger controversy, and thus be a clue to an evolving dispute that has consequences for you and your community. Understanding how evidence is practically used, misused, or underused will equip you to recognize and understand various ways audience opinions can be unduly influenced by adversaries that discredit, and distract from the strength of, evidence. Simultaneously, we seek to encourage you to engage your audiences with the best evidence available, so that you are not contributing to this problem. The subject of evidence is especially timely, as so many contemporary public issues involve challenges to public confidence in authorities, "gaslighting," and—particularly in the context of our source-specific consideration of the news media—the popular heft of the concept of "fake news."

(7) Good public policy advocacy benefits from an advocate's respect for, and understanding of, the concerns of a target audience.
A community experiences the effects of the status quo, and advocates belong to that community. As such, good public policy advocacy is crafted from and for the community, which is also the "target audience" for your advocacy. From that starting point, you must define your target audience and set reasonable advocacy goals. Inherent in this effort is the temptation to use information about your audience to craft messages that are motivated more by the desire to "win" than to develop (or maintain) effective solutions to societal problems. This ethical dilemma permeates the entire universe of an advocacy campaign, from beginning to end, but it is best addressed at the beginning when you are setting goals for what you might reasonably achieve with your advocacy based on an analysis of who is likely to care about the issue, how much they know about it, what opinions they might have formed about it already, and how close they are to agreeing with the outcome objectives of your advocacy.

Answers to these types of questions emerge from skillful issues analysis and the setting of reasonable goals for whom you might convince to support your position, and to what degree you might convince them. That analysis is often aided by techniques that give you a more precise profile of your target audience and assist you in crafting messages that appeal to them.

(8) Good public policy advocacy effectively navigates the limitations and opportunities of the advocacy setting, including the norms associated with settings.
Good public policy advocates reflect on, and dynamically consider, the way the advocacy setting affects the range of available advocacy strategies. In addition to being a physical setting, the context for your advocacy is a rhetorical situation. It is the product of your decisions to focus on an issue and make others aware of it. Norms associated with the advocacy setting are ubiquitous, offering limitations and opportunities, including opportunities to change the norms by pushing against them, whether your setting is a traditional in-person speech in which an audience is physically present or you are engaged in mediated advocacy.

In the next chapter we discuss determining the policy issue at the center of a controversy through an analytical process that locates advocacy under a policy proposition and assesses the main issues under consideration (stock issues). In Chapter 2, we will also discuss the utility of analyzing public discourse as an intellectual, critical endeavor.

Public Policy Advocacy as Political Communication

Since 2009, Suffolk County in New York has been operating a red light camera program, a program that photographs the license plates of drivers who run red lights. The cameras function as an automated law enforcement mechanism; photographs are taken and fines are assessed in the mail. Many receive such tickets for rolling right turns or for crossing an intersection just as, or seconds after, the red light appears. The Suffolk County program, like many similar red light programs nationwide, is widely unpopular. Proponents claim enforcement deters risky behavior and prevents accidents. Opponents claim sudden stops to avoid a ticket can be unnatural and unexpected by drivers behind those seeking to avoid a ticket, causing accidents that would otherwise not occur. Opponents also claim that safety claims by proponents are insincere, that the real motive is generating municipal revenue. According to a *Newsday* article from August, 2019, the cameras generated $20 million in revenue annually for Suffolk County.[24] As the county legislature communicates to defend the program, its detractors work to organize opposition. Consequently, the controversy provides a vivid illustration of the difference between government-generated policy communication and citizen-driven public policy advocacy.

Government policy communication is communication originating from government agents to constituents, and is often characterized by its support for the status quo, or for popular positions. Elected officials and their appointees are concerned with self-preservation and do not often perform the kind of coalition building that turns the tide on issues. Regarding the red light cameras, the Suffolk County government supports the status quo, and finds itself needing to justify the cameras to a public that is increasingly critical of the program. Government officials stress the cameras' value as a safety device. Jason Elan, a spokesperson for the Suffolk County Executive, explains, "We agree with the research, evidence and national safety experts that cite red-light cameras as an effective tool that enhances public safety and saves lives."[25] Elan references a study conducted by AAA evaluating the efficacy of red light camera laws throughout the state of New York. That study's results were mixed, however. While reducing traffic speed and collision-related fatalities, data also shows that the cameras may have contributed to an uptick in rear-end collisions at red lights.[26] The mixed results have helped enflame public opposition to the cameras.

Regardless of the noted benefits, public advocates—those engaging in public policy advocacy—argue that the cameras must be removed. As they do so, they work to build a critical mass of constituents that will eventually influence office holders, or support the replacement of such public officials. They cite several key reasons, the most prominent of which is the assertion that the tickets issued by the cameras function solely as a revenue generating mechanism for a cash-strapped county. Hector Gavilla, a Long Island real estate agent, has made the red light camera issue a centerpiece of two campaigns for the Suffolk County Legislature. In a 2019 letter to a local online newspaper *The Patch*, Gavilla explains, "The County spent $250,000 for a study of the red-light cameras. When the report proved accidents increased, they threw the report in the garbage and voted to extend this scam for five more years. The cameras generate $30 million in revenue."[27] The assertion that the report was thrown in the trash is hyperbole, but the suggestion that the fines are used to offset budget shortfalls is a plausible conclusion. Elsewhere, Gavilla adds that the cameras unfairly target low income neighborhoods.[28]

While government policy communication in this case seeks to maintain the system, the advocacy of opponents seeks to build a public that opposes the status quo. Given modern communication techniques and technology, a government unopposed by the public could likely maintain the status quo until it was unbearable. Consequently, citizen-driven public policy advocacy, in this case, is an essential mechanism that balances the power and influence of government.

Exercise: Considering Public Controversies as Arguments

Access the Internet and go to a major news media webpage. Consider the issues of the day and identify an issue that you care about personally. First, give the issue a creative name ("The trouble with Obamacare," "The warming earth," "Children on the border," for instance). Second, describe the problem as you understand it. For the people concerned, what's going wrong and why is it bad? Or, what existing program, policy, activity, or behavior is being questioned or criticized, and what are the consequences that, according to some, will follow efforts to change the way society addresses that program, policy, activity, or behavior? Third, assume the issue has at least two sides, and one is calling for a change, and the other is arguing that things should not be changed. What change is the first side calling for? Finally, identify some of the key players in the controversy. Give each side a name ("Proponents of [insert the change sought]" and "Opponents of [insert the change sought]") and describe some qualities of each (nations, political parties, community groups, labor unions, people who purchased a particular product, people who do not have health insurance, etc.).

Notes

1 " 'Stay Black and Die': One Woman Reflects on Her Path to Protesting Police Brutality," *The Daily* (podcast), August 5, 2020, https://www.nytimes.com/2020/08/05/podcasts/the-daily/protests-racism-police-brutality.html. Sharhonda Bossier was interviewed by *New York Times* reporter Caitlin Dickerson; *The Daily* host is Michael Barbaro.

2 Zimmerman, the neighborhood watch coordinator for the gated community where Martin was visiting his relatives, was acquitted of Martin's murder in 2013 after claiming self-defense.

3 There are many excellent sources to consult about Black Lives Matter. For a comprehensive history of the movement, see Christopher J. Lebron, *The Making of Black Lives Matter: A Brief History* (New York: Oxford University Press, 2017). For an excellent study of how Black Lives Matter and related movements have used online tools and the general capacity of such tools to facilitate social and political change, see Deen Freelon, Charlton D. McIlwain, and Meredith D. Clark, *Beyond the Hashtags: #Ferguson, #Blacklivesmatter, and the Online Struggle for Offline Justice*, a report of the Center for Media & Social Impact (American University's School of Communication), 2016, https://cmsimpact.org/wp-content/uploads/2016/03/beyond_the_hashtags_2016.pdf.

4 *Oxford English Dictionary*, s.v. "Orientation," https://www.lexico.com/en/definition/orientation.

5 John Milton, *Milton's Areopagitica* (London: Spottiswoode & Co., 1873), 65.

6 John Stewart Mill, *On Liberty* (Boston: Ticknor & Fields, 1863), 41.

7 *Abrams v. United States*, 250 U.S. 616 (1919).

8 Elisabeth Noelle-Neumann, *The Spiral of Silence: Public Opinion – Our Social Skin* (Chicago: University of Chicago Press, 1993).

9 David Helfert, *Political Communication in Action: From Theory to Practice* (Boulder: Lynne Rienner Publishers, 2018).

10 James Bohman, *Public Deliberation: Pluralism, Complexity, and Democracy* (Cambridge: MIT Press, 1996), 4.

11 Ibid., 59.

12 Ibid., 2.

13 Jurgen Habermas, *The Structural Transformation of the Public Sphere* (Cambridge: MIT Press, 1989).

14 Nancy Fraser, "Rethinking the Public Sphere: A Contribution to the Critique of Actually Existing Democracy," *Social Text*, no. 25/26 (1990), 56–80.

15 In addition to Fraser, "Rethinking the Public Sphere," see Robert Asen and Daniel C. Brouwer, eds., *Counterpublics and the State* (Albany: SUNY Press, 2001).

16 Randy Shilts, *And the Band Played On: Politics, People, and the AIDS Epidemic* (New York: St. Martin's Griffin, 2007), 596, 311.

17 "T&D Teach In," *Act Up NY*, https://actupny.org/documents/T&DTI.html.

18 Peter Staley, interview by Sarah Schulman, Act Up Oral History Project, December 9, 2006, transcript, http://www.actuporalhistory.org/interviews/images/staley.pdf. To learn more about Peter Staley, see *How to Survive a Plague*, directed by David France (2012; New York, NY, Public Square Films), https://surviveaplague.com/.

19 For more on the legacy of ACT UP in terms of expanded access, see Marie-Amélie George, "The Fight Against AIDS Has Shaped How Potential Covid-19 Drugs Will Reach Patients," *Washington Post*, April 29, 2020, https://www.washingtonpost.com/outlook/2020/04/29/fight-against-aids-has-shaped-how-potential-covid-19-drugs-will-reach-patients/.

20 Martha Cooper, *Analyzing Public Discourse* (Long Grove, IL: Waveland Press, Inc., 1989), 50.

21 David Zarefsky, "Forward: Speech and Debate as Civic Education: Challenges and Opportunities," in *Speech and Debate as Civic Education*, eds. J. Michael Hogan, Jessica A. Kurr, Michael J. Bergmaier, and Jeremy D. Johnson (University Park, PA: The Pennsylvania State University Press, 2017), xii (italics in original).

22 G. Thomas Goodnight, "The Personal, Technical, and Public Spheres of Argument: A Speculative Inquiry into the Art of Public Deliberation," *Journal of the American Forensic Association* 18, no. 4 (1982), 214.

23 Kathryn M. Olson and G. Thomas Goodnight, "Entanglements of Consumption, Cruelty, Privacy, and Fashion: The Social Controversy Over Fur," *Quarterly Journal of Speech* 80, no. 3 (1994), 249 (emphasis added).

24 Rachel Blidner, "Suffolk Panel Passes Red-Light Cameras, But Balks at Recommendation for Legislature," *Newsday*, August 29, 2019, https://www.newsday.com/long-island/politics/red-light-cameras-suffolk-1.35622821.

25 Ibid.

26 Marla Diamond, "Red Light Camera Programs in NY Show Mixed Results," WCBS Newsradio 880, November 19, 2019, https://wcbs880.radio.com/articles/news/red-light-camera-programs-ny-show-mixed-results. A similar study was conducted in Chicago on that city's red-light camera program by the *Chicago Tribune*, with similar results (see David Kidwell and Alex Richards, "Tribune Study: Chicago Red Light Cameras Provide Few Safety Benefits," *Chicago Tribune*, December 19, 2014, https://www.chicagotribune.com/suburbs/lake-county-news-sun/ct-red-light-camera-safety-met-20141219-story.html). Several public officials in Illinois have been investigated for accepting bribes for their support of red light cameras within the state and Illinois municipalities (see Jon Seidel, Robert Herguth, and Mitch Dudek, "Ex-Sen. Martin Sandoval Said He Was Going 'balls to the walls' for Red-light Camera Company for Thousands in Bribes: Feds," *Chicago Sun-Times*, January 28, 2020, https://chicago.suntimes.com/crime/2020/1/28/21111932/state-senator-martin-sandoval-red-light-camera-bribery-charge; and Joe Mahr, "South Suburban Mayor Charged in Red-light Camera Bribery Scheme," *Chicago Tribune*, August 7, 2020, https://www.chicagotribune.com/news/breaking/ct-crestwood-mayor-presta-federal-corruption-charges-red-light-cameras-20200807-lemzwqtdfngqzh75j5h6c6dv74-story.html).

27 Michael DeSantis, "Letter to the Editor: Hector Gavilla Responds to Susan Berland," *Patch*, Half Hollow Hills, NY Patch, October 16, 2019, https://patch.com/new-york/half-hollowhills/letter-editor-hector-gavilla-responds-susan-berland.

28 David Luces, "Suffolk Legislature Votes to Extend Red-Light Camera Program," *TBR News Media*, September 5, 2019, http://tbrnewsmedia.com/tag/red-light-camera-program/.

2

ANALYZING ISSUES AND POLICY PROPOSITIONS

Takeaways

(1) An *analytical process* is needed to help you identify the policy issue at the center of the controversy, where you stand in relation to that controversy (which "side" you are on and any policy goals you may have), and the issues addressed by your advocacy.

(2) It is helpful to that process to understand the way academic debaters locate their advocacy under a *policy proposition*—a statement that announces a general preference for a change that invites debate—and assess *stock issues*—what is the alleged significance of a problem, the alleged cause of a problem, the proposed solution to the problem, and the alleged beneficial outcomes of the proposed solution?

(3) Once you locate your advocacy within the controversy, you will be able to better follow the intention and significance of information that is part of the ongoing controversy.

(4) These analytical tools can also help you analyze public discourse with the intention of producing scholarly analyses.

The way many people engage in public policy advocacy is generally reactive. They may encounter an assertion they disagree with, and counter it. Or, they may learn some bit of information and feel compelled to share it with others. Understanding how such information contributes to the controversy helps you know "where" you are in a public policy controversy, which is crucial to understanding the purpose of your advocacy and determining your advocacy goals.

In this chapter, we focus on (a) deciphering the policy issue being debated and (b) encouraging you to determine where you stand on that issue (which "side" you are on). As an aspiring advocate, it is important for you to define the boundaries of a controversy and delineate what is and what is not germane to the public policy controversy. In traditional academic debate settings, debaters kick off (and in many ways simplify) this *analytical process* through the development of a *policy proposition* that announces a general preference for reform and allows for clear distinctions between sides. Advocates for the proposition (the affirmative side) typically introduce a specific plan and assert that their plan will result in advantages; those against the proposition (the negative side) typically introduce reasons why the affirmative side's plan will have undesirable consequences—or disadvantages—and introduce challenges, such as whether the affirmative side has assessed the problem correctly, whether there are factors in the status quo that will prevent the affirmative's plan from working, and so on. In some circumstances, determining the policy issue at the center of a controversy and which side you prefer may not require as much analysis. Advocates may be very clear about their end goals and explain in detail how they think their plans improve matters. It may be as simple as considering the consequences of proposals to determine what the general proposition is, and whether you are *for* it or *against* it.

We have already noted several differences between public policy advocacy and academic debate. A debate in a classroom or at an intercollegiate debate tournament is an event with a clear beginning and end; one side wins and the other loses. Public policy advocacy is an ongoing phenomenon, as many issues take considerable time to resolve—if they are ever resolved. Across the span of the time the public devotes to the on-again, off-again engagement of an issue, the contributions of discussions here or there can be ambiguous. Astute observers recognize that different people and organizations arrange themselves around reform proposals, calls to change the status quo, in response to alleged problems—or policy propositions. While propositions often go unstated, the exercise of identifying them, and understanding the positions taken by others in relation to them, is an essential starting point to strategizing and developing your advocacy.

In this chapter, our main goal is to help you navigate these constructive goals by instructing you to determine the policy issue at the center of a controversy and establish a clear sense of what positions you wish to take in relation to that issue and any existing proposals. Determining the policy issue at the center of a real-world controversy and establishing a position within that real realm requires analysis. The starting point of that analysis, we contend, should be a one-sentence summary of the central policy issue that is structured like a traditional proposition in the realm of academic policy debate (an affirmative assertion that some agent of change should engage in some action which would alter the status quo). Finding the locus of the central disagreement, or the proposition, is only the first step. Continuing with our spatial metaphor, knowing *where you are* requires a point of reference. To this end, we also begin our consideration of policy *stock issues*. Stock issues can help you locate more precisely where you are within a public controversy while you are engaging in advocacy. At any point in your discussions and debates with others, *are you disputing the significance of a problem? Are you reasoning about the cause of a societal problem? Are you maintaining that someone's proposal is unworkable?* If you do not know *where you are* when you argue, you risk losing focus on what you seek to accomplish.

We also hope to inspire you to appreciate the usefulness of understanding and critically engaging claims made in the context of a public policy controversy even if you don't choose to enter the controversy as an advocate. Determining the proposition and stock issues also forms an analytical protocol to aid you in identifying the fundamental disagreement and where you (and/or others) stand on issues of your historical era, how society is addressing those issues, and—in the spirit of all great intellectual endeavors—*why*. We will get to this loftier goal later in this chapter; for now, let's begin by learning about policy propositions.

Policy Propositions

Policy propositions are affirmative assertions that *some agent of change should engage in some action which would alter the status quo.*

"[Agent of change] should [engage in some action which will alter the status quo]."

Typically, in public policy advocacy, the agent of change is an entity with the power to enact and enforce the change across the broadest range of human and organizational activity. This is most often, but not always, a governmental body (local, state, national, or international). Most argumentation and debate textbooks compare policy propositions with fact and value propositions, noting how they operate within the same controversy. "Typically," writes Martha Cooper, "the possible points of issue in controversies about public issues" concern all three: "What is and how do we define it?"—fact; "Of what value or importance is it?"—value; and "What course of action should we take toward it?"—policy.[1] We proceed assuming that recognition of policy objectives is an essential starting point to your emergence as a public policy advocate, but we also believe it is important to expect that you might encounter factual claims ("Vaping causes users to become addicted to nicotine," for instance), or value claims ("It is wrong for vaping product manufacturers to target adolescents in marketing vaping products," for instance) as fragments of those larger policy objectives. In actual practice, neither the most skilled nor newly initiated advocates tend to make explicit the policy propositions that give rise to their advocacy. This lack of propositional clarity is particularly evident in public controversies that consist of numerous episodes of argument—as most public policy controversies do.

Consider, for instance, a member of Congress pointing to a heinous crime in a major city committed by someone they call an "illegal immigrant." The claim itself likely functions to reinforce the perception that either a disproportionate amount of crime is committed by persons who have entered, live in, or work in the United States without proper authorization or that such persons are prone to particularly violent acts. The audience to the claim misses a much more important point, however, if they fail to notice that the member of Congress is asserting this point in the context of a larger controversy about the merits of other policy goals, such as a southern border wall and other impediments to make border crossing more challenging. During his presidency, Donald Trump advocated for a border wall as a means of reducing or largely eliminating unlawful crossings along the United States' southern border and the consequences of such crossings (crimes committed by those persons who make it across the border, deaths due to drugs smuggled across the border, and more). The member of Congress in this example would be contributing to the former president's advocacy, arguing both that the problem is significant and that the cause is known. As a consumer of this advocacy, your ability to tie this episode of argument to the unstated policy proposition under which it belongs would be very useful.

Without determining the proposition, advocates risk failing to fully iden-tify and evaluate their argumentative burdens and points they might wish to make. Imagine yourself reading a blog post that you relate to the topic of global warming. You might conclude a blogger is arguing about global warm-ing, but *what* about global warming? *Is the planet warming? Is global warming part of a natural cycle? Is global warming caused by humans? Is global warming bad? Can global warming be prevented? Are the benefits of preventing or reversing global warming outweighed by the costs?* After some analysis, you might determine that the blog's author is claiming that,

> The U.S. federal government should significantly limit the production of greenhouse gases.

This proposition is a clear expression that allows you to determine where your beliefs lie in relation to it, and what evidence and reasoning issues may arise as this proposition is debated.

Textbooks on argumentation and debate outline rules for developing formal propositions for academic debate, which we believe are also helpful to aspiring advocates outside of the classroom. These rules are helpful for academic debaters because they make certain that opposing sides are being treated fairly before the debate even begins, by ensuring there is fair ground for everyone to argue and that neither side is left arguing for or against some-thing absurd. We are confident much of the confusion this academic process prevents can also be of practical use to you as you seek to determine where your advocacy fits within a real controversy. This is because good public policy advocacy emerges from a thoughtful identification of the general controversy, the side you are on, and your policy goal. If, at first, you have not determined the particulars of your advocacy, you might start by recognizing there is a dif-ference of opinion, or dispute, between you and another, and it follows a basic formula: *someone wants a change, and someone doesn't.*

A Brief Word on "Sides" and Responsibilities in Advocacy

Before we outline some of the traditional requirements of propositions, and get too far into the analysis of public controversies, we want to devote some space to the notion of "sides" and the responsibilities we believe come when you "take a side." It might be that, as you read this, your side is being assigned to you in an argumentation and debate class. It might be that you are reading this book because you have an already-established position on a public issue, and you wish to build your message from that point. It might be that you are not sure where you stand on a range of public issues and want to improve your ability to consume information about problems and controversies you're learning about.

Whatever your reason, determining which side you are on might appear to work against constructive dialogue and open-minded analysis of public discourse, a dilemma about which we have this to say: we are strong believers in the effectiveness of academic speech and debate training, which places students in repetitive hypothetical conflict and competition, often requiring them to debate both sides of an issue as a means of developing their capacity to invent and deliver messages and contend with opposition. Through that experience *we* learned how to debate and have applied those skills to a variety of disagreements and problems we have encountered in our careers and public lives. As educators and practitioners, however, we also recognize the limits of adversarial communication and the potential for dialog that encourages participants to abandon their attachment to a side in order to consider common goals within a community and avoid the pitfalls of what Deborah Tannen has termed, "the Argument Culture."[2] Tannen, Josina M. Makau, Debian L. Marty, and others have offered students and practitioners of advocacy frameworks for what is often referred to as "cooperative argumentation."[3] In particular, while acknowledging the success of teaching programs wherein students "are taught to select a disputed topic and develop 'cases' for 'both' sides," Makau and Marty warn that "adversarialism in the classroom" points students away from "exploring a multiplicity of perspectives required for understanding and resolving complex issues responsibly and wisely."[4]

We welcome such emphasis on advocacy that responsibly addresses the problems faced by communities through consensus-seeking dialogue and deliberation. Contemplation of traditions of coaching and administering academic speech and debate programs have produced reform agendas and initiatives that take Makau and Marty's concerns seriously.[5] By no means do we wish to discourage you from entering into constructive dialogue with others to determine if there are areas of mutual agreement and consensus which might lead to an outcome that is satisfactory to people with varying perspectives. We have incorporated into our classrooms and advocacy practices (within organizational development and movement realms, particularly) cooperative approaches, and hope that our readers will as well, as they build their capacity to responsibly respond to disagreement and controversy.[6] *Our goal at this point in the book, however, is to help you determine where you stand because that action, as far as we are concerned, is a highly effective first step in developing your advocacy—what you plan to say.* Moreover, you may have little choice in the matter of whether a controversy can be addressed through more cooperative and collaborative problem solving frameworks, as those who oppose your position may be unwilling to enter into dialogue with you. For these reasons, we will continue with guidance designed to help you thoughtfully identify the general controversy, the side you are on, and your policy goal.

Four Requirements of a Proposition

Advice given to students within argumentation and debate textbooks on how to develop propositions can commence a process of analyzing issues that interest you. Students are advised to develop a one-sentence proposition, about one issue, using unbiased language, that advocates a change in policy within the current system.

We recommend that you consider each requirement from the standpoint of "invention." Invention is one of what Roman orator Cicero termed the "canons of rhetoric." The canons—including also delivery, organization, memory, and style—were developed to improve advocates' persuasive faculties. Cicero defined invention as the "discovery of valid or seemingly valid arguments to render one's cause probable."[7] You should therefore consider the requirements of a proposition for ways each helps you think more clearly about the controversy you are engaging and what you plan to say about it. Determining the policy proposition thus works as an analytical process that helps you address questions such as: *What exactly is it that you want to achieve with your advocacy? For what exactly are others advocating? Does this evidence really help your case? Does arguing a point really advance your side of a dispute?* The proposition acts as an anchor point, from which you can make more reasoned determinations about these and many other points.

(1) A proposition is a complete sentence.
Ideally, a proposition encapsulates a whole thought within a complete sentence. The central issues of a public controversy and an indication of the endpoint of advocacy are captured in this single sentence. When you cannot craft a single sentence, it is often a sign that your thinking is not yet clear on the matter or that you are blending arguments about two or more related topics that do not fall within the parameters of a single proposition. The sentence will typically include an agent of change as the subject, followed by

the verb "should," followed by some general description of a policy direction that differs from the status quo (for instance: "The U.S. federal government should deploy the Illinois National Guard to assist with law enforcement in Chicago.").

We often find that students who require two or more sentences to describe a proposition are simply moving beyond a general description of desired reform into a more-specific plan for reform, or are prematurely affixing to their proposition a reason to favor their position. This is how lines begin to blur between a general statement that *invites* debate or discussion to one that *debates* and *discusses*. For instance, if you followed the above proposition with "in order to protect communities from looters and avoid the collapse of law and order," you'd be well into laying out a more-defined plan and its advantages.

(2) A proposition is about one policy issue.

A policy proposition encapsulates a public issue. Martha Cooper defines an "issue" generally as "a contemporary situation with a likelihood of disagreement," and "public issue" as "a situation with a likelihood of controversy that arises from our sense of ourselves as members of a community, that affects the community's interest, or requires community involvement."[8] While there may be many reasons for public policy disagreements, opposing sides typically disagree about a single larger matter. "The State of New York should ban religious exemptions for vaccines" is a proposition about one policy issue. Advocates supporting (or affirming) the proposition may have plenty of reasons for calling for such an action and several specific policy scenarios; those opposing (or negating) the proposition, on the other hand, may oppose every possible action that reasonably fits under this call for action. Statements made by advocates on either side amount to either support *for* or *against* a proposed action. For the purposes of public policy advocacy, the knowledge that a proposition focuses on one policy issue is most helpful when determining the single larger matter of disagreement, or controversy, within a community.

In your effort to narrow down the dispute to one single matter of disagreement, you may find yourself grappling with multiple issues. Consider the following proposition: "The U.S. federal government should adopt policies that reduce the use of carbon fuels and encourage innovation in green energy solutions." Instead of one thought, this proposition includes *two* disputable points, and, as such, is poorly conceived. You can *agree* that carbon fuels should be reduced but *disagree* that green energy solutions should be "encouraged." Because you disagree with one point, you technically disagree with the proposition, *but do you?* Maybe you support green energy solutions but believe they should be mandatory, not merely "encouraged" (to illustrate further, consider the public issue of mask wearing to protect against the spread of COVID-19, and how disagreement over encouraging vs. mandating figures in that controversy). Such an attitude would put you squarely in support of a proposition requiring reductions in carbon emissions, but not in support of policies that merely encourage green energy innovation. Proceeding from the assumption that a public policy controversy centers around one policy issue suggests to us that advocacy for green energy solutions probably functions as a sub-argument in the larger public controversy encapsulated by the following proposition: "The U.S. federal government should adopt policies that reduce the use of carbon fuels."

(3) A proposition is a proposal to change the status quo.

For the sake of clarity and developing the ability to craft effective messages, we believe it is useful for you to assume that *all public policy propositions should call for a change in the status quo.* This assumption provides for clear and reliable division of responsibilities for which advocates can prepare and makes identifying the proposition for the purposes of such preparation much easier. To understand this assumption better, think of the status quo in the context of a courtroom. Just as the accused person in court is presumed innocent until proven guilty, the status quo too is considered sufficient until a compelling argument can be made to change it. Like a courtroom's prosecutor, affirmative advocates must explain what is *wrong* with the status quo. This is often referred to as the "burden of proof" or "burden of evidence." For instance, Americans presently live in an economy that relies heavily on energy derived from fossil fuels. Fossil fuel consumption and its accompanying disadvantages (pollution, depletion of natural resources, damage to land and water quality, etc.) are mostly acceptable within communities across the United States. If you support laws designed to reduce carbon emissions resulting from fossil fuels, for instance, you would be proposing a change to the status quo. You would have the burden of proving that the status quo causes a significant problem, one worth solving. Using this example, an ideal proposition might be:

> The U.S. federal government should enact laws that mandate the reduction of fossil fuel use in America.

This proposition clearly calls for a change in the status quo. A proposition that fails to call for a change in the status quo ("The U.S. federal government *should adopt no additional laws* that mandate the reduction of fossil fuel use in America," for example) makes less sense as an initiation point for advocacy. Advocates supporting such a proposition have no reason to call for or support any new action, as the status quo already favors their position. Returning to the courthouse situation, a proposition supporting the status quo would be the equivalent of an unaccused person appearing in court to plead their inno-cence when, in fact, they have not been charged with any wrongdoing.

(4) A proposition provides room for both sides to argue.
The proposition is *not* a persuasive appeal used to influence how audiences feel about one or the other side of the policy issue; it is an instrument that helps advocates better understand the nature of the disagreement. An effort to explain the controversy in a neutral way will require you to transcend the controversy, to try to remove yourself from the controversy and think of it in an unbiased way. Transcending the controversy means being mindful of the fact that the language and terminology you use in a public controversy may reflect bias, intentional or not, toward your own points of view. Attempts to neutrally describe a controversy in a proposition usually involve learning enough about the public issue to select terminology that is not inherently evocative of support for one side or the other. Much attention of late has been given to terminology used by opponents of reform that would grant pathways to citizenship to persons who have entered, live in, or work in the United States without proper authorization.[9] Propositions that refer to such persons as "illegal aliens," "criminal aliens," or references to such persons' "unlawful" or "criminal" presence, might be viewed by proponents of citizenship pathways as an unbalanced wording of a controversy under which they would struggle to craft proposals interpreted as reasonable (imagine, for instance, the unfairness of the proposition, "The U.S. federal government should enact legislation to substantially increase the number of criminal aliens granted U.S. citizenship").

Others may launch into advocacy when the task is intended to be limited to constructing an accurate and fairly worded assessment of the controversy. An example of a proposition that overreaches might be something like, "The State of New York should repeal bail reform legislation that prevents judges from protecting our communities from criminals." While those seeking the repeal of bail reform may be right that some people released before trial may recommit crimes, that assertion has no place in the proposition. Instead, it belongs in the body of the advocacy supporting the proposition. An easy way to check for this form of proposition overreach is to look for conjunctions such as "because," "that," "so that," or similar. If this type of extended explanation is present, there is likely overreach.

Locating Your Place in the Controversy

During a controversy over a proposal to change the status quo, many arguments pertaining to an unstated proposition may arise. Consequently, untrained advocates may, as it is said, fail to "see the forest for the trees." Recognizing a controversy and understanding precisely where sides oppose each other allow you to understand where *you* are entering the controversy, as well as the implications of your advocacy on the larger proposition. This allows you to answer the question, *What is my contribution to this controversy?*

The controversy over national infrastructure helps us illustrate these points. Infrastructure is a term used to refer to all the built elements of our environment we take for granted while going about our daily lives. These elements include roads, bridges, water treatment and supply systems, sewers, pipelines, and more. Much of the infrastructure across the United States is aged, not having been replaced since it was originally built decades ago. Because of the risk of catastrophic failure of these assets, infrastructure became an issue in both the 2016 and 2020 presidential races. People researching this topic will find public essays, op-eds, blogs, and press releases from politicians and think tanks, among other sources, discussing whether there is a need, how pressing the need is, who has the responsibility to fund maintenance, where the funding will come from, how quickly it should be done, and whether some public assets should be privatized. If you read any one piece in isolation from the others or without a firm grasp of the proposition, you may not understand how the information or opinion expressed in an individual news item or opinion column matters to the larger controversy. For instance, if it is a fact that interstate bridges are at risk of collapsing, then there is reason to act to fix or replace such bridges. The assertion that local bridges might soon collapse (perhaps in an opinion column, blog, or section of a candidate's stump speech) has implications for the larger controversy. After substantial consideration of these matters, you would likely determine that the proposition is something like the following: "The U.S. federal government should upgrade national infrastructure."

Looking at a specific instance that focuses on a different issue, we consider *The New York Times* op-ed piece from April 21, 2020, by Daniel Markovits. In this piece, Markovits clearly advocates for a robust response by the U.S. federal government to the COVID-19 health crisis. But, as you read further and consider his argument, and its timing, you can discern that solutions for the larger problem that concerns him have already been written and adopted. He notes that three COVID-19 relief packages had been passed; what remains, argues Markovits, is a viable source of funding for those relief plans. Markovits' answer: a wealth tax: "[a] 5 percent tax on the richest 5 percent of households could thus raise up to $2 trillion."[10] In the absence of his proposed solution, he points out, the only plans the government has for funding these packages is to borrow the money. Considered one way, you can conclude that he is affirming the following proposition: "The U.S. federal government should provide relief to people suffering from COVID-19." In that larger controversy, you might conclude he is calling for more funding, and believes it is possible through funds raised with a wealth tax. Considered another way, in light of the fact that relief legislation was already enacted and funded by loans prior to *The New York Times'* publication of Markovits' op-ed (meaning, the programs and funds resulting from the legislation make up part of the status quo), you might conclude that Markovits is advocating his own proposition or change to the system: "The U.S. federal government should adopt a wealth tax." Considering the proposition this way, you can understand that one advantage of a wealth tax, according to Markovits, will be to provide the needed funds to respond to the COVID-19 pandemic. By performing this analysis, you gain a clearer idea of what the policy issue is, and on what side of that issue you find yourself and other members of your community. *Would you support a wealth tax to fund a national response to an unexpected and devastating public health crisis?*

Specific Locations Within the Controversy: Stock Issues

Daniel Markovits' op-ed piece allows us to illustrate what we mean by locating your place in a public policy controversy. While the proposition tells you what a general controversy is about, the stock issues of policy enable you to find specific locations within that controversy—where smaller disagreements often reside—and permit you to determine your personal interests in the controversy. In Chapter 3, we discuss the stock issues at length. We introduce them here as instruments for locating your place within a controversy. Stock issues are just that—"stock," generic, or typical arguments that emerge within public policy disputes. They are:

(a) **Problem**: An assertion that a problem within the status quo is significant enough to warrant change.

(b) **Cause**: An assertion that a cause has been identified, and/or that the status quo is incapable of fixing the problem without a change.

(c) **Solution**: A policy proposal, or specific policy goal, describing what actions will remedy the problem.

(d) **Advantages**: Assertions about the beneficial outcomes of the solution's adoption.

As we have noted, the order in which these points emerge in the material you are consuming may vary, but we present them in this order to illustrate the persuasive logic of first generating a desire for a remedy (problem) and then presenting the remedy (solution). Relying on this order as a public policy advocacy template of sorts can help you pinpoint where advocates are in the controversy—how a specific argument contributes to the larger public issue.

Using the stock issues, we can identify the location and function of Markovits' op-ed within the larger controversy over what the U.S. federal government should do to respond to the COVID-19 health crisis. As you consider Markovits' advocacy, you can determine that he is not disagreeing with the problem cited by most advocates of a robust relief plan (that COVID-19 poses a serious threat to public health and the stability of the U.S. economy). Instead, because of this analysis, you can recognize that he is critical of the mechanism for funding the proposed solution (borrowing the money), which leads him to offer another proposal, another means of generating funds to cover the cost of COVID-19 relief packages. Because the relief plans have already become law, Markovits' new proposal would result in the configuration of a new set of stock issues (in which the problem is the effects of borrowing trillions of dollars; the cause is the borrowing; the solution is the wealth tax; and the advantages flow from not having to pay back the borrowed funding—for generations).

Determining the policy issue and constructing a proposition, and your perceptive observance of dispute along any one of the stock issues, begins an analytical process that leads to a holistic understanding of a controversy, and where your advocacy and the advocacy of others fits within that controversy. Locating your advocacy is an important step in the emergence of advocates. In much the same way that a math problem or proof proceeds in stages, and flaws early on hinder the completion of an accurate outcome, it is important to form a clear view of the public issue, or controversy, determine which side you are on, and develop a sense of how your advocacy contributes to the controversy.

Analyzing Public Issues and Controversy

In addition to helping you determine what to argue, analyzing public issues can be performed as an act of intellectual engagement. That intellectual engagement, moreover, can have far-reaching impacts on your life and your community. If you are reading this book as part of a college course, you may encounter professors using terms and phrases to describe such endeavors, including "analyzing public discourse," "rhetorical criticism," "criticism," and more. Here we will briefly address such analytical pursuits because we have found that some students' interests in the skills of debate appropriately cross over to an interest in critical analysis of public policy advocacy. As a paleontologist may reconstruct a likeness of a long-extinct animal from just one tooth, as they have done with the megalodon, a keen observer of public policy advocacy can often envision the entire contour of a public policy controversy from a single news story, meme, speech, advertisement, or advocacy mailer. And, as they do so, they may find themselves drawn into an intellectual engagement with a controversy that increases understanding and appreciation of matters such as: what advocates are asking the public to support; where public agreement or consensus starts and stops; what significance might be made of this moment in history; and whether any of the arguments being made illustrate something interesting about how argument occurs, how disputes are addressed, how norms and values within a community change over time; etc.

Argumentation and debate educators have long sought to not just assist students in the development of effective communication skills, but also to generate and share knowledge about how humans use argumentation to address social problems.[11] In addition to being practitioners, teachers, and coaches, many speech and debate educators—like us—also study how disputes within the public sphere are settled or extended through communication. We engage in this activity not necessarily because we have a particular side in a controversy (although we may have), but because we are keenly interested in messages that express perspectives and positions, the sources of those messages, and the audiences and settings those messages impact. As teachers of argumentation and debate, we have also found this particular mix of practical, strategic analysis and critical contemplation is an excellent opportunity to maintain the interest of students who struggle to join the advocacy fray, but nevertheless find social controversy fascinating.

Analyzing Public Discourse

The analytical processes that are central to inventing compelling public policy advocacy are also ideal starting points for the analysis of public controversies. In her text, *Analyzing Public Discourse*, Martha Cooper provides an analytical framework for the study of controversies playing out in the public sphere.[12] Cooper seeks to blend her readers' interests in analysis *and* activism, attempting to "integrate the critical tools common to the study of argument and rhetorical criticism with the political perspective common in the study of public opinion and free speech."[13] Her project encourages the study of controversies (over single moments of public address, or speeches), which invites analyses of disputes, including contemporary public issues that interest analysts. Importantly, and a point she makes clear, her approach "explores public discourse from the audience's point of view," which aligns more accurately with "a far more typical role for most people."[14]

Cooper's hope to encourage more critical engagement of controversies is regularly realized within the discipline of Communication Studies, particularly among a community of rhetorical critics who have focused on controversies.[15] Seasoned critic of public argument Robert P. Newman writes that projects that study public controversies "usually come about when someone begins to wonder, 'Now why in the world did *that* happen?'"[16] That certainly may be enough of a spark to light a fire; it has been for us a time or two. Especially interesting to us have been controversies animated by the demands of marginalized communities whose advocacy strategies are determined to a significant extent by advocates' lack of access to "prominent channels of political discourse and a corresponding lack of political power," what have become known in the discipline of Communication Studies as "counterpublics."[17] Many of the contemporary controversies involving citizen-driven public policy advocacy involve advocates we would consider to be counterpublics, including many social justice movements that are of contemporary interest to many aspiring advocates (LGBT activists, advocates of bail and prison reform, communities protesting deportations, and the Movement for Black Lives are some examples of counterpublics).

Many studies of controversies are driven by critics' intense personal connection to the subjects of disputes, the people and organizations under examination, and/or the communities in which disputes play out. As such, if you are interested in the analysis of public discourse pertaining to such controversies, you need not abandon your desire to be an agent of change to perform such analyses. You will not be asked to turn in your "activist badge" if you are seeking to *study* a controversy. This is especially true of situations in which you might actually be a participant at some level in the controversy (although there might come a time when a more objective stance is helpful in assessing certain aspects of a public issue). Such personal participation may be due to your direct involvement in a policy issue (you are on one side of an issue); or it may be due to your belief that some level of participant-observation is needed to understand the events you are studying. Indeed, several who study public discourse have approached their engagement with controversies "ethnographically," utilizing close observation, interviews of individuals and groups, and— along the way—gaining access to materials and information that they can only get "in the field."[18] Sara L. McKinnon, Robert Asen, Karma R. Chavez, and Robert Glenn Howard make a strong case for approaches of this kind in their introduction to *Text+Field: Innovations in Rhetorical Method*, a collection of essays by researchers who use fieldwork in concert with other methods of analysis.[19] Noting the challenge of examining "the rhetorics of marginalized and excluded groups," in particular, they describe the usefulness of interviewing and focus groups to "engage otherwise inaccessible texts, like local, marginal, and/or vernacular discourses."[20]

Debate's Outward Turn: Forensics as Scholarship

Speech and debate educators continue to contemplate a vibrant future for their subject, including how such training can serve as a driver of civic engagement.[21] For many generations, participants in speech and debate activities have found themselves engaged in the analysis of public discourse as a result of becoming intensely interested in a public issue they are debating in an academic setting (or perhaps the subject of a competitive speech they have written and are performing), and that interest pulls their attention outward toward the external practical political world where people and organizations are actively considering related public issues. This is often fertile ground for the development of a scholarly interest. Gordon Mitchell (who we featured briefly in the Preface) believes more needs to be done to inspire argumentation and debate students to engage in actual advocacy.[22] Part of his project is to get students into the field where advocacy is really happening. But, another part of his project is to encourage debaters to perform primary research that allows them to "reconfigure themselves as producers of knowledge, rather than passive consumers of it," what he refers to as "action research."[23] This could include, among other modes of research, such things as "contact[ing] social movements, government officers, and citizens involved in the controversy for their viewpoints on the debate," and "interaction ... that enables academic debaters to learn from people living in impacted communities."[24]

Collaboration between teachers and students toward the deeper analysis of public issues would advance the cause of what Mitchell and G. Thomas Goodnight also refer to as "forensics as scholarship."[25] In light of several significant advancements in the use of digital technology by intercollegiate competitive debaters, the two consider the potential for "academic debate as a vehicle to transport the theory and practice of argumentation to wider society."[26] They envision "bottom-up publication" of information and peer reviewed scholarship across multiple media platforms that are accessible to a wide range of stakeholders.[27] Mitchell and Goodnight's debater/scholar can essentially commence an examination of the controversy, beginning an analytical process like what we have described as the work of the analyst or critic. Debaters can enter the realm of the actual controversy, prompting their consideration of policy alternatives supported by existing knowledge. They might then gain access to influential thinkers and decision makers as they join organizations and interact with others over various platforms for the exchange of information, ideas, and opinions.

In the next chapter, the beginning of Part II of the book, we shift our attention to the process of building thoughtful and effective advocacy in pursuit of good public policy. The movement into arguing involves an expanded consideration of stock issues and clearer delineation of affirmative and negative advocacy.

The Case for Association Health Plans

Using what we know about propositions and stock issues, we are equipped to provide a unique analysis of the public debate surrounding the Affordable Care Act (ACA), or what is popularly known as "Obamacare."

After a lengthy public debate, the ACA became law in 2010. Those advocating for the law's adoption conceived of it to solve problems caused by a lack of affordable healthcare coverage. Few denied the existence of a problem. Instead, more clash centered around the cause and the solution. Pinning the cause on the insurance industry's greed, Democrats argued that government's failure to properly regulate the insurance industry caused the problem. Meanwhile, Republicans countered that government regulation was the cause. Consistent with the cause as they considered it, Democrats took advantage of their control of Congress and the White House and proposed several key regulations they believed would decrease the number of uninsured people.

The solution that became the ACA involves numerous working parts. First, it requires everyone to purchase health insurance. This reduces and stabilizes health insurance rates by requiring people less likely to make insurance claims (younger and healthier people) to pay for coverage. Second, it standardizes coverage, detailing a list of essential health benefits that must be provided by qualifying insurance plans, and requiring all American taxpayers to purchase "minimum essential coverage" or face a penalty when they file their income taxes. Third, it provides subsidies to those who need them to afford the coverage while expanding Medicaid to cover those who can't afford it at all. Finally, it guarantees that nobody will be denied coverage and that everyone, regardless of health history, will qualify for the same low-cost premiums (the amount paid monthly for health insurance). Minus any one of these components—if lawmakers permit health plans to operate that fail to meet these standards, for instance—the ACA will become significantly less effective, if not unworkable altogether.

Immediately after President Obama signed the ACA into law, it became the target of its critics who sought to repeal it altogether or maim it so badly it ceased to be effective. In 2018, after failing to repeal the ACA, the administration of President Donald Trump, an avowed opponent of the ACA, proposed new rules governing Association Health Plans (AHPs). Instead of a plan for one large single employer, AHPs band employers together across an industry, and design insurance plans for the group's membership. AHPs, under new rules proposed by the Trump Administration, would qualify as minimum essential coverage under the ACA but could exclude some of the more expensive benefits considered essential under the law. AHPs would also be permitted to "risk select" to some degree, or make coverage available exclusively to groups with lower risk (employers with younger employees, for instance).

Analysis of the ensuing controversy might proceed from the posing of some questions, such as: *What practical impact might AHP advocacy have on the success of the ACA if AHPs were to become a widely used system of health plan design? What then is the general proposition under which the expansion of AHPs might be introduced as a policy goal, or plan?* and *What does AHP advocacy reveal about the argumentation strategies of ACA opponents?* Controversy over the Administration's objectives for AHPs is an extended dispute unfolding over the course of what will likely be several years. Much of the public policy advocacy concerning AHPs occurs within government documents, beginning with an Executive Order on October 12, 2017, in which the President directed the Secretary of Labor to write regulations and revise guidance to allow more employers to form AHPs.[28] This was followed by the issuance of a Final Rule by the U.S. Department of Labor (USDOL) on June 19, 2018, which would have made it possible for AHPs to begin offering coverage on April 1, 2019.[29] Before that date, on March 28, 2019, Judge John D. Bates of the U.S. District Court for the District of Columbia invalidated the Final Rule in response to a lawsuit filed against the USDOL by the State of New York (and others).[30] The USDOL issued a response to the ruling the next day,[31] and announced its intention to appeal on April 29, 2019.[32]

Posing the above questions and examining the official documents (commentary offered in a variety of settings by the President and other Administration officials could also be examined in a comprehensive study) would likely reveal that AHP advocacy was a hostile move against the ACA disguised as a solution to the problem of healthcare affordability. The tack taken by ACA opponents appears to be to loosen the ACA's market restrictions (what the law insisted must be minimally covered) through actions packaged as efforts to address the original problem— the need to make healthcare more affordable (in fact, Trump eventually presented several Executive Orders related to healthcare as his healthcare plan in the 2020 election[33]). While AHPs may make relatively more affordable plans available to small employers or the self-employed, such plans may not meet the coverage needs of their participants, leaving covered individuals vulnerable to catastrophic healthcare expenses. Moreover, allowing risk selection can siphon healthier people out of the risk pool of those buying insurance through the ACA marketplace, weakening a key component of the ACA. Removing healthier (less expensive to cover) people from the larger risk pool leaves less healthy (more expensive to cover) people with nowhere to go for coverage other than the ACA marketplace. Older and more inclined to illness, these people will lead to more expensive claims and more expensive premiums for plans following the ACA standards. In other words, the expansion of AHPs undermines the solution sought through the ACA, one designed to reduce costs for *everyone*. Indeed, in one notable moment in the controversy, D.C. District Court Judge Bates, in his ruling that invalidated the Final Rule, concluded that the USDOL's new rules were "clearly an end-run around the ACA."[34] As such, a reasonable proposition under which those opposed to the ACA might advocate for AHPs might be something like: "The U.S. Federal Government should repeal and replace the Affordable Care Act."

Analysis of the AHP controversy with this proposition in mind illuminates the way ACA opponents may no longer seek to win the debate about the ACA on its merits. Instead, their advocacy strategy seeks to exploit the ambiguity implicit in the ACA's mission to lower the cost of healthcare. AHP advocates clearly want to lower the cost of healthcare, but not healthcare writ large—they seek to lower costs for employers who hope to avoid the costs associated with the essential health coverage mandated by the ACA. But without a careful analysis of problems and causes under consideration in the original ACA advocacy, the implications of the AHP proposal becomes murky. In such an advocacy environment, those opposing expansion of AHPs are erroneously framed as opponents of affordable healthcare, when, more accurately, they are protecting a status quo policy designed to reduce costs across the board. Using your knowledge of propositions and stock issues, the proposal to expand AHPs is revealed for what it is. Health insurance is expensive, but expanding AHPs only lowers insurance costs for some while increasing it for others. Pan back and you see *AHP advocates* are actually ACA *opponents*, chipping away at a solution designed to expand coverage and slow nationwide increases in healthcare costs.

Exercise: Proposition Recognition Assignment

Select one editorial, or extended blog posting, or other primary document from one side of a current public policy controversy, and identify the proposition. Keep in mind the writer may never state the proposition and/or may be opposed to the proposition. Develop a sentence for the proposition consistent with the four requirements outlined in this chapter (the proposition will follow the formula: "[Agent of change] should [engage in some action which will alter the status quo]."). Then identify which side the writer is on. *Is the writer a proponent of the proposition or an opponent?* As far as you can tell, *is the writer offering a specific plan in support of the proposition, and what are the reasons the writer believes the proposition should or should not be supported?*

Notes

1 Martha Cooper, *Analyzing Public Discourse* (Long Grove, IL: Waveland Press, Inc., 1989), 42. See also Robert James Branham, *Debate and Critical Analysis* (Hinsdale, NJ: Lawrence Erlbaum Associates, 1991), who notes that "[a]ll propositions of policy necessarily subsume propositions of fact and value" (37); and Jeffrey P. Mehltretter Drury, *Argumentation in Everyday Life* (Los Angeles: Sage, 2020), who notes how policy propositions "involve sub-debates about facts and values" (159).

2 Deborah Tannen, *The Argument Culture: Moving from Debate to Dialogue* (New York: Random House, 1998).

3 Josina M. Makau and Debian L. Marty, *Cooperative Argumentation: A Model for Deliberative Community* (Prospect Heights, IL: Waveland Press, 2001); and Josina M. Makau and Debian L. Marty, *Dialogue & Deliberation* (Prospect Heights, IL: Waveland Press, 2013).

4 Makau and Marty, *Dialogue & Deliberation*, 12–13.

5 For example, see J. Michael Hogan, Jessica A. Kurr, Michael J. Bergmaier, and Jeremy D. Johnson, eds., *Speech and Debate as Civic Education* (University Park: The Pennsylvania State University Press, 2017).

6 Those interested in such models may wish to consult the accessible guidance on the "Coordinated Management of Meaning" (CMM) approach found in W. Barnett Pearce, *Making Social Worlds: A Communication Perspective* (Malden, MA: Blackwell, 2007); and, for a highly practical framework for addressing conflict and decision-making more cooperatively within organizations, see Sam Kaner, *Facilitator's Guide to Participatory Decision-Making*, 3rd Ed. (San Francisco: Jossey-Bass, 2014). Regarding the incorporation of CMM in debate programs, see Edward H. Hinck, "Debate Activities and the Promise of Citizenship," in Hogan et al., *Speech and Debate*, 177–190.

7 Cicero, *De Inventione* (Book I), trans. H. M. Hubbell (London: Heinemann, 1949), vii.

8 Cooper, *Analyzing Public Discourse*, 6.

9 Stephen Hiltner, "Illegal, Undocumented, Unauthorized: The Terms of Immigration Reporting," *New York Times*, March 10, 2017, https://www.nytimes.com/2017/03/10/insider/illegal-undocumented-unauthorized-the-terms-of-immigration-reporting.html.

10 Daniel Markovits, "A Wealth Tax is the Logical Way to Support Coronavirus Relief," *New York Times*, April 21, 2020, https://www.nytimes.com/2020/04/21/opinion/coronavirus-wealth-tax.html.

11 For an excellent review of this consensus, see G. Thomas Goodnight and Gordon R. Mitchell, "Forensics as Scholarship: Testing Zarefsky's Bold Hypothesis in a Digital Age," *Argumentation and Advocacy* 45, no. 2 (2008): 83–85. See also James H. McBath, ed., *Forensics as Communication: The Argumentative Perspective* (Skokie, IL: National Textbook Company, 1975), 11.

12 Cooper, *Analyzing Public Discourse*.

13 Ibid., ix-x.

14 Ibid., x.

15 Space does not permit a thorough review of representative scholarship. We direct you to the essays collected in Robert Asen and Daniel C. Brouwer, eds, *Counterpublics and the State* (Albany: SUNY Press, 2001); the exceptional additional body of work of Robert Asen, including his extensive analysis of local school board deliberations (*Democracy, Deliberation, and Education* [University Park: The Pennsylvania State University Press, 2015]); the essays and book-length studies of Robert P. Newman; the extraordinary essay by Valeria Fabj and Matthew J. Sobnosky ("Aids Activism and the Rejuvenation of the Public Sphere," *Argumentation and Advocacy* 31, no. 4 [1995]: 163–184); and, if you want to read more from the authors of this book, see John Butler, "Transgendered DeKalb: Observations of an Advocacy Campaign," *The Journal of Homosexuality* 45 (2003): 277–296; and Philip Dalton and John Butler, "Getting Clipped: Denial and Masculinity Politics in the 2002 US Senate Race in Montana," *Western Journal of Communication* 74, no. 3 (2010): 226–248.

16 Robert P. Newman, *Enola Gay and the Court of History* (New York: Peter Lang, 2004), xi.

17 For critical analyses of this kind, see Asen and Brouwer, *Counterpublics and the State*.

18 For a recent collection of essays by rhetorical scholars on the incorporation of field work into rhetorical criticism, see Sara L. McKinnon, Robert Asen, Karma R. Chavez, and Robert Glenn Howard, eds., *Text+Field: Innovations in Rhetorical Method* (University Park: Pennsylvania State University Press, 2016). See also Michael Middleton, Aaron Hess, Danielle Endres, and Samantha Senda-Cook, *Participatory Critical Rhetoric* (New York: Lexington Books, 2015).

19 McKinnon et al., *Text+Field*, vii.

20 Ibid., 3 and 6.

21 Hogan et al, *Speech and Debate*.

22 Gordon R. Mitchell, "Pedagogical Possibilities for Argumentative Agency in Academic Debate," *Argumentation and Advocacy* 35, no. 2 (1998): 41–60.

23 Ibid., 47 and 45.

24 Ibid., 49 and 51. Included in Mitchell's three "stages" of action for debate programs, "public advocacy" refers to activist projects that might emerge from well-constructed policy plans introduced (and tested) in debate competition that debaters later advocate for outside of the tournament realm.

25 Goodnight and Mitchell, "Forensics as Scholarship."

26 Ibid., 94. In short, the use of digital technology to support academic debate is generating new ways of culling, archiving, and distributing high quality evidence gathered for tournament debate competition and measuring the credibility of sources (particularly online sources that do not emerge through the traditional process of hard-copy publication).

27 Ibid., 92.

28 U.S. President, Executive Order, "Promoting Healthcare Choice and Competition Across the United States, Exec. Order 13813 of October 12, 2017," *Federal Register* 82, no. 199 (October 17, 2017): 48385, https://www.govinfo.gov/content/pkg/FR-2017-10-17/pdf/2017-22677.pdf.

29 Katie Keith, "Final Rule Rapidly Eases Restrictions on Non-ACA-Compliant Association Health Plans," *Health Affairs*, June 21, 2018, https://www.healthaffairs.org/do/10.1377/hblog20180621.671483/full/.

30 *State of New York et al. v. United States Department of Labor*, U.S. District Court for the District of Columbia, Civil Action No. 18–1747 (March 28, 2019), https://ecf.dcd.uscourts.gov/cgi-bin/show_public_doc?2018cv1747-79. See also Katie Keith, "Court Invalidates Rule on Association Health Plans," *Health Affairs*, March 29, 2019, https://www.healthaffairs.org/do/10.1377/hblog20190329.393236/full/.

31 United States, Employee Benefits Security Administration, "Department of Labor Statement Relating to the U.S. District Court Ruling in State of New York v. United States Department of Labor," March 29, 2019, https://www.dol.gov/agencies/ebsa/laws-and-regulations/rules-and-regulations/completed-rulemaking/1210-AB85/ahp-statement-court-ruling.

32 United States, Employee Benefits Security Administration, News Release, "U.S. Department of Labor Statement Relating to the U.S. District Court Ruling in State of New York v. United States Department of Labor," April 29, 2019, https://www.dol.gov/newsroom/releases/ebsa/ebsa20190429.

33 Chris Cillizza, "How President Trump's Surprise Gift to '60 Minutes' Completely Backfired," CNN, October 26, 2020, https://www.cnn.com/2020/10/26/politics/donald-trump-60-minutes-book-lesley-stahl-health-care/index.html.

34 *State of New York et. al. v. United States Department of Labor*, 2. See also Keith, "Court Invalidates Rule."

Part II
Arguing

3

UNDERSTANDING STOCK ISSUES
IN PUBLIC POLICY ADVOCACY

Takeaways

(1) Not all public debate occasions will conform to the concepts and techniques outlined in this book, and advocates and audiences will not always focus on the merits of policy proposals; nevertheless, the concepts and techniques will help you develop compelling messages for an unpredictable policy environment.

(2) Stock issues are matters of potential dispute that help you develop messages when debating a policy proposition (that there is a problem, a cause of that problem, a solution, and that advantages will accompany that solution).

(3) Initially these are burdens of advocates proposing a change in the status quo—affirmative advocates. Advocates supporting or defending the status quo—negative advocates—will also find that stock issues offer important entry points for their advocacy.

(4) It is unlikely that all stock issues will be specifically addressed in a single advocacy event, but recognizing these key components of advocacy helps you locate where your advocacy fits within a controversy and construct effective messages.

Karate students learn "forms," or combinations of moves (strikes, kicks, turns, advances, and blocks) that display knowledge of, and the ability to perform, techniques. While being evaluated by their instructor, the karate student adheres to the forms they are taught. In an actual fight, however, the rules change, though some of the moves may resemble what was learned in training. An adversary will not wait to view a fighter's form, or express admiration for its precision—they'll simply try to win. For the karate fighter, the situation, not the form, will determine what moves are best to employ in their own self-defense.

While we usually like to avoid metaphors that equate debate with fighting (this is a common feature of argumentation's bad reputation and a concern that inspires some innovation in debate instruction we appreciate[1]), we are going to dwell here for just a moment to make an important point: *not all fights are fair.* Particularly, we observe in our present era many instances in which people insinuate themselves into controversies with little regard for what we might call the norms of civility—lack of respect for others' opinion, rejection of people altogether because they disagree with them, refusal to let others speak, ignoring the merits of a proposal, name-calling over engagement with policy positions, assertions with no basis in fact, distorting evidence to support a desired outcome, and more. Because so many well-intentioned advocates find themselves on the receiving end of these "blows," let us consider for a moment the expectation of a "fair fight" and how that relates to the practical experiences of advocates.

No matter how well trained you are as advocates, you may find your opponents are, at least initially, determined to win at all costs. This determination may structure their strategic choices and predispose them to seek their victory and your defeat. Like the karate student, formal training in argumentation and debate equips you to formulate a particular approach based on formulas and systems educators have constructed and taught you; it prepares you to apply certain techniques; and, ideally, it enables you to address a range of contingencies. Like the trained karate student, however, what you do based on your advocacy training will not always guarantee an equal or secure footing in the situations you encounter.

Imagine you decide to lead an advocacy effort to build a new library in your city, and a referendum for a modest property tax increase to pay for it. Imagine you've spent months lobbying city council members and preparing your thoughtfully crafted arguments. Following all the rules of good public policy advocacy, you've gathered the most relevant and accurate evidence and anticipated the logical arguments against your proposal. You're ready! But when you arrive at the city council meeting, imagine you find someone opposed to your proposal passing out leaflets accusing you and your spouse of not paying the right amount of property taxes, calling you a "tax cheat." Imagine also that you learn your opponents have filed an ethics complaint against two city council members who support your proposal, accusing them of having an ownership stake in construction companies that might someday win the bid to perform work on the library (imagine your opponents are calling it a "criminal conspiracy"). Imagine a local newspaper reporter approaches you immediately asking you to defend yourself before anyone has made any remarks. Welcome to an unfair fight!

Debate educators who discuss and write about their craft often consider the challenges of transferring skills learned in academic/classroom debate to the forums of public policy advocacy.[2] One central lesson for the student of debate is that the actual rules that apply to classroom debates are rarely followed in wider society. Only if parties in conflict agree to follow certain rules might they be followed (such as in the case of a formally structured public debate or forum, for instance). But, another important lesson that hopefully is conveyed through debate education is that knowledge of the rules of argumentation enables advocates to make more complex and informed persuasive choices, and develop strategic messages.

This is the aspirational nature of public policy advocacy. While not all fights are fair, you are more likely to successfully navigate a complex (and unfair) argumentative situation, possibly even turn it into a more structured debate or discussion, if you learn the foundational techniques that allow you to develop good reasons for your position. This does not mean that structured debate, even when such is possible, will always produce logical ends (indeed, observers of American political processes and argumentation scholars often consider situations when reasoning fails, why such failures occur, and how such situations can be better addressed). However, we firmly believe that any hope that controversies can be resolved in a manner that serves the particular interests of a community requires that we assume wise policy proposals *can* emerge from high quality public debate. Argumentation theorist Frans H. van Eemeren underscores this aspirational approach when he contemplates whether his defense of "dialectical rules for argumentative discourse" (essential to "participatory democracy") may be "a little bit Utopian."[3] "Maybe indeed a little bit," he notes, adding: "I really wonder whether there is any other acceptable way of trying to cope with the overwhelming problems of change than by promoting a culture of critical discussion."[4] In this and subsequent chapters, this optimism will hopefully surface as we focus our attention on developing compelling messages for an unpredictable policy environment.

This chapter is the first of five chapters we place under Part II of our text, titled "Arguing." Here we shift our attention to the process of building thoughtful and effective advocacy in pursuit of good public policy—what we will more simply refer to as *message development*. The movement into arguing begins with the subject of this chapter—identifying the unique burdens you have when you seek to change or defend the status quo.

Invention and Stock Issues

Message development is a type of invention. We have already introduced you to the concept of *invention* in Chapter 2, the process of developing arguments to support one's cause. When you begin to identify the unique burdens you have when you seek to change or defend the status quo, you have begun the process of invention in the realm of public policy. The main subject of this chapter, stock issues, is critical to this process, as stock issues inform content choices in public policy advocacy.

In this chapter, we expand on the stock issues so they may be used together as a detailed system for understanding the standard components of public policy advocacy. Elsewhere, you may encounter stock issues under the alternative term, "burdens." The language of burdens implies correctly that an advocate calling for change to the status quo has a responsibility to adequately address each of these issues. An advocate *of* the status quo therefore can rightly hold a proponent of change accountable if they fail to meet the following burdens:

(a) **Problem:** Establish that a problem within the status quo is significant enough to warrant change.

(b) **Cause:** Identify a cause of the problem, and/or that the status quo is incapable of fixing the problem without a change.

(c) **Solution:** Provide a policy proposal, or specific policy goal, describing what actions will remedy the problem.

(d) **Advantages:** Establish the beneficial outcomes of the solution's adoption.

Most advocates in the realm of public policy advocacy will technically fail to meet all four of these burdens in any *one* public appeal. An advocate may either address one or more of them, or dodge one or more of them if they are not prepared to provide them. As an inventive tool, the stock issues tell you what has been argued and what has not. From an analysis of stock issues, you learn *what you and others are arguing, what might be taken for granted, what needs to be argued*, and *how and where to best counter an argument*.

We have already introduced the idea that the status quo is presumed to be sufficient. We have also introduced you to the common academic debate terminology to describe the two sides of a policy debate: "affirmative advocates"— those who seek to change the status quo—and "negative advocates"—those who seek to maintain or defend the status quo. This terminology is especially helpful as you contemplate the stock issues and how they impact your message development efforts.

Affirmative Advocates	Negative Advocates
• They "affirm" the proposition, seeking to change the status quo.	• They "negate" the proposition, seeking to maintain/defend the status quo.
• They have the burden to show that the status quo is insufficient and warrants change (an insufficient status quo).	• They have the burden to defend the status quo policy (a sufficient status quo).

We believe it is useful to think of stock issues as the building blocks of a *map*—a landscape of sorts—that helps you locate where you might best begin your journey or which direction to head when you encounter an unexpected or undesirable development. Without the map, you are limited to seeing what is immediately in front of you. With the map, you can situate your advocacy within the larger terrain of the controversy and chart a sensible pathway toward your destination. When you map out directions, not only do you consider the most efficient route, you also simultaneously rule out other paths that make little practical sense. In the realm of public policy advocacy, you begin charting your course when you either wish to propose a change to the status quo (become an affirmative advocate) or if you encounter a proposal with which you disagree (become a negative advocate). It is possible that you might head in the wrong direction, the equivalent of engaging in a challenge that you will "lose" when you might have otherwise achieved a partial or even full "victory." You might also get distracted and lost, the equivalent of being lured into responding to arguments that, were you to "win" or "lose," have no real bearing on whether your policy goal is wise or achievable. Moreover, there are choices along the way, priorities you might adopt or options you might consider, the equivalent, from a persuasive standpoint, of determining you are better off addressing a stronger position of your own or a weaker position of your adversary.

Imagine you believe the Tax Cuts and Jobs Act of 2017 was bad public policy because there was less economic growth than the Act's supporters predicted, the lost federal revenue will require cuts in government programs that are important to you, federal deficits as high as $1 trillion annually are expected, and more. One night out with a group of friends, you learn that one of those friends supports the Act, when they claim the new taxing scheme led to the lowest unemployment rates in recent history (at least until the COVID-19 health crisis). Without a map, you might simply focus on what's in front of you, and counter, "That's not true!" Before you know it, you might be drawn into a debate in which you assert that the unemployment numbers were much higher than claimed when military enlistments and college enrollments are considered, or that the gains consisted mostly of low wage jobs and thus offered little advantages to the formerly unemployed. *Is this a practically useful route for you to travel?*

Considering what you now know about propositions, and looking at the stock issues map, you would recognize that you are a proponent of repealing the Act or replacing it with measures that restore the tax policy in place before the Act went into effect. The stock issues provide a path for you to travel other than to focus on your friend's specific claims. You might determine, for instance, that the Act has caused significant harms, and these harms outweigh the gains in employment cited by your friend. Had you continued to travel in the direction of unemployment numbers, you would have continued to argue that the numbers weren't as strong as your friend suggests. Doing so would have encouraged your audience to think that your proposal to repeal/replace the Act should be accepted or rejected on the basis of employment gains or losses. *What if your friend is right, or close to right, and they can convince your audience that there were significant job gains?* By taking the route determined by your friend, and not considering the map on your own terms, you forego an opportunity to weigh such employment numbers against significant harms, such as the ones that caused you to oppose the law all along. In fact, this alternative route might have been *so* helpful to your position that you could have even conceded your friend's points about employment gains altogether.

As the above example illustrates, understanding stock issues is helpful both as a means of furthering your analysis of public issues and of laying out a pathway and expanding choices for your advocacy. Approaching stock issues from the standpoint of invention, we consider the multiple ways each might inform efforts to affirm or negate a policy proposition.

The Burdens of Advocacy

Stock issues are—initially—matters of importance for affirmative advocates, but once affirmative advocates outline their concerns with the status quo, stock issues become useful for negative advocates also. Formal argument training instructs affirmative advocates to argue all four stock issues convincingly; negative advocates engage in refutation that addresses the stock issues in an effort to convince the audience that the affirmative's analysis of one or all of those issues is flawed.

Problem

Similar to a defendant who is presumed innocent until proven guilty, advocates can safely assume the public is inclined to view the status quo as sufficient. This is reasonable. The public might be indifferent about an issue because they are either unaware of the problem or perceive the problem as insignificant, remote, unchangeable, deserved, or too costly to change. On the other hand, you can assume that, if the public viewed the status quo as harmful, something would have been done about it already. Even in cases in which the public has adopted the attitude that a change is necessary, if advocates have not convinced the public of the need to act, you can still safely conclude that the public is tolerant of the current system.

The first responsibility of the affirmative advocate then is to impress upon the public that the concern they wish to address is significantly harmful to warrant the public's attention, disappointment, and/or action. The point at which a problem (sometimes termed a "need") is harmful enough to address is subjective. Affirmative advocates must evaluate the problem in a manner that is relevant to the target audience. Convincing the public, for instance, that federal action is needed to regulate parasailing is going to be more challenging than convincing the public of the need to evacuate an expectant volcano's blast zone. To convince an audience of a problem's significance, you must possess knowledge of the extent of the problem and/or vivid descriptions of the potential or actual harm.

Introducing an audience to a *significant* problem will rarely be enough to move them if they have already established habits and strategies of ignoring it. Consequently, significance must be compelling. Leon Festinger's theory of cognitive dissonance posits that humans seek to avoid psychological stress caused by opposing—or incommensurable—beliefs, facts, and/or behaviors.[5] Overcoming such avoidance requires advocates to describe the problem in a manner that resonates with those who have not yet been persuaded. Consider advocacy in favor of "Medicare For All," an effort to nationalize the health-care system and end the private insurance that, proponents argue, has left millions without insurance coverage. While this proposal enjoys some support, many do not believe the problem is significant enough to warrant a nationalized healthcare solution. In addition to what is often publicly emphasized (numbers without insurance, premature deaths, health-related bankruptcies, and so on), proponents might ask: *How is the target audience negatively affected by the status quo? How are their premiums affected? How is their own healthcare delivery affected? How is their neighbors' healthcare affected?* Sometimes the problem is better cast as an *impending dilemma*—an imperfection that will escalate over time and present serious consequences worth avoiding if possible. The push for soda taxes within some major U.S. cities, for example, focuses on the long-term harms of cheap sugary drinks, such as obesity and diabetes, and the financial consequences that result from treatment of such maladies.

The scale and relevance of the problem in these cases are often evaluated in terms of significance. If you are an affirmative advocate, you must argue persuasively that a significant need exists to solve a problem. How significant a problem must be to warrant a change is a subjective judgment. For some, a problem is viewed as an abstraction. They may not have experienced it themselves, and their willingness to intervene to address the problem relies on good will or empathy, which may not always surface. Problems can also be described for audiences in concrete ways intended to demonstrate their significance and relevance to the audience. Quantitative measures can, for example, demonstrate how widespread a problem is. You could establish the problems related to healthcare bankruptcy, for instance, as a significant problem by numerically showing the large number of people affected, and how such bankruptcies are distributed across household income levels, race, gender, and so on. Doing so might demonstrate that the problem is widespread and particularly impactful on communities with which your audience identifies. Skillfully communicated, with graphics, comparisons, and contrasts, such numbers can be perceived as significant enough to warrant change.

Advocates need to overcome audience perceptions that problems are acceptable or simply "the way things are." Worldwide, people suffer from hunger and political oppression, and yet many people do nothing about it, either individually or as a society. *What if a billion people worldwide suffer from hunger? Would such a number motivate the citizens of nations with ample food supply to seek a solution to the problem?* Problems such as these, for many, are too remote or abstract. In such cases, qualitative assessments (descriptions and illustrations) may be far more compelling. Television advertisements appealing to U.S. residents to give money to help the world's impoverished do not limit their arguments to numerical assessments of the problem's size, if they mention size at all. Including so many hungry, poorly clothed, and seemingly unhealthy children in their advertisements, these images can cause audiences to empathize in ways that numerical descriptions do not. Because an injustice affects someone else, getting an audience to perceive it as a significant problem can be challenging. A qualitative description of it, however, can trigger the empathy and sympathy of a target audience.

In many cases, the significance of a problem is just assumed by advocates. Not explicitly stating the problem might sometimes engage and involve an audience that is inclined to agree (a form of argument often referred to as an "enthymeme"). Another tactic may be to assume that identifying the cause can stand on its own as statement of the problem. An advocate might establish the problem of college debt, for instance, assuming their audience already buys into all of the concordant harms (disparities by race, difficulties with home purchasing, job disqualification due to lower credit score, and more), even though college debt is really the cause of these harms. Something similar is occurring when an advocate wishes to gloss over the problem by substituting it with a concept for which the audience already has an established antipathy. Consider arguments by some for a border wall to block immigration along the southern U.S. border. Advocates might refer to "illegal immigrants," "criminal aliens," "undocumented workers," or "anchor babies" to excite concerns about immigrants and invite negative associations that some audiences may readily make, while valid evidence describing concrete harms uniquely caused by Central and South American immigration is difficult to find. Advocates on either side of the proposition must be alert to the manner in which the stock issue of a problem is managed.

Cause

Knowing the cause of a problem is often essential to developing, support-ing, and/or opposing policy proposals. While evidence of a problem can be pointed to, questions of cause have to do with the *relationship* between prob-lem and cause, or (in reverse) cause and effect. While affirmative advocates may identify the cause by presenting evidence establishing a link between the problems and their cause, quite often the cause is implied and suggested in the solution. For instance, advocacy in favor of a sugar tax implies that the affordability of high-sugar foods is responsible for the problems of obesity and diabetes. *Is the connection between cheap sugar and these illnesses established? Is acceptance of that connection warranted by evidence?* Affirmative advocates who move quickly to discuss a proposed solution, without careful consideration of cause, might fail to develop effective policy as well as an effective message in favor of reform. Negative advocates, likewise, might exploit these assump-tions by offering alternative causes of a problem that a proposed solution fails to address.

Defining the Cause

There are both practical and ethical reasons why affirmative advocates should identify for themselves and/or the audience the cause of the problems they seek to solve. First, the failure to identify the correct source of the problem when developing and advocating a solution can result in—figuratively—putting a band-aid over a gunshot wound. While the bandage may have the short-term effect of making society feel like it has remedied a problem, in the long run, this failure may be wasteful and distracting, and may prolong or exacerbate the problem. From a strategic point of view, an advocate's failure to address the cause may be a sign that they are seeking to exploit fears about the status quo to bypass audience scrutiny of a solution.

Second, one side's notion of the cause prompts a debate about a cause-effect relationship that is necessary. Relationships between cause and effect are theoretical—advocates are maintaining that a proven phenomenon (prob-lem) was brought into existence or made more prevalent by a cause. Even in cases where advocates might be inclined to think incontrovertible factual evidence of cause can be provided, causal relationships almost always involve inference. We pay special attention to cause-effect relationships because their reliance on informed guesswork, trust in authority, and consensus often render them soft spots in otherwise strong advocacy.

For these reasons, at the point affirmative advocates are developing policy, identifying the cause as a separate issue is an important responsibility. Policymakers are often criticized, sometimes harshly and for long periods of time, for failing to appropriately support what they allege is the cause. A common scenario for this criticism is to allege that a particularly awful event (described as the problem), or other activity that results in outrage, permits advocates to ignore altogether the question of cause without much pushback or scrutiny.

The public discussion about the causes of the 9/11 attacks on the World Trade Center and the eventual decision of the U.S. government to invade Iraq as part of the "War on Terror" is a commonly referenced example of a failure to properly scrutinize an alleged cause. Frightened by the perception of extremist Islamic animosity toward the United States following the 9/11 attacks, critics argue, decision makers accepted the invasion of Iraq as part of a solution to protect the United States from another attack.[6] Iraq possessed one of the least religious governments in the Muslim world and had no demonstrable link to the 9/11 attacks, and evidence supporting its alleged possession of weapons of mass destruction (and probable use of them against the United States) was highly suspect. In other words, critics claim there was insufficient evidence to support the notion that Iraq was part of the cause of the 9/11 attacks or constituted an imminent threat to the United States. The preemptive invasion that removed Iraq's mostly secular government arguably helped spawn disdain for the United States, its international allies, and factions within Iraq who aligned with U.S. forces to rebuild Iraq's damaged nation. Indeed, many argue this disdain created the conditions for the rise of ISIS (the Islamic State of Iraq and al-Sham), which emerged and declared itself a caliphate or Islamic state in 2014.[7] The public's appreciation of the stock issue of cause could have been the impetus for generating a more robust public discussion of the Bush Administration's Iraq-as-cause assertion. The United States spent over $1 trillion to fight the war, over 4,400 U.S. soldiers have died, over 32,000 U.S. soldiers have been wounded, and hundreds of thousands of Iraqi citizens have perished.[8]

Even where there is no outrage, often advocates on either side do not seriously concern themselves with an analysis of the cause. This may be due to the time limitations of an advocacy event, because an advocate assumes their audience is of like mind on the cause, and/or because advocates expect audiences will fill in the cause as they consider the problem and solution. On a practical level, for affirmative advocates, the takeaway is that the particular controversy or advocacy setting may not always require the identification and discussion of the cause; however, the potential for flawed policymaking should offer you ample motivation to consider the cause in the development of (or assessment of) a proposed solution, and to always be prepared to address it. For all these reasons, it is also imperative that negative advocates attend closely to affirmative advocates' consideration of the cause (whether expressly identified, implied, or unstated).

How you define the cause is critical to whether you can convince an audience your solution will address the problem. Argument scholar Lee Hultzen uses the term "reformability" instead of "cause" to name this stock issue.[9] His choice of language captures an important facet of cause as a stock issue—that some problems are defined in ways that make reform impossible. An affirmative advocate's job is to convince the audience that the cause of the problem can be effectively addressed. But no public policy can stop imminent hurricanes, floods, or volcanoes, for instance. Problems caused by hurricanes, however, *are* products of flooding and wind damage. Thus, the cause could focus on reformable conditions, permitting solutions that address preparedness for flooding and wind damage (moving people from flood prone areas, strengthening building codes, for instance).

Barriers and Inherency

Identifying the cause of a problem can sometimes be aided by what, in academic debate environments, is referred to as "inherency analysis." Inherency analysis asks *which aspects of the status quo contribute to (that is, cause) the problem's present existence?* You will find that common *barriers* are structural, attitudinal, and existential conditions that are "inherent" (thus the term "inherency") to the status quo. Understanding these barriers helps you draw attention to the relationship, or lack thereof, between the problem and the proposed solution. Assessing the potential effectiveness of a proposed solution, you can also ask whether a solution can overcome the barriers within the status quo. Barriers are typically discussed by affirmative advocates as part of their analysis of the cause of the problem or something that is preventing the status quo from correcting itself. Negative advocates can also draw attention to barriers not seriously contemplated by affirmative advocates which, they claim, might be sufficient enough to prevent the claimed advantages from occurring.

Structural barriers are systemic realities that prevent the status quo from solving the problem on its own. You should ask *what structures are in place that support the continuation of the problem, and is there a solution that can overcome these structural barriers?* Imagine you and your neighbors wish to expand the geographic service region of a local water district, thus the volume of water it treats. You've determined funding is available for the facility expansion and there is strong public support. But, you discover the charter of the water district defines the geographic boundaries it can serve, and so it is prohibited from expanding services without an act of the county legislature redefining the water district's boundaries. The charter is a structural barrier that prevents the status quo from solving the problem.

Some barriers are a function of the collective choices or preferences of the community—matters that can't easily be altered by legislation. We consider these types of barriers as *attitudinal barriers*. Attitudinal barriers may manifest as unexamined habits, preferences, or biases. Attitudinal barriers prevent the status quo from self-correcting. They are trickier for you to address because the system cannot legislate attitude. You should ask *what attitudes are in place that support the continuation of the problem and can you design a solution that antici-pates and addresses the attitudes in some way?* Imagine you are opposed to the recreational use of marijuana in a state that has recently legalized it. You continue to be concerned about widespread substance abuse and the dangers that come from operating vehicles under the influence of drugs and alcohol. To address these problems, you advocate for a reduction in the amount available for recreational sale and the restoration of tougher penalties for the possession and distribution of marijuana beyond these limits. You quickly discover that the most significant barrier to your proposal is a widespread attitude among most of your target audience who believe that, even if marijuana were to again become illegal, people just like it and will continue to use it. They believe it is generally harmless and resent prior efforts to prevent its use, which have caused so many to face harsh consequences within the criminal justice system. In this case, you are dealing with a preference for the status quo based on a portion of the public becoming comfortable with the legal use of marijuana; for them, legalization just makes sense and avoids problems.

Some attitudinal barriers are based on attitudes that are more formally connected to ideas or theories that members of the public may have accepted as truths that guide their decisions and responses in certain areas of their personal and professional lives. Awareness of such barriers may help you sharpen your advocacy or assess the reasoning and evidence used within a controversy. Because it is the audience's hierarchy of values, or strongly held philosophical principles, that needs to be overcome or reprioritized, you will need to target more precisely the ideas or values that form the basis for their beliefs. Now imagine you live in a state that continues to prohibit the use of marijuana other than for medical purposes, and you are on the side of legalizing recreational use. Your analysis of your target audience (perhaps through surveys or focus groups) uncovers a recurring theme you eventually determine is more philosophical, or ideological, in nature (as opposed to the pragmatic "I just like it and making it illegal won't work" attitude above). You learn that legalization opponents embrace certain "Puritanical" values that prize hard work and industriousness over recreation, and have formed the idea that marijuana users are anti-social, or counter-cultural—generally unwilling to accept personal responsibility for addressing their own needs and unwilling to participate in the economic and political success of their community. As far as they are concerned, you conclude, legalizing marijuana is tantamount to giving up on the American way of life, surrendering to the demands of a generation that refuses to take care of itself. Your strategies for addressing this barrier would differ from more general preferences and opinions, because you would need to address the root values and strongly held belief systems of some within your audience.

In the practice of public policy advocacy, causes cannot always be precisely identified, or the harms of the status quo may have continued unencumbered for such a long time that advocates of reform may just assume that *something* is blocking society from addressing the problem. When an advocate for reform observes a sustained injustice or urgent crisis that society appears to have let develop, they may assert they are dealing with an *existential barrier*. After establishing that a significant problem either has not historically solved itself or demands immediate action, your advocacy might proceed with the built-in assumption that the effect itself (the problem) is proof enough that a cause must exist, regardless of whether you have identified it. In such a case, you might acknowledge that a barrier *exists* and a solution must be adopted regardless of whether the cause is fully examined to the satisfaction of your audience. Consider the social ill of poverty and its closely attendant harms (violence, hunger, and malnutrition) or that particular conditions predictably combine to produce a widespread famine that places hundreds of thousands, if not millions, of people in danger. Likewise, there are some reformers targeting longstanding social inequities and persistent injustices who might assert that the U.S. economic, political, and legal systems are inherently unable to self-correct, that the barriers to effective reform are too entrenched within the larger system to even permit a cogent analysis. From our perspective, including existential barriers as a type of barrier is useful insofar as it recognizes one way advocates might contemplate the failure of policymakers to address intractable problems. However, we encourage advocates to delve deeply into the history of their proposals, ask who may have advocated similar actions in the past, and determine whether there is support for such actions that contends with structural and attitudinal barriers that may offer a clearer path to overcome the forces preventing reform.

A serious contemplation of barriers helps affirmative advocates develop effective solutions and negative advocates assess those solutions, but that is not all. Such contemplation also allows you to question whether the *entire* cause has been identified or if the cause that has been identified works in combination with other contributing causes. *Will addressing one structural barrier eradicate the problem at all if other factors are also responsible? Will removing one barrier simply reduce the problem, and if so, will the amount of reduction of the problem be worth the cost of the solution?* These are questions worthy of consideration, particularly because affirmative advocates will tout the achievements of their remedy even if it addresses only a small portion of the problem they set out to solve.

Solution

The components of a solution, or plan, are often referred to as "planks." Generally, four planks are subject to debate: agency, mandates, funding, and enforcement. If you are an affirmative advocate, the nature of the plan and the circumstances of the advocacy event help determine what you need to include in your efforts to influence the public. There are some situations in which advocates conclude comprehensive plans are not needed. For example, before the Defense of Marriage Act (DOMA) was effectively nullified by the U.S. Supreme Court in 2013, if you believed that efforts to prevent discrimination against LGBT Americans were continually obstructed by DOMA, then your proposal may be, quite simply, to repeal DOMA (you are getting rid of something, not adding something). Considering this from the standpoint of invention, the simplicity and elegance of producing so many advantages by simply repealing a law is an ideal situation—so many advantages with so little effort (although negative advocates would have likely argued that other causes of discrimination against LGBT Americans would persist after DOMA). If you are a negative advocate, the planks function as a guide for what you ought to expect from the affirmative, and—as such—what might be missing. *Why might those advocating change ignore the cost of their proposal? Why haven't they included any mention of enforcement?* Perhaps, the answers to these questions reveal that cost and enforcement are the least attractive part of their proposal, important clues as to how their proposal might link to a number of unintended consequences or disadvantages.

Some complex proposals for change necessitate detailed description. An example of a public policy that necessitated a more detailed plan is the Affordable Care Act (ACA). The ACA consisted of 955 total pages outlining new agencies, mandates, taxes, and enforcement mechanisms. No public forum existed, however, that would withstand a thorough description of this legislation. *How did proponents of the ACA whittle 955 pages of legislation down to manageable speeches or op-eds?* That is the challenge faced by many involved in public policy advocacy. What follows is a brief consideration of the four planks in the context of this complex solution.

Agency. Agency is a description of the apparatus that will implement and administer the solution. The proposed agent in the case of the ACA—government or private insurers—attracted serious attention during the public debate over the ACA. Democrats seeking to solve the problem of people without healthcare coverage debated the issue of agency before proposing their solution. Some believed a government-run or "single-payer" plan would work best, while others thought private insurers would be better. The single-payer option would have had the government take over the entire health insurance industry, making it the single or only agency compensating doctors for the care. Instead, the ACA proposed a plan that used the private insurance markets as the agent of health insurance coverage. Publicly identifying the agent preempted anticipated counter-arguments, likely by negative advocates, warning against "government takeovers" of "one sixth of the nation's economy," or "socialized medicine."

Agency, as with the other planks, needs to be more than workable; it needs to be acceptable. The central role of private insurance companies in the design of the ACA puts a fine point on the importance of the agency plank. Owing to a great deal of distrust about the ability of government bureaucracies to solve problems, particularly in healthcare, the ACA agent addressed attitudinal and philosophical barriers related to faith in the free market as the most effective means of reducing the costs of healthcare.

Mandates. Mandates are descriptions of authority and directives given to agencies to execute a policy. The ACA has more mandates than can be described in any single public message (we outlined four of them in our case study in Chapter 2). Advocates need to balance several factors when deciding how to describe the mandates of their solution. You should make the specific mandates clear and, to the greatest extent possible, understandable to your target audience. You should consider how the public will perceive the mandates in light of attitudes and philosophies. And, affirmative advocates should consider what negative advocates will argue about each mandate of an affirmative plan (mandates are often key links negative advocates cite for disadvantages they claim will arise as a result of the solution).

Funding. Funding is an explanation of how the solution will be paid for. Funding for the ACA became an important point of contention during the debate that led to its adoption, and it continues to generate concern among opponents of the law. The requirement to purchase health insurance obligates the federal government to subsidize the insurance purchases for those in need. This aspect of the ACA was to be funded, in part, by new taxes and, it was argued, anticipated savings. Expecting resistance to the proposal of new spending and tax increases, the Obama Administration made an argument that was complex: the trajectory of the present healthcare system was going to make current federal healthcare obligations an unaffordable burden; the status quo (before adoption of the law) would, therefore, become more expensive when compared to the proposed changes. Thus, it was reasoned that more involvement by the government in this industry (usually associated with greater costs) would help reduce forecasted cost increases. The new law, claimed its proponents, would cost money, but it would also result in savings elsewhere (such as lower cost projections for Medicare and Medicaid).

In the hypothetical environment of argumentation and debate classes, educators instruct students to argue that their proposals will be funded "through normal means," which implies that new plans will require increased revenue through some form of new money. Likely, such new money will require increased taxes and/or fees. Funding is certainly fair game for rigorous debate, although it should not be either side's sole concern (see below discussion of "fiat"). If a problem is worth solving and the solution is effective, affirmative advocates should not hesitate to defend what is required to fund their proposals. Advocates' hesitance to propose tax increases, even in an artificial debate setting, however, reflects the strength of the philosophical resistance to taxes (and spending) held by many. In some cases, the funding mechanism can function as a persuasive opportunity for affirmative advocates. Such instances include those in which proposals are either revenue neutral or result in a net savings. We mentioned earlier that affirmative advocates will often emphasize those stock issues that play to the strengths of their advocacy. Not unlike an infomercial pointing out "all you get at a low-low price," affirmative advocates may find it particularly appealing to their target audience to point out just how little the solution costs. Even better, in some cases enacting a plan may cost less than the amounts being devoted to addressing the problem in the status quo.

Knowledge of affirmative advocates' responsibility to describe their funding mechanism gives negative advocates a valuable opening to challenge proposed solutions. Not only are many audiences averse to increased taxes, but negative advocates can reasonably argue that advantages cannot likely emerge from unfunded mandates. President Trump may authorize the construction of a border wall, for instance, but without Congressional funding it cannot be completed.

Enforcement. Enforcement mechanisms are means by which the mandates are executed. Sometimes the enforcement mechanism is the most complex or controversial part of the plan. After the ACA was passed, the enforcement mechanism became the centerpiece of the opposition's strategy to eliminate the new law. *If the success of the legislation hinges on a requirement to buy health insurance, how does the government compel people to do it?* The government proposed enforcing this rule by having the IRS charge a penalty, theoretically removing any incentive to avoid the purchase. Several states later challenged the constitutionality of requiring citizens to buy *anything*. During the summer of 2012, the Supreme Court issued its *National Federation of Independent Business v. Sebelius* decision, indicating that the penalty was actually a tax, deeming it constitutional under the government's authority to levy taxes.

Affirmative advocates' enforcement mechanisms are important because they ensure that the proposed solution will be executed. The public, convinced of the need to solve a problem and poised to pay for the solution, will want assurance that the proposal will work as planned. Whether a detailed description of an enforcement mechanism is necessary often depends on the nature of the solution and the challenges raised by the opposition.

Advantages

The stock issue of advantages addresses the problems the solution aims to solve. Often, affirmative advocates include multiple advantages. Advantages perform two functions: first, they demonstrate that the solution fulfills its intended purpose of fixing the harm (this is also referred to as "solvency"); second, they provide a description of the solution that intensifies a target audience's desire for it. While it seems logical that a workable solution that solves a significant problem is desirable all on its own, demonstrating solvency is an opportunity to increase the persuasiveness of your appeal by convincing your target audience that your solution will make their lives better.

We noted earlier that affirmative advocates are highly exposed when they assert a causal relationship between status quo forces (the cause) and the effects of those forces (the problem). Assertions that X *causes* Y are dependent on informed guesswork, trust in authority, and consensus. The same is true about solvency. If you are an affirmative advocate, you should strive to find and present your strongest and most compelling evidence to support this relationship. If you are a negative advocate, you will likely find solvency to be a particularly vulnerable moment for affirmative advocates, due to the uncertainty that is a natural feature of such causal claims.

Solvency is the affirmative advocate's demonstration that the problems warranting a change are solved by the proposed solution. If, for instance, two significant problems are outlined by affirmative advocates, both problems should be addressed with corresponding advantages. Consider, for instance, arguments about public schools. Many people agree that poor academic performance and high dropout rates are problems for many high schools and their students. If you were an affirmative advocate focused on these problems, you would order these concerns in a manner similar to this outline:

Significant problems exist with the nation's high schools.

A. High school academic performance is too low.
B. High school dropout rates are too high.

Your solution should fix or measurably reduce both problems. Because it is assumed that you would, if you could, establish that your solution would likely solve the discussed problems, failure to demonstrate that a reduction or eradication of the problems might reasonably suggest that one of them was included just to embellish the problem or perhaps frighten the audience into accepting the proposed solution. In this case, the solvency of your solution must demonstrate that it improves performance *and* reduces dropouts. Thus, you would state and support the following:

The proposed solution reduces the problems.

A. The solution will improve high school academic performance.
B. The solution will reduce high school dropout rates.

In this manner, you would be providing reasons to believe that your proposal will have the intended effect and on a scale that justifies the change.

The second function of advantages is that they intensify desire. Occupying the minds of the audience with impressions of a remedied world has persuasive power. Monroe's Motivated Sequence introduces and explains what Alan Monroe terms the "visualization" component of a persuasive appeal. In *Principles of Speech*, Monroe explains that the goal of visualization "is to intensify desire."[10] "Its purpose is to make your listeners really want to see the belief accepted by everyone or to see the proposal adopted and carried out."[11] If the stock issue of solution is the equivalent of Monroe's "satisfaction" step, advantages are the equivalent of Monroe's visualization step. Monroe's emphasis on visualization punctuates the power of advantages to persuade beyond the measured and logical description of a particular solution's ability to solve a problem. Helping people vividly imagine your solution in action, like allowing them to test-drive a car, enables your target audience to approximate the feel of the new and improved world.

President Obama illustrated this phenomenon in his healthcare address on September 9, 2009, to a joint session of Congress, when he outlined a vision of the future for the American people:

> What this plan will do is make the insurance you have work better for you. Under this plan, it will be against the law for insurance companies to deny you coverage because of a preexisting condition. As soon as I sign this bill, it will be against the law for insurance companies to drop your coverage when you get sick or water it down when you need it the most. They will no longer be able to place some arbitrary cap on the amount of coverage you can receive in a given year or in a lifetime. We will place a limit on how much you can be charged for out-of-pocket expenses, because in the United States of America, no one should go broke because they get sick. And insurance companies will be required to cover, with no extra charge, routine checkups and preventive care, like mammograms and colonoscopies—because there's no reason we shouldn't be catching diseases like breast cancer and colon cancer before they get worse. That makes sense, it saves money, and it saves lives.[12]

In plain language, the tangible and immediate benefits of healthcare reform are laid out by its chief advocate.

Thoughts on Fiat in Public Policy Argumentation and Debate

If you've spent any time on a debate team, you've learned about "fiat." Fiat, in its most basic sense, means a formal authorization, a decree or order. If something is done "by fiat," it is not subject to debate. Particularly in classroom and tournament debating, fiat is an *understanding* or *agreement* between the two competing sides that they will assess the merits of a proposed plan, not the political feasibility of adopting a proposed solution or other such practical matters that might suggest the solution would never come into existence. "Will the Affordable Care Act produce the desired advantages?" is a question for policy debate, while "Will Congress actually pass the Affordable Care Act?" is not. The intent of "granting fiat" to an affirmative advocate is to assume the proposal will garner the needed support and funding so that the debaters can consider fully, and weigh, the advantages against the disadvantages, and other matters that relate to whether the solution will solve a problem. Were debaters to focus only on whether a legislature would pass, and an executive would sign, a piece of legislation, whether the proposed policy could bring about the advantages claimed by affirmative advocates (or the disadvantages claimed by negative advocates) would never be thoroughly considered.

While fiat keeps the debate focused strictly on testing the workability of the proposed policy changes, limiting public policy debate to this focus is neither practical nor always desirable. In the realm of public policy advocacy, negative advocates will challenge the notion that a policy proposal will achieve the support needed for implementation. That is, if you are an affirmative advocate, you *will* encounter opposition who argues, "this will never pass," or, "there isn't enough money available to fund this solution, so it's not worth our time considering it." People will also disagree about whether an idea can possibly get traction with the public or a legislative body. Perhaps a policy idea is sound, but the context or timing makes it politically toxic. Perhaps, at the moment of your advocacy, other politically sensitive proposals are being considered, and your proposal will throw off the political balance. For example, while there has been a great deal of discussion in the United States about immigration reform, congressional Republicans have often made clear that they will not discuss so-called pathways to citizenship for immigrants who entered the country illegally. The refusal to consider pathways to citizenship has little to do with evidence-based consideration of its merits—*will pathways to citizenship produce advantages?* Instead, many Republicans are concerned about primary challenges from conservatives within their own party—*will passing pathways to citizenship anger party leadership, donors, and voters?*

While defenders of the status quo are unlikely to focus exclusively on the practical merits of a proposal, if you are proposing reforms you should still attempt to convince your target audience that your proposal will solve the serious problems you are setting out to solve (that is, you should attempt to transcend exclusive talk of political feasibility). If you do this, negative advocates may soon discover that they are not offering their target audience an attractive defense of the status quo, or any viable alternative means of addressing the problem you have established.

In the next chapter, we begin our consideration of reasoning in public policy advocacy, with a particular focus on causal claims that support essential elements of affirmative and negative advocacy. We also begin our use of critical questions to effectively develop and assess messages.

Exercise: Identifying Stock Issues

Typically, you can identify stock issues by stepping back from a single advocacy event and surveying the controversy more broadly and historically. Your task with this exercise is to (a) choose a controversy, (b) determine and write the proposition under which advocacy is taking place within the controversy, (c) identify the stock issues (problem, cause, solution, and advantages) associated with at least one problem claimed by affirmative advocates, and (d) provide three quotations (and citations) from affirmative advocates. Use their words directly, when possible. Explain which stock issue each quotation supports.

Notes

1 Allusions to "fair fights" resonate with our students and colleagues. Still, we hope to neutralize the potential damage such a metaphor may have by simultaneously critiquing it. See Daniel H. Cohen, "Argument is War ... and War is Hell: Philosophy, Education, and Metaphors for Argumentation," *Informal Logic* 17, no. 2 (January 1995), and the authors

we cite in Chapter 2 to highlight some of the innovations in forensics pedagogy that seek to depart from adversarial and competitive models.

2 See William Rehg, "The Argumentation Theorists in Deliberative Democracy," in *Discourse, Debate and Democracy: Readings from Controversia: An International Journal of Debate and Democratic Renewal*, eds. David Cratis Williams and Marilyn J. Young (New York: International Debate Education Association, 2009), 17; Gordon R. Mitchell, "When Argumentation Backfires: The Motivated Reasoning Predicament in Speech and Debate Pedagogy," in *Speech and Debate as Civic Education*, eds. J. Michael Hogan, Jessica A. Kurr, Michael J. Bergmaier, and Jeremy D. Johnson (University Park: The Pennsylvania State University Press, 2017), 94; and Gordon R. Mitchell, "iSocrates: Student-led Public Debate as Cultural Technology." *Controversia* 7, no. 2 (2011): 68.

3 Frans H. van Eemeren, "Democracy and Argumentation," in Williams and Young, *Discourse, Debate and Democracy*, 47.

4 Ibid., 49.

5 Leon Festinger, *A Theory of Cognitive Dissonance* (Stanford: Stanford University Press, 1985) (originally published in 1957).

6 For a challenging version of this criticism, see Robert C. Byrd, *Losing America: Confronting a Reckless and Arrogant Presidency* (New York: W. W. Norton & Company, 2004).

7 For a recent detailed study of the events and implications of the war in Iraq, see Robert Draper, *To Start a War: How the Bush Administration Took America into Iraq* (New York: Penguin Press, 2020).

8 See Daniel Trotta, "Iraq War Costs U.S. More Than $2 Trillion: Study," Reuters, March 14, 2013, https://www.reuters.com/article/us-iraq-war-anniversary-idUSBRE92D0PG201 30314; Kimberly Amadeo, "Cost of Iraq War, Its Timeline, and the Economic Impact," The Balance, updated August 05, 2020, https://www.thebalance.com/cost-of-iraq-war-timeline-economic-impact-3306301; Gilbert Burnham et al., "The Human Cost of the War in Iraq: A Mortality Study, 2002–2006," Bloomberg School of Public Health, December 12, 2012, https://web.mit.edu/humancostiraq/reports/human-cost-war-101106.pdf; and Amy Hagopian, Abraham D. Flaxman, Tim K. Takaro, Sahar A. Esa Al Shatari, Julie Rajaratnam, Stan Becker, Alison Levin-Rector, Lindsay Galway, Berq J. Hadi Al-Yasseri, William M. Weiss, Christopher J. Murray, and Gilbert Burnham, "Mortality in Iraq Associated with the 2003–2011 War and Occupation: Findings from a National Cluster Sample Survey by the University Collaborative Iraq Mortality Study," PLOS Medicine, October 15, 2013, https://journals.plos.org/plosmedicine/article?id=10.1371/journal.pmed.1001533 (estimating 405,000 Iraqis would die as a result of the 2003 invasion). The Iraq Body Count (IBC) Project maintains a detailed public database of violent civilian deaths since the 2003 invasion, as well as separate running total which includes combatants (https://www.iraqbodycount.org/).

9 Lee Hultzen, "Status in Deliberative Analysis," in *The Rhetorical Idiom: Essays in Rhetoric, Oratory, Language and Drama*, ed. Donald C. Bryant (Ithaca, NY: Cornell University Press, 1958).

10 Alan Monroe, *Principles of Speech* (Glenview, IL: Scott, Foresman, and Company, 1943), 97.

11 Ibid.

12 "Obama's Health Care Speech to Congress," *New York Times*, September 9, 2009, https://www.nytimes.com/2009/09/10/us/politics/10obama.text.html.

4

REASONING I: REASONING ABOUT CAUSE

Takeaways

(1) Evaluating reasoning permits you to uncover the often-invisible logic that drives all advocacy—the assumptions and evidence upon which advocates base their claims.

(2) Evaluating *causal reasoning* is the most productive means of assessing policy goals and appeals.

(3) There are relatively simple *critical questions* that may make you more efficient at interrogating the reasons advocates offer in support of policy proposals.

(4) The critical questions you pose form the tenets of a common rationality that will help you develop compelling messages.

The amount of carbon trapped in an ancient air pocket in a deep layer of Arctic ice does not argue for the existence global warming, or for the need to adopt carbon neutral energy policies. An assault in San Francisco by a person residing in the United States illegally does not make the case for stricter immigration enforcement, or for a border wall. The slowed economy during the COVID-19 pandemic identifies neither COVID-19 nor a state's shutdown order as its cause. Carbon measures, assault incidents, and the economic performance measures are facts. As facts, they are persuasively inert. To bridge evidence with an advocate's conclusion requires reasoning. In this chapter we begin our consideration of reasoning: *how advocates link ideas and evidence they believe their audience will accept to conclusions they hope their audience will draw.*

In his book *On Rhetoric*, Aristotle distinguished between what are termed "inartistic" and "artistic proofs."[1] This is a useful distinction that makes clear *how* evidence is essential to persuasive outcomes. Inartistic proofs are facts we cite when we make an argument. *How* they are employed is an outcome of the artistic proofs—ethos, logos, and pathos. "Ethos" is the persuasiveness that results from advocates themselves, and is usually associated with charisma, credibility, and authority. "Logos" involves how we use words to reason our way from evidence to conclusion. "Pathos" refers to the emotional state of the audience. This chapter focuses on logos—or reasoning—in public policy advocacy. Students encounter lessons about reasoning in a variety of college classes, most intensely perhaps in philosophy classes where they learn about formal and informal logic. We are not seeking to replicate that body of knowledge; instead, our goal in this chapter is to direct your attention to where it is most needed in the successful execution of public policy advocacy.

If there is a place in the public policy advocacy map that is most vulnerable to scrutiny, it is in the *causal assertions* made by advocates. While various forms of reasoning are used throughout public policy advocacy, persuasively linking a problem to a cause and a solution to its advantages is pivotal to the success of affirmative advocates. In both places, advocates are asserting an inferred causal relationship. Consequently, this chapter focuses on causal reasoning and a set of *critical questions* you can apply to public policy advocacy (yours and that of others) as you develop and assess messages. We focus on locations in the stock issues map where causal reasoning is particularly important, drawing attention along the way to the reasoning infrastructure that lies behind public policy appeals.

Reasoning and the Infrastructure of Advocacy

The way advocates reason to arrive at their conclusion is the infrastructure, or internal strategy, that holds up a reason for believing something. Advocates seek to discover the substance behind a call for reform or defense of the status quo, and that substance is an appeal's essential architecture or its infrastructure. If you think of a building that seems to effortlessly stand against opposing forces (gravity, weather, natural and human-made disasters), you know that something behind the façade holds the building together. A common revelation among new students of argument is that unveiling the existence and inadequacies of an argument's infrastructure is often a significant step in the process of improving or countering an argument.

Understanding the infrastructure of an argument is also important because so much advocacy in the public sphere is presented in an incomplete manner. We make the point throughout the prior chapter that an argument presented at a particular moment, or place, in an advocacy situation is almost always only a part of the larger landscape of a public controversy. Advocates may offer only a brief concern or complaint and leave it to the audience to fill in the remaining logic. Some advocates are simply outraged. People are being shot near their homes or schools and they want it to stop. Their relatives are being deported and they want it to stop. Their business is being overburdened by taxes and fees and they want it to stop. These dynamics may cause advocates to make demands of people in positions of power; but as powerful as outrage is as a driving force for activism, it does not naturally result in a clear articulation of policy objectives. Understanding the infrastructure of arguments helps you form a more complete picture of the larger issues and what you want to say about them.

To appreciate the infrastructure of advocacy appeals, and fill in what's missing, students of argumentation and debate are often taught complex and rigid rules of formal logic to determine whether arguments are well-reasoned. But, everyday advocacy rarely involves such a systematic presentation of elements such as major and minor premises; one or more key points are typically missing when advocates express their position within ordinary, everyday advocacy settings. Thus, *evaluating reasoning involves a mental assembly of what is stated and what is not stated.*

Consider the "Fight for $15," a campaign to increase the minimum wages from the national minimum wage (at time of writing) of $7.25 per hour to $15.00 per hour. Those opposing this increase (in our rubric this would come from negative advocates) make a version of the following causal claim:

> When prices go up, demand goes down. Increasing the minimum wage will raise prices, and so will reduce demand.

This is a *disadvantage*, which we will explain in more detail below; here we simply analyze it to demonstrate the way analysis reveals the components of advocacy. The argument is an economic principle; if things cost more, those who pay for those things will buy less of it. Applied to wages, the principle means if it costs more to employ people, employers will employ fewer people and unemployment will increase. Here is the argument as it appeared in a 2009 *Forbes* article:

> This is a standard application of basic economic principles. Demand curves slope downward, which means that people wish to buy more of something as it gets cheaper and less of something as it gets more expensive. Supply curves slope upward, meaning people are willing to do more of something as the rewards increase and less of something as the rewards decrease. In competitive markets, minimum wages create unemployment: While they draw more people into the labor market, they reduce the amount of labor companies wish to hire.[2]

The claim that, if employers need to pay more for labor, they'll hire fewer people, is a generally accepted premise among economic conservatives. Processing the $15 proposal through this principle follows the structure of what logicians would call a "categorical deductive syllogism," which we will consider in more depth in Chapter 5. One can "deduce" the claim that something or someone belongs to a category from the major and minor premises. Following the rules of logic, *if* the major premise and minor premise are true, *it follows logically that* the conclusion will be true. As such:

Major premise: All minimum wage increases reduce demand for labor.
Minor premise: The "Fight for $15" will increase wages.
Conclusion: The "Fight for $15" will reduce demand for labor.

However, if you follow the advice of philosopher Steven Toulmin, you will seek a simpler means of identifying the components of arguments.[3] Premises, argues Toulmin, can rarely be assessed as "true" or "false," and only advocates in the most formal of argument settings speak in a structure closely approximating a syllogism. Toulmin draws attention to how advocates bridge "data" and a "claim" with a "warrant," in his well-known model:

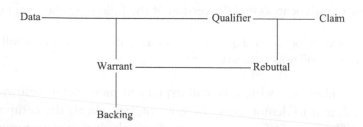

The "claim" is the conclusion advocates wish the audience will draw. "Data" is another term for "evidence," but it might also involve more simply an explanation or idea that supports the claim. The "warrant" links the data and the claim and thus serves as a basic term labeling the reasoning strategy of advocates. Here is the argument about the disadvantages of a minimum wage increase laid out in Toulmin's model:

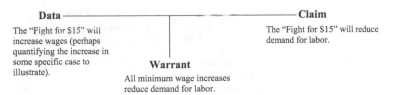

Data ———————————————————— **Claim**

The "Fight for $15" will increase wages (perhaps quantifying the increase in some specific case to illustrate).

Warrant
All minimum wage increases reduce demand for labor.

The "Fight for $15" will reduce demand for labor.

Often a warrant is further bolstered with additional data or information, which Toulmin refers to as "backing." Backing for the above claim might include evidence such as provided in the *Forbes* piece: "a comprehensive survey research on minimum wages by David Neumark and William Wascher finds that minimum wages do, in fact, reduce employment."[4] Taken together, the warrant and its backing offer an indication of *how advocates link claims and evidence they believe their audience will accept to conclusions they hope their audiences will draw.* The two additional components Toulmin provides (qualifier and rebuttal) offer additional insights into the potential weaknesses of an argument.[5]

Toulmin's scheme can also illustrate the way certain assumptions that link facts or data to a conclusion are often implied/unstated. For example, perhaps an advocate merely asserts that "this raise in the minimum wage will hurt the working class," or that "this increase in minimum wage is going to cost my employer a lot of money and many people will lose their jobs where I work." These would both constitute incomplete arguments. In the academic field of argumentation, these incomplete arguments are referred to as *enthymemes*. Enthymemes are arguments with missing premises or a situation in which some aspect of an argument is withheld either intentionally or unintentionally. The missing component of the larger argument is (theoretically) filled in by the audience to form a conclusion, and this tendency of the audience to complete the incomplete argument offers advocates an opportunity to strategically connect with the audience. What's missing is typically an idea advocates assume will be shared by a large portion of a target audience. Consider the example above—"this increase in minimum wage is going to cost my employer a lot of money and many people will lose their jobs where I work." Missing is the critical assumption: "All minimum wage increases reduce demand for labor," as well as any subsequent backing that indicates why the maker of this argument believes any minimum wage increase necessarily reduces labor demand. Here is a diagram of the argument with the missing components in italics:

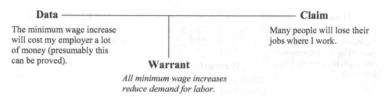

Data ———————————————————— **Claim**

The minimum wage increase will cost my employer a lot of money (presumably this can be proved).

Many people will lose their jobs where I work.

Warrant

All minimum wage increases reduce demand for labor.

    Confronting this argument, you can engage what is said and/or what is implied. By contending with the implied or unstated assumptions—in this case the warrant—you can consider reasons why it might not always be true that minimum wage increases decrease labor demand. Maybe there are notable exceptions. Maybe research backing the warrant reflects the biases of its researchers or those who funded the research. Perhaps there are examples of minimum wage increases that did not lead to reduced labor demand. Each of these factors could be presented to challenge the claim and expand the depth and range of the debate. However, if you engage only what is stated, you may not pose productive objections and the resulting debate might be considerably less rigorous. You might assert, "your boss would never fire you because you're too important to the company," or other responses that fail to contend with the fundamental assumptions behind the claim. If you were to counter only what is stated, you might also inadvertently concede (appear to agree with) the implied warrant.

    This is the briefest introduction to how reasoning works on a very general level. One way to move rapidly into the reasoning infrastructure and productively address the reasoning of public policy advocates is to focus on the causal claims being made by advocates. This is where we will turn our attention now and through the remainder of this chapter.

Predictions in Public Policy Advocacy: Evaluating Causal Reasoning

Imagine yourself wanting to be supportive of a good friend who just went through a breakup. You arrive at your friend's home and find him or her lying around, with no plans, obviously very depressed and with little apparent hope for the future. You suggest the two of you go see a movie, a comedy romance that's doing well at the box office.

> *You claim:* "It will get your mind off the breakup."
> *Your friend replies:* "I'd rather not. Going to see that movie will just depress me."
> *You respond:* "There are other movies, of course, but it seems to me you're already depressed, so the movie isn't going to cause that problem. It might actually make you more hopeful about the next chapter of your life."

While this is not a policy argument specifically, it illustrates an engagement in causal reasoning and challenges related to causal reasoning.

Notwithstanding how policy arguments are initially presented by one or more persons, public policy controversies are essentially two or more sides predicting the future based on cause-effect claims—*if we do* X, Y *will most likely occur,* or more simply, X *will lead to* Y. You are claiming in the above hypothetical that going to the movies will make your friend more hopeful. The advocate opposed to the minimum wage increase claims increased wages will cause many at their work to lose their jobs. We have already discussed how public policy advocacy is "deliberative" speech, which means it is speech about the *future.* Recognizing that most claims debated in the realm of public policy are predictions focuses attention on the end point, or hypothetical consequences asserted by advocates.

In the above example involving your invitation to a friend, you make a proposal based on a prediction that seeing a movie may *cause* your friend to feel better (thus you are an affirmative advocate). Your friend doubts your prediction and counters with an alleged potential disadvantage: that a movie may *cause* him or her to become depressed (thus he or she is a negative advocate). The exchange continues with asking critical questions about your friend's causal reasoning, leading to your response that any depression in the aftermath of the movie could not be blamed on the movie on the grounds that he or she is *already* depressed, reasoning that the major cause of that depression is the breakup. Indeed, you claim that the movie may produce an advantage: to *cause* your friend to be more hopeful about their future.

In our experience, newcomers to the activity of advocacy are quite capable of objecting to faulty causal reasoning. This is perhaps due to the way humans learn through causal reasoning: *If I do* X, *I will be fed. If I avoid* Y, *I will be safe.* There are many well-known examples of controversies over causal reasoning (whether global warming constitutes a long-term or permanent threat to humans and other life on earth, whether violent video games cause young users to become violent themselves, whether marijuana use leads to more dangerous substance abuse, to name a few).

Causal Reasoning and Stock Issues

Target audiences in the relam of public policymaking might not consciously follow conventions for reasoning, relying instead on intuition or common sense. Nevertheless, we believe deliberative decisions are made based on specific inferential leaps that can be impacted by your advocacy. Places in a public policy advocacy where the most consequential inferential leaps are made include:

1. Problem → Cause
2. Solution → Advantages

In the first instance, advocates reason that a specific cause produces a specific problem. Consider an argument about global warming. Imagine that you argue that global warming, and its associated harms, are caused primarily by the combustion of fossil fuels. The direct, irrefutable relationship between global warming and carbon has never been witnessed. However, the relationship between carbon and heat can be observed in experimental conditions. Increases in atmospheric carbon and planetary temperatures can be recorded and tracked over time. Planet temperatures can meet predictions based on atmospheric carbon concentrations, confirming theories. Plant growth records can be combined with historic carbon measures to show that prehistoric carbon levels coincided with lower temperatures. In each of these instances, proving this causal claim can benefit from past factual evidence; if in fact the relationship between problem and cause (i.e., temperature and carbon) is factual and true, it will have left evidentiary traces or knowable facts. How those facts, however, are reasoned to the conclusion that fossil fuels cause or contribute to global warming depends, in large part, on the persuasiveness of your reasoning.

Much the same applies to the second sequence: Solution → Advantages. Advocates reason that a solution will cause advantages. This is made more complicated by the fact that the inferential leap involves speculation about the future. Affirmative advocates reason that a not-yet-adopted solution will result in worthwhile advantages. Returning to the global warming example, if you propose the adoption of renewable energies such as solar and wind power, you are asserting that widespread adoption will necessarily reduce carbon emissions, and slow, stop, or reverse the effects of atmospheric carbon. Your target audience cannot know with certainty this will happen. Nevertheless, you can make an argument that this outcome is likely, and worth the risk or expense, especially if the status quo is especially problematic. Perhaps authorities vouch for this causal relationship. Perhaps adoption of these proposals elsewhere has demonstrated the desired effects. Perhaps the target audience for your advocacy will simply reason that reduced dependence on fossil fuels will necessarily reduce carbon emissions.

Regardless, these two places in public policy advocacy are especially vulnerable because it is in these places where essential components of a call for reform are most easily weakened. If you ultimately want the audience to support your solution, you must convincingly argue the cause of the problems and the advantages of the solution. Those opposing the solution should focus on these places to evaluate the strength of your reasoning. These are "soft spots" or the "soft underbelly" of public policy advocacy, where affirmative advocates might find themselves most productively challenged by advocates of the status quo. Fortified with care, these places may also withstand objection and ring true with target audiences.

Bridging the Gaps with Reasoning: In Practice

It is useful now for us to consider a public policy controversy that illustrates how reasoning is performed to connect key stock issues. Recall that seldom is each stock issue argued in a single argument event; during a given argument event, an arguer may believe that only a part of the overall argument needs to be addressed. Ideally, you can reconstitute the larger arguments in order to form a fuller picture of the controversy.

President Trump's Border Wall: Problem → Cause

When Donald Trump declared his candidacy for President of the United States on June 16, 2015, he announced his plan to build a wall along the Mexican border to help control immigration. Three and a half years later, on January 8, 2019, the President delivered a speech from the Oval Office arguing his case for funding his embattled proposal to, among other things, construct a southern border wall. In this matter, Trump is an affirmative advocate, because he is advocating for something that does not yet exist in the status quo. *Focusing first on the relationship between problem and cause*, the president provides a provocative description of the problem's scope, which he terms a "humanitarian crisis." He adds:

> It strains public resources and drives down jobs and wages.

And:

> Every week 300 of our citizens are killed by heroin alone, 90 percent of which floods across from our southern border.

And:

> One in three women are sexually assaulted on the dangerous trek up through Mexico. Women and children are the biggest victims by far of our broken system.[6]

Veracity aside, if the description of the problem functions to create a desire to remedy the status quo, Trump's argument could hardly be more compelling. The next burden of the advocate, however, is to demonstrate the cause of that problem. *Are public resources, wages, drugs, and sexual assault linked to immigration?* Cases might be made for each claim, but the president doesn't make them. Instead, the audience is left to fill in the blanks. For instance, *is there reason to believe illegal immigration reduces available jobs and wages?* The audience may reason that more available labor results in lower wages, but *is any evidence being offered to support that conclusion? Is there any evidence to support the conclusion that relates to recent patterns of immigration? Are there historical instances of this phenomenon that might apply in this case? Is there supporting economic data? Do authorities make these connections?* Certainly, Trump does not offer information along these lines. The target audience is left with little more than to assume the absence of the solution is the cause, which may be enough for some experiencing his message.

While a public audience might find this argument adequate upon first encountering it, zeroing in on the gap between problem and cause is an opportunity for negative advocates—those seeking to maintain a status quo that does not include a wall spanning the length of the U.S. southern border. Advocates often focus their arguments where they are strongest and leave out of their analysis stock issues that they have more trouble substantiating.

Those negating the president's proposal are probably better off criticizing what the president *doesn't* do—he doesn't establish a compelling case that recent unlawful border crossings are the cause of the cited problems. The opposition could offer counter explanations for the problems described. *Is drug trafficking, for instance, caused or enabled by the absence of a wall?* The demand for drugs doesn't exist because of the ease of trafficking. So, if the absence of a wall isn't the cause of illegal drug use in the United States, a wall quite likely won't prevent it. A savvy advocate might find instances when very serious physical barriers failed to limit drug trafficking (such as, for instance, in the case of prisons).

President Trump's Border Wall: Solution → Advantages

The next gap the president addresses is *the gap between the solution and the advantages.* His reasoning here addresses the question, *Will the proposed solution solve the problem?* or *Will the proposed solution result in the advantages the president appears to be claiming will come with his solution?*

We begin first by considering the solution: in addition to a wall spanning the entire US-Mexico border, the president requests new technology, agents, border judges, and bed space for those detained. *How does he reason these proposals will produce advantages? How will $6 billion for the wall alone reduce the problems the president outlines?* Arguably, the president reasons from his solution to his implied advantages in three ways. First, you are encouraged to take it on good authority, as he explains the proposals were developed by "law enforcement professionals and border agents." You are also encouraged to assume problems with jobs, drugs, and assaults will decline because representatives from these communities developed these proposals. Second, you are told the border wall, the single-most controversial component of his proposal, is "just common sense." It may seem likely, or you might conclude "it stands to reason," that a physical barrier would restrict or limit the movement of drugs and people across the border. Third, the president reminds you that "wealthy politicians build walls, fences and gates around their homes." While this analogy does nothing to establish the efficacy of such walls, it reminds some folks who might question a barrier's efficacy that they themselves use walls to keep threats out.

All told, the president's advocacy relies on the assumption that walls keep people out. The strength of that assumption with audiences may explain why he did not offer further reasoning to bridge the gap between solution and advantages. It bears noting also that he does not provide much reasoning or evidence to establish that the advantages will produce more employment opportunity, less drugs, and less crime. These matters of "solvency" (as they are referred to in academic debate) are only implied. Regarding solvency, he merely says it would be immoral "for the politicians to do nothing and continue to allow more innocent people to be so horribly victimized." The speech wraps up with a description of four tragic events that he implies would not have occurred if his approach to immigration control had been adopted earlier.

The gap between solution and advantages is a distance that must be traveled by affirmative advocates who do so by offering evidence that the proposed plan will produce the advantages (and those advantages will address the problem). Other than on the basis of common sense, the president provides little to establish a link between his proposals and their alleged outcomes. Perhaps he might have referred to examples of walls actually succeeding in stopping movement between borders (we will discuss the use of examples, or "inductive reasoning," in this manner in Chapter 5); however, the two most famous examples of immigration-abating walls—the Berlin Wall and Israel's security fence—carry with them strong negative associations. Trump's reasoning is more "deductive," based on the hope that his premises will seem logical to his target audience (more on this form of reasoning also in Chapter 5). *Do walls stop immigration and drugs?* People intent on crossing the southern border make the distant trek across a country (at a minimum), through a desert, sometimes with their children, without water, often without money, to reach a nation whose elected president was determined to stop them from entering, where they do not likely speak the native language. *Are they going to elect to stay put because of a wall?* Very often, these are people in desperate situations who cannot turn back. *Will the demand for, or supply of, drugs decline because of a steel border barrier?* Drug traffickers use vehicles, tunnels, submarines, and drones to bring drugs to the United States. *How would a 20-foot fence stop that flow?* Meanwhile, the president never establishes that those immigrating to the United States are more inclined to commit violent crimes. *Because it was never established that immigration necessarily contributed to criminal behavior in the first place, are you convinced that restricting immigration would reduce crime?*

Into this reasoning gap, if you are opposed to the president's solution, you might reason from the solution to one or more disadvantages you allege result from the solution. As we shall explain, among the options available to negative advocates is the argument that disadvantages caused by a proposed solution will outweigh its advantages. An argument along these lines is that, while walls may reduce some undesired commerce (such as the drug trade), walls also reduce desired commerce (such as travel and shopping).[7] Whether these arguments, or Trump's, establish significant reasons to support or oppose the building of a wall on the U.S. southern border is an ongoing and open question.

Introducing Critical Questions for Public Policy Advocacy

Much of the analysis of causal arguments above is driven by a set of critical questions which we shall now outline. Because we will be providing critical questions to assist you in addressing more than just causal claims, we begin by discussing critical questions more generally.

Why Critical Questions?

There are many excellent systems for evaluating reasoning that accommodate the practical characteristics of public policy advocacy. To give you confidence that you can affect the outcome of a dispute without extensive training in debate, we favor an approach that poses a limited set of *critical questions* designed to assist your own critical thinking and discover flaws in the reasoning of others. This approach is similar to the goals of other argumentation and debate teachers and scholars who seek to—in the words of William Rehg—avoid "a detailed knowledge of formal rules or standards," in favor of "a comprehensive critical attentiveness to the general aspects of reasonable argumentation" through "a capacity for raising a few critical questions."[8]

The deployment of critical questions is a system of evaluating reasoning—and, in the next chapters, evaluating evidence—that imagines how advocates' reasoning will be evaluated by their target audience. As we explain in more detail in Chapter 8, when it comes to evaluating reasoning, for all practical purposes, you should consider yourself part of the community you are addressing and seeking to convince. In so doing, it is helpful to your message development goals—determining *what to say*—for you to assume that those who are part of this community share with you an affinity for common patterns of thinking or ways of constructing claims that are rational. Certainly, we know that your target audience may not always conform to the rational expectations that undergird the critical questions (recall that we also advise you to be prepared for unfair engagements). However, we have already noted how advocates rely on audiences to share certain sentiments, resulting in implied and assumed warrants, and (in the case of enthymemes) fill in missing elements of advocacy. If you are proposing a policy change, you should assume that these critical questions are inevitable responses of your audience even if you have failed to pose them yourself regarding your own advocacy.[9]

As a practical matter, if any of these critical questions are to become convincing refutation, they must be reformulated into statements refuting the claims of either affirmative or negative advocates. For example, if you are a negative advocate, you will want to know the answer to the critical question: *Will the proposed solution cause additional problems not already occurring in the status quo?* If your answer is "yes," it might be best for you to reformulate the question into a statement for the purposes of refutation: "The proposal causes a problem that is not already occurring," or you might move directly to articulating the specific problem caused by the proposal, which would have the same impact: "Building on that land will cause flooding," or "The proposal to go to war will lead to long-term destabilization of the region."

As you will learn in the next chapter, isolated arguments are supported by a variety of reasoning infrastructures, but we strongly recommend that you *begin* your analysis by asking whether the policy goal is well-reasoned—*whether the proposed policy solves a problem without causing other new problems that are more troubling than the original problem?* The above minimum wage advocacy is an example of how an advocate might get distracted by other questions and issues. To focus, for instance, on whether a particular company will lay off a particular person, could easily lead you to an unproductive dispute that steers your attention away from your analysis of the problem (many people who work full time cannot afford housing, food, transportation, education, etc.), identification of its causes, your plan for mitigating the problem, and a thorough consideration of advantages of your plan. We advise you to make the critical questions below your *first* priority (see **Appendix** for a list of all critical questions recommended for the evaluation of reasoning and evidence). These initial questions focus attention on the central burdens of advocacy in the realm of public policy; an appreciation for the mechanics of other forms of reasoning will complete an essential toolkit for critical thinking and problem solving.

Those evaluating the causal reasoning of a policy proposal should ask the following six critical questions:

(1) Is the identified cause significant enough to produce the problem?
(2) Are there other probable causes that might reasonably produce the problem?
(3) Will the proposed solution solve the problem?
(4) Is there something about the status quo that will prevent the proposed solution from working?
(5) Will the proposed solution cause additional problems or disadvantages not already occurring in the status quo?
(6) Is an identified disadvantage the likely result of the proposed solution, or might it be caused by other factors?

These questions deal directly with the stock issues discussed in Chapter 3 and, as such, represent the most common concerns of those wishing to construct compelling affirmative positions or inclined to defend the status quo. Once these questions have been asked and answered to some degree, they also become components of a framework of refutation.

Applying Critical Questions to Affirmative and Negative Advocacy

We have already applied the critical questions to examples of policy proposals above to some extent. Consider them now more systematically applied to a single hypothetical case—imagining you are an activist concerned with the spread of HIV/AIDs in a particular war-torn foreign nation. You argue the problem is caused by the failure of that nation's government to promote the use of condoms and call on the U.S. federal government to provide more funding for condom distribution efforts. The *first critical question* concerns the cause of the problem. Imagine those opposed to your solution argue that the failure of the target nation's government to promote condom use (what you allege is the cause) may explain only a small portion of the problem or may not be a reasonable explanation at all. The opposition may provide evidence that the nation's government is already involved in an extensive condom promotion effort. This leads to the *second critical question* concerning other probable causes of the spread of HIV/AIDs in the nation. Imagine the opposition argues there is a widespread cultural aversion among males in the region to the use of condoms and an unwillingness of male leaders to address this widespread reluctance. Concerning the *third critical question*, you are fairly confident that the U.S. federal government has the capacity to fund (their actions would lead to, or *cause*) a large-scale condom distribution effort in the target nation; however, the opposition provides evidence to indicate that increased funding by the United States has led to no measurable decrease in the spread of HIV/AIDS in that nation. There's a reason for this, argues the opposition, raising the *fourth critical question*. This concerns a particular dynamic of a civil conflict in the region: a propaganda campaign by one of the leading factions that is convincing men and women that contraceptives provided by foreign governments are unsafe and potentially damaging to users. While misguided and inaccurate, this information will prevent sexually active individuals in the region from using the condoms provided by your plan. You argue that a U.S.-sponsored intervention may work to change the thinking of the people of the region, but the opposition poses the *fifth critical question* and argues there is a significant disadvantage to providing more funds to the government of this nation. Evidence indicates this government has been channeling donated funds intended to reduce the spread of HIV/AIDs to weapons purchases that are fueling an ongoing civil war. Experts claim any additional weapons added to the conflict will exacerbate the situation, leading to a fear among the population of impending violence, widespread famine, and a refugee crisis. Finally, concerning the *sixth critical question*, you argue that the civil conflict was well under way before your proposal and, therefore, the policy you have proposed could not be said to uniquely cause the disadvantage.

This hypothetical example illustrates the way the six critical questions can pose major challenges to the causal infrastructure of a proposal. If you are an affirmative advocate, your primary reason for believing that your proposal is warranted requires a series of believable causal claims, which negative advocates will challenge. Knowing you will face a challenge, you have an initial opportunity to pose these critical questions yourself, anticipating the concerns of negative advocates and preparing for them. Likewise, if you find yourself in the role of a negative advocate, these six critical questions should serve as a starting point for your evaluation of the causal claims of an affirmative advocate.

While the first three critical questions concerning causal reasoning recall the stock issues and represent essential burdens of affirmative advocates, the second three form *a framework for negative advocacy* that requires more explanation. Below we provide that explanation and match the critical questions to some common argument types that surface in public policy advocacy settings.

Now imagine yourself as a negative advocate. The fourth question—*Is there something about the status quo that will prevent the proposed solution from working?*—can lead you to discover what are sometimes referred to as **counteracting causes** or **barriers** that will prevent the solution from working. Counteracting causes and barriers are realities of the status quo that you allege the policy proposal does not seek to, or cannot, change, which will continue to cause the problem. Counteracting causes and barriers may also be aspects of the status quo or the proposal you claim will interrupt the effectiveness of the proposal.

Consider the example of the "Fair Tax" proposal in Illinois. Voters were asked to approve or reject this proposal in the 2020 General Election. The proposal sought to address significant funding needs (the problem) by changing a longstanding requirement in the Illinois Constitution (the cause) that demands that all residents be taxed at the same tax rate.[10] Allowing for different tax rates based on income levels, or a "fair tax" system (the solution), supporters of the change argue, would permit the state to implement higher tax rates for wealthier residents. The resulting additional state income could be used to address significant funding needs (the advantages), particularly funds needed to shore up the critically underfunded pension programs for public employees.

You may be unfamiliar with the challenges faced by governmental bodies (including state governments, municipalities, school districts, colleges and universities, and so on) across the United States who have long provided public employees with retirement plans, or pensions. Most pensions promise the employee a set amount when they retire that can be reasonably relied on for the remainder of their life. These are guaranteed benefits that result in a monthly payment. Such plans must continue to receive regular contributions from the public employer to accumulate enough money to cover future benefits. When public employers do not contribute the necessary funds, or there is a significant loss of funds due to a loss of investment earnings during an economic downturn, pension funds fall below the amount they need to have on-hand to cover future benefits. Severely underfunded funds are at risk of running out of money (insolvency), in which case current retirees may face reductions in their monthly pension amount.

Those in Illinois opposed to the Fair Tax proposal have a variety of concerns with the proposal. One is that the proposal does not address a *barrier* that would remain even if the proposal was adopted—another provision in the Illinois Constitution which forbids any action that would "diminish or impair" public pensions (that would reduce earned benefits owed to retiring state employees).[11] In effect, opponents of the Fair Tax argue that this second Constitutional provision—what is referred to as the "pension protection clause"—will ultimately prevent meaningful reform of the public pension systems, as any proposed differential or graduated tax scheme envisioned by proponents of the Fair Tax proposal will not produce enough additional income to address the magnitude of the underfunded pension funds.[12]

While the identification of barriers is a particularly common strategy of negative advocates, if you are an affirmative advocate, you can also introduce barriers or counteracting causes in response to disadvantages claimed by a negative advocate. In this circumstance, you might claim that some aspect or outcome of the proposed solution will counteract the alleged negative consequences of the solution. As an affirmative advocate, you might also introduce a counteracting cause to claim that the causal relationship that allegedly produces the disadvantage will be interrupted by some counteracting force of the status quo (see more below on how disadvantages are linked to solutions).

A policy proposal may also be criticized for not being appropriately structured to deal with the problem. That is, if you are a negative advocate, you might argue that *the proposal itself may be a barrier* due to, for instance, its inadequate funding or limited time frame. Opponents of the Fair Tax plan in Illinois could argue that increasing the amount of revenue that can be collected from wealthier taxpayers will not produce enough funds to address the most significant expenditure threatening the state's financial solvency: the unfunded liability of the public pension systems in the state. Because the Fair Tax plan leaves the "pension protection clause" in effect, opponents argue, it offers no means of restructuring benefits offered by these pension plans—thus it is structured to perpetuate the problem.[13]

The fifth and sixth critical questions concerning causal reasoning deal with potential **disadvantages**. The fifth critical question—*Will the proposed solution cause additional problems or disadvantages not already occurring in the status quo?*—is a standard question raised by those considering a public policy proposal, although you may experience different versions of this question (one of the most common is: *Will there be unintended consequences?*). Disadvantages are asserted by negative advocates in defense of the status quo. They are causal claims—*policy X will cause disadvantage Y*, argues the negative. Most disadvantages assume that the proposal will be enacted and ask *what will occur after enactment* (see our discussion of "fiat" in Chapter 3).

Disadvantages are structured in a wide variety of ways. Ideally, if you are a negative advocate, disadvantages you construct should accomplish the following:

(1) Identify something about the policy proposal that will cause an undesirable effect (often referred to in academic debate as a *link*).

(2) Claim that the effect is significant (often referred to in academic debate as an *impact*).

Before these essential components are provided, you would typically name your disadvantage in some way. Ideally, you will make a full sentence claim, such as, "Preemptive war with Iraq will have devastating and irreversible consequences for the people of Iraq, America, and the world." Or, you will name your disadvantages in a manner that highlights the consequences specifically, such as, "Worldwide recession will occur if we go to war with Iraq." The overriding objective of arguing a disadvantage is to establish that the disadvantages outweigh any advantages of the proposed solution.

If one or more disadvantages are offered by negative advocates, the sixth question will place the same reasoning burdens faced by affirmative advocates onto negative advocates. By asking, *Is an identified disadvantage the likely result of the proposed solution, or might it be caused by other factors?* affirmative advocates begin a process of uncovering a wide range of potential flaws in the reasoning on which a disadvantage relies.

This begins with questioning whether negative advocates have identified a particular aspect of the affirmative policy proposal that will cause the consequences. Affirmative advocates are essentially posing the causal challenges that may have been posed against their advocacy against negative advocates' causal claims, beginning with the first critical question: *Is the identified cause [in this case, the affirmative policy proposal] significant enough to produce the problem [the disadvantage]?* If affirmative advocates' answer is no, which it is likely to be, they will argue that negative advocates failed to prove that the policy proposal contains any specific element that will cause the disadvantage.

Consider again our example of the Fair Tax plan in Illinois. There are several disadvantages opponents of Illinois' Fair Tax proposal might assert (recall in Chapter 3 our discussion of funding and how new or increased taxes are regularly opposed), but the most effective would stop the proposal before it succeeds at the ballot box, by breaking off a substantial portion of the "yes" votes and turning them into "no" votes. As the vote neared, opponents of the

Fair Tax plan began to argue that passage of the plan would lead to the taxing of retirement income (in Illinois, retirement income is not taxed in the status quo). The argument is that the Fair Tax plan will permit differential tax rates based on income, and that would open the door to the taxing of retirement income, because lawmakers could include such taxation as part of a larger revenue strategy (remember, the state needs new revenue to fix the public pension systems). If you were a proponent of the Fair Tax plan, you would be on sensible ground to argue that there is nothing specific in the solution (no link) that would cause the decision of lawmakers to begin taxing retirement income in Illinois. To establish a link between the proposal and the disadvantage, opponents initially pointed to public remarks of the Illinois Treasurer, a proponent of the Fair Tax plan, who appeared to suggest that an advantage of the plan is that it would allow for the taxing of the retirement income of some taxpayers whose retirement income is significant.[14] Opponents would later rely more on general cynicism and distrust among the public of promises made by "politicians."

Sometimes negative advocates overstate or exaggerate the impact of a disadvantage. It is a common criticism of intercollegiate competitive policy debaters that they take relatively small impacts and extrapolate larger, more severe outcomes (threading together otherwise disconnected evidence to claim, for instance, that a frustrated Russian government will initiate a nuclear strike against its enemies). In defending a proposal against an alleged severe negative consequence that lies at the end of a complex chain of causal events, it is often sufficient to demonstrate that a chain of causation is not sufficiently backed by evidence. For negative advocates, it is generally acceptable, and perhaps wise, not to go too far along the causal chain. Offering generally undesirable impacts (closure of small businesses, increased unemployment, economic recession, regional conflict, drought, and so forth) is often sufficient. In the case of the Fair Tax plan, for instance, the new imposition of taxes on retirement income would be perceived, for many Illinois retirees, as a significant negative impact, even if the actual net increase resulted in a relatively modest loss to their income.

The second critical question—*Are there other probable causes which might reasonably produce the problem?*—can also be asked by affirmative advocates to discover that another cause within the status quo is *already* producing a claimed disadvantage. The logical conclusion, argue affirmative advocates, is that their policy proposal cannot be said to be the only, unique, or even a significant cause of the disadvantage. For example, the concern of opponents of the Fair Tax plan—that the plan will result in the taxing of retirement income—is not uniquely caused by the solution. *Uniqueness* is an important principle in policy advocacy. For a proposed solution to be rejected because of a disadvantage, the solution must be the sole cause of the disadvantage. If anything else might cause the taxing of retirement income, then the solution cannot be said to uniquely cause the disadvantage. The best way to establish "non-uniqueness" is to prove that the disadvantage can happen, or is happening, in the status quo. *Can legislators tax retirement income—in the status quo—before the Fair Tax plan is passed?* If they can (*and they can*) negative advocates will struggle, at least logically, to tie this disadvantage to the proposal.

There are two common defenses negative advocates offer in favor of the causal claims that make up their disadvantages. The first is to simply argue that, even if the status quo is already experiencing the problem, that problem is made worse by a policy proposal. The second is to be more precise about the timing of the alleged disadvantage, arguing that the consequences are close at hand and the affirmative proposal will produce the conditions that cause them to occur.

Another argument form that is a common causal argument in public policy advocacy is referred to as a *turn*. When a negative advocate claims that *the proposed solution will cause disadvantages*, affirmative advocates can "turn" the analysis around, claiming that the logical effect of a disadvantage may, in some way, *just as likely* help the values and interests of the affirmative, or claiming that not implementing the proposed solution would enhance the consequences that concern negative advocates. Consider again the Fair Tax plan. Without the ability to set varying rates (and limited effective means of generating additional revenue), if you were a Fair Tax proponent you might argue that taxing retirement benefits would have to happen. You would argue, if the Fair Tax does not pass, everything gets worse for retirees. With no ability to set varying rates, participants in both public and private pension programs with lower monthly pensions will end up paying whatever the flat tax rate is, since that would be the only way to tax that income without a permissible graduated tax plan. Public sector retirees might also lose a significant portion of their benefits if their pension plans dip further into insolvency. Private pensions that depend on contributions tied to work hours—like construction trade labor funds whose participants work on state infrastructure and public works—will suffer too when the governmental bodies no longer have the money to spend on capital improvements.

Turns are clever and dynamic arguments. Technically, a turn against a disadvantage ends up becoming another reason to vote for the solution, because once a disadvantage is effectively *turned* it becomes another advantage of the solution (the advantage being that you avoid the disadvantage). In real-world advocacy, turns are often complicated to explain and confusing. They need to be explained in simple terms.

Finally, seeking to avoid the disadvantages of a proposed solution, negative advocates often introduce *counterplans*. We will discuss counterplans in more detail in Chapter 5, as they bear on another type of reasoning common in public policy advocacy. It is important, however, to define them here as a tactical strategy used by negative advocates to offer a target audience another option that, at least they claim, will avoid the disadvantages they believe will be caused by affirmative advocates' solutions. Returning to our Fair Tax plan example, one obvious alternative solution—and one favored by many opponents of the Fair Tax plan—is to rescind the structural barrier to reforming pension programs in the state: the provision in the Illinois Constitution that forbids any action that would reduce earned benefits owed to retiring state employees. This is a highly controversial proposal that, were it seriously considered, would likely alter the fundamental political landscape of the state of Illinois. Counterplans regularly carry this sort of weight, and are often thought to be insincerely offered, owing to their political and ideological impracticality.

In the next chapter, we continue our discussion of reasoning by considering three common forms of reasoning (deductive reasoning, inductive reasoning, and reasoning by analogy) and related critical questions.

Exercise: Reasoning in a Newspaper Opinion Piece

Select a letter to the editor, column, or editorial wherein the writer is addressing a public controversy. Identify the controversy and which side of the issue the writer is on, if possible. Determine the cause of the problem the writer is addressing, as he or she might define it, and ask and answer the first two critical questions for causal reasoning (see above or **Appendix**). Note: The writer may not address the cause explicitly or clearly. You may need to determine the cause the writer implies from the way the writer describes the larger public controversy.

Notes

1 George Kennedy, *Aristotle, On Rhetoric: A Theory of Civic Discourse* (New York: Oxford University Press, 1991).

2 Art Carden, "Repeal the Minimum Wage," *Forbes Magazine*, October 16, 2009, https://www.forbes.com/2009/10/16/minimum-wage-labor-economics-opinions-contributors-art-carden.html#4363f09291d2.

3 Stephen Toulmin, *The Uses of Argument* (New York: Cambridge University Press, 2008).

4 Art Carden, "Repeal the Minimum Wage."

5 Toulmin's "qualifier" consists of any clear indication of the level of commitment advocates have for their claim ("probably," "likely," "certainly," and so on). The "rebuttal" imagines a counter position, and functions as a counter to the warrant, best imagined as a statement beginning with the term "unless." The rebuttal might also serve to counter the data (unless the evidence is flawed).

6 "Full Transcripts: Trump's Speech on Immigration and the Democratic Response," *New York Times*, January 9, 2019, https://www.nytimes.com/2019/01/08/us/politics/trump-speech-transcript.html.

7 Jack Wang, "Border Walls Could Have Unintended Consequences on Trade, Study Finds," *Phys.org*, January 3, 2020, https://phys.org/news/2020-01-border-walls-unintended-consequences.html.

8 William Rehg, "The Argumentation Theorists in Deliberative Democracy," in *Discourse, Debate and Democracy: Readings from Controversia: An International Journal of Debate and Democratic Renewal*, eds. David Cratis Williams and Marilyn J. Young (New York: International Debate Education Association, 2009), 18–19. Martha Cooper offers a similar path, noting the difficulty of applying logical fallacies to "everyday argument," offering instead "lines of objection" that "represent objections that are fairly typical in the course of discussions regarding public issues" (*Analyzing Public Discourse* [Long Grove, IL: Waveland Press, Inc., 1989], 119).

9 This is Cooper's point when she writes, "the analyst can imagine the types of objections that would be raised by an ideal audience, that is an audience that was trying to be reasonable and respond to the message with reasoned skepticism" (*Analyzing Public Discourse*, 120).

10 "Everything You Need to Know about the Proposed Graduated Income Tax," *Chicago Sun-Times*, Feb 20, 2020, https://chicago.suntimes.com/2020/2/19/20999063/graduated-income-tax-illinois-referendum-everything-you-need-to-know.

11 For more on this barrier, see Elizabeth Bauer, "What the Illinois Supreme Court Said About Pensions—And Why It Matters," *Forbes Magazine*, Jan 8, 2020, https://www.forbes.com/sites/ebauer/2020/01/08/what-the-illinois-supreme-court-said-about-pensionsand-why-it-matters/#2d337b783666; and Elizabeth Bauer, "Was the Illinois Constitution's Pensions

Clause Meant To Be A Suicide Pact? Three Important Pieces of Historical Context," *Forbes Magazine*, January 15, 2020, https://www.forbes.com/sites/ebauer/2020/01/15/was-the-illinois-constitutions-pensions-clause-meant-to-be-a-suicide-pact-three-important-pieces-of-historical-context/#10ef5646659d.

12 For an example of this argument, see Joe Cahill, "Voters Should Send this Message on Pritzker's 'fair tax'," *Crain's Chicago Business*, September 3, 2020, https://www.chicagobusiness.com/joe-cahill-business/voters-should-send-message-pritzkers-fair-tax.

13 For an example of this advocacy see Adam Schuster, "Pension Apocalypse? COVID-19 Exposes Long-Running Fragility of Illinois Public Pensions," Illinois Policy, September 3, 2020, https://www.illinoispolicy.org/reports/pension-apocalypse-covid-19-exposes-long-running-fragility-of-illinois-public-pensions/. (Note: Illinois Policy is consistently critical of the Democratic state officials and their policy proposals).

14 See Richard Klicki, "Chamber Chief: State Needs to Modify Reopening Plan," *Daily Herald*, June 17, 2020, https://www.dailyherald.com/business/20200617/chamber-chief-state-needs-to-modify-reopening-plan. See also Greg Bishop, "Treasurer Clarifies Position on Taxing Retirement Income," The Center Square, Aug 5, 2020, https://www.thecentersquare.com/illinois/treasurer-clarifies-position-on-taxing-retirement-income/article_c81f5072-d75a-11ea-b5bd-5f53b0ffc3b8.html (Note: The Center Square is a news source with clear ties to entities opposed to the Fair Tax plan).

5

REASONING II: REASONING BY DEDUCTION, INDUCTION, AND ANALOGY

Takeaways

(1) You should be cautious not to get distracted by appeals that move you too far from a focus on the main causal claims supporting or opposing a proposed solution.

(2) You may be better able to defend your policy positions and remain on a productive path to your intended policy goal by understanding the flaws to which deductive, inductive, or analogical claims are susceptible.

(3) Such competency advances your ability to understand and appreciate the nuances of thought behind causal claims and predictions, and the additional infrastructure of claims made in support of, and opposition to, policy proposals.

(4) Critical questions specific to these forms of reasoning can assist you in calibrating your advocacy.

We have discussed how imbalances within the democratic system can sometimes make it challenging to focus on the stock issues. Your first line of strategy should be to focus on the most substantive question: *whether a proposed policy solves a problem without causing other new problems that are more troubling than the original problem.* However, many other claims are made along the way to substantiate affirmative advocates' policy proposals, and negative advocates often pivot and shift attention away from the policy goals to which they are opposed, and the issues that should be central to how a policy proposal is evaluated. Returning to our metaphor of a stock issues map, advocates can find themselves in confusing surroundings, even lost, as the infrastructure of claims becomes the equivalent of a dense matrix of one way streets and unexpected closures. There is still a viable route, but navigating that route requires some additional information.

In this chapter, we delve more deeply into specific forms of reasoning used in asserting causal relationships and other claims commonly advanced in public policy controversies: reasoning by deduction, induction, and analogy. The flaws to which deductive, inductive, or analogical claims might be susceptible will provide additional content for scrutiny. As a result, you should learn more about these common forms of reasoning to better equip you to defend your policy positions and remain on a productive path to your intended policy goal.

When you have completed your consideration of these main forms of reasoning, our hope is that you will have an enhanced appreciation for the various kinds of claims that will have overarching implications on the appeal of your advocacy, and more isolated and specific implications on the structural integrity of your advocacy. Causal claims can be asserted within arguments that are deductively, inductively, and analogically structured, so you will need to determine when it is most appropriate to focus on the strengths or weaknesses of reasoning structures that support these causal and other claims we consider in this chapter. We are also encouraging you to consider that some challenges to deductive, inductive, and analogical arguments that make up aspects of your advocacy may be distractions intended to push you off course and shift the audience's attention to issues that have little bearing on the public problems under consideration.

Reasoning by Deduction

Deductive reasoning is reasoning in its most classical or traditional sense. We noted in the previous chapter that advocates can make causal inferences using deductive reasoning. Recall the minimum wage argument in which it was argued that a specific minimum wage increase would result in a loss of jobs. This conclusion was *deduced* as a logical outcome of the premise that minimum wage increases lead to job losses. In this section, we provide some basic lessons that will assist you in evaluating the quality of deductive reasoning.

The structure of deductive reasoning is illustrated below with premises that, taken together, deduce knowledge about a specific instance from acceptance of a general principle:

Major Premise: *All humans are mortal.*
Minor Premise: *Lucy is a human.*
Conclusion: *Therefore, Lucy is mortal.*

This argument includes three important terms—"humans" (A), "mortal" (B), and "Lucy" (C)—and the validity of the conclusion is dependent on these terms remaining relatively stable in placement and meaning throughout the presentation of the argument. This leads to the following mathematically sound formula:

$A = B$
$C = A$
Therefore $C = B$

In logic classes or more formal considerations of argumentation theory, you may learn there are several errors advocates can commit by not keeping each significant term in its correct place or if the meaning of one of the terms changes between its first and subsequent uses. While these standards, if committed to memory, will assist you in evaluating reasoning, explaining the violations may not result in the most appealing messages (that is to say, it would come across as rather formal).

Nevertheless, a deductive structure may serve as a common vehicle for a variety of arguments considered within a public policy controversy. Consider the proposition that: "The federal government should mandate health insurance companies to provide health insurance to all customers, regardless of preexisting conditions." There are many deductive arguments that emerged when healthcare reform advocates proposed the Affordable Care Act (ACA) as a solution under this proposition. As we have noted throughout this text, public policy advocacy more likely involves incomplete arguments. An advocate of the ACA wishing to argue, "We can't expect insurance companies to cover people with preexisting conditions unless an effective law is passed that mandates it," could advance a number of arguments. Conceived deductively, here is one example:

Major Premise: Only a comprehensive law that addresses profit concerns and reform goals (combines mandatory purchase of health insurance and coverage of preexisting conditions) (A) can change profit-driven decisions not to cover individuals with preexisting conditions (B).

Minor Premise: The ACA (a collection of government mandates) (C) is a comprehensive law that addresses profit concerns and reform goals (combines mandatory purchase of health insurance and coverage of preexisting conditions) (A).

Conclusion: The ACA (a collection of government mandates) (C) can change profit-driven decisions not to cover individuals with preexisting conditions (B).

In the above argument, the major premise is a general principle that is central to the debate over the ACA, and the minor premise is a specific claim that links the major principle to the conclusion. If the general principle and minor premise are acceptable to the audience, the conclusion should be acceptable.

Two main types of arguments rely on deductive reasoning and are especially common in public policy advocacy: *categorical* and *disjunctive*. As noted above, we always advise asking first whether the policy is one that solves a problem without causing other new problems that are more troubling than the original problem. Once you consider the policy objectives in this manner, the critical questions we offer for the evaluation of deductive reasoning may *further* assist your effort to reveal key assumptions and flaws in reasoning.

Categorical Deduction

The first type of deductive reasoning is *categorical deduction*, which introduces a general conclusion about a set or category of something and then makes a claim about a specific case that arguably fits into that category. Both the above arguments are categorical deductions. To make this form of deduction even simpler, the previous minimum wage example illustrates this well:

General rule: All minimum wage increases (A) reduce demand for labor (B).
Specific case: The "Fight for $15" (C) is a minimum wage increase (A).
Therefore: The "Fight for $15" (C) will reduce demand for labor (B).

The conclusion drawn about the category (minimum wage increases) should apply also to the specific case (the policy goal of the "Fight for $15"). It begins with a general rule, or major premise, and follows with a specific case, deducing a conclusion. The general rule is essential to the persuasiveness of a categorical argument. Advocates deploying categorical reasoning count on their target audience to accept the general rule as true in all cases (you might refer to this as "categorical consistency"). Once accepted, the audience is expected to apply the same general characteristics to a specific case.

The history of American public policy is rife with examples of categorical reasoning undergirding some of the most controversial public debates. An example used by Martha Cooper is the claim that "abortion should be illegal."[1] The claim relies on the classification of abortion as murder, facilitated by the application of the general rule—murder should be illegal—to abortion (the specific case), as illustrated below:

General rule: Murder (A) should be illegal (B).
Specific case: Abortion (C) is murder (A).
Therefore: Abortion (C) should be illegal (B).

Once the audience learns that an advocate plans to exploit the target audience's acceptance of the general rule—to cause them to deduce that the act of abortion (the specific case) should be illegal—those who disagree with the conclusion will focus on whether abortion reasonably belongs to the category or class of human behavior called "murder." Categorical consistency is not *per se* a good reason to support the conclusion that naturally follows; instead of interrogating the reasoning, a public policy proposal might be shown to be repugnant or harmful, regardless of its consistency. In response to the above categorical argument, questions such as, *Should the American legal system conclude that abortion is murder?*, or *What would be the consequences of classifying abortion as murder?*, would address the claims as matters of public policy.

Still, you may find that identifying the flaws to which categorical reasoning is susceptible is another useful approach to interrogating the public policy implications of a proposal. The following critical questions will equip you to evaluate categorical reasoning in public policy advocacy:

(1) Is the specific case or instance under consideration true in all cases?
(2) Does the specific case or instance under consideration belong to the general category or rule?
(3) Are the meanings of the terms used throughout the argument consistent?

The first two critical questions focus your attention on the action, behavior, occurrence, and so forth, that advocates believe should be treated in the same manner as the general category or rule. Many advocates encourage audiences to accept principles, mottos, axioms, or common sense presumptions as necessarily true in all cases. "Abortion as murder," even for ardent pro-life advocates, is often complicated in cases where the mother's life is at risk without termination of the pregnancy. In terms of minimum wage, you might ask whether minimum wage increases *always* lead to reductions in labor demand. The second critical question has you considering whether there are qualities of the instance (policy or context) that exempt it from the rule. *Might there be something unique about this moment in history that suggests a $15 minimum wage would not result in reduced labor demand?* In such an instance, the specific case may not belong to the general category or rule.

The third critical question for categorical arguments concerns the meaning of terms used to describe the actions, behaviors, occurrences, and so forth, throughout the description of the general rule, specific case, and conclusion. A flaw occurs when a term shifts in meaning from its original use to something different later in the argument. This is often referred to as *equivocation*, the tendency to rely on the ambiguous nature of certain terms to avoid commitment to a position or to assemble a justification that "sounds" sensible. In the abortion example used to illustrate a categorical argument, the terms are consistently used; they have agreed-upon or at least uniformly understood meanings that are maintained throughout the articulation of the argument. But not all deductive arguments utilize consistent terminology. Anthony Weston, in his review of common fallacies in argument, cites the following particularly complex example of a moment of equivocation:

> Women and men are physically and emotionally different. The sexes are not "equal," then, and therefore the law should not pretend that we are [equal].[2]

Weston makes clear that "[b]etween premise and the conclusion this argument shifts the meaning of the term 'equal,'" where it initially means "identical," to its latter, inferred meaning, where the intended meaning of "equal" (in the bracketed instance) is what women might expect to be entitled to under the law—the same rights and responsibilities as men.[3] Equivocation is tricky business and can take many forms. In the above example, the term "equal" was mentioned only once; its second meaning was implied in a reference to "the law" (thus placed in brackets).

Disjunctive Deduction

A second type of deductive reasoning is called *disjunctive deduction*. "Disjunctive" means expressing a choice between mutually exclusive possibilities. "Mutually exclusive" means you cannot accept both at the same time. One cannot vote for both the Democratic and the Republican presidential candidate or hire two people for one job, for example. The concept may also be used to identify a nonsensical choice, one in which one option would produce negative effects that would counteract the positive effects of another option. Advocates deploying disjunctive reasoning offer alternatives and systematically reject the alternatives that do not make sense. The terms "either" and "or" signal a disjunctive argument, but the choices may not always be presented in such obvious ways.

Disjunctive argument in public policy advocacy is very common. Here is an example of a disjunctive argument that you might encounter at the meeting of any college or university board of trustees:

> The members of the board have long dealt with the challenges associated with finding the resources to invest in some of our strategic technological initiatives. We could increase our revenues by lowering our admission standards and increasing our enrollment. That has real downsides, though. And, we must keep our tuition affordable if we are to remain a viable option for new and existing students, even though increasing tuition would increase our revenue. There is real merit to the idea of adding a fee for courses that involve technology, however.

It is only after you receive the entire message that you understand the advocate's intent to argue in favor of a new technology fee. Here is how the above argument might be presented as a disjunctive argument:

> In order to raise funds needed to improve technology, we can either lower our admission standards to increase our revenue (A), raise tuition to increase our revenue (B), or charge a new fee for courses that involve technology (C).
>
> We cannot lower our admission standards (A) or raise tuition (B).
>
> Therefore, we must charge a new technology fee for courses that involve technology (C).

More simplistically, this argument can be presented as follows:

> *Either A, B, or C.*
> *Not A or B.*
> *Therefore C.*

In our experience, disjunctive arguments are especially common in professional settings, when leaders introduce several possible solutions to a problem. The disjunctive message structure follows closely the generally agreed upon process of problem solving that calls for the systematic consideration and review of multiple recommendations. However, like the concern expressed above about categorical reasoning, the inadequacy of other options is not *per se* a good reason to support a recommended policy. Just as with categorical deduction, before you consider the common flaws of disjunctive reasoning, our recommendation is to evaluate whether the proposed action actually solves a problem. In the above example, the policy proposal will likely address the immediate need for funds; however, certainly there are some who would argue that increasing costs to students might have a negative impact on enrollment and other major sources of operating revenue for a university (disadvantages).

Once you have subjected the favored policy proposal at the end of a disjunctive argument to debate, you may find it useful to assert the common flaws of disjunctive reasoning. These flaws can be discovered by asking the following critical questions:

(1) Is the advocate considering all reasonable options?
(2) Is the advocate offering good reasons for rejecting options?
(3) Are combinations of considered options or other options more reasonable?

In terms of the first critical question, advocates who use disjunctive reasoning often fail to include all reasonably available options. You may find that reasonable options are not actually limited to A, B, or C; *there may be a D and an E.* In the above example, there are relatively obvious alternatives a university board of trustees can take to fund their technology needs, such as efforts to improve the efficiency of information technology resources. In this case, the advocate may be presenting the audience with a "false choice" fallacy (referred to as a "false dichotomy" when two options are considered). When employing a false choice, advocates may give the audience the perception that they are fairly considering the options. This may be a strategic rhetorical choice, or may reflect a failure to consider additional options or whether the options presented are truly mutually exclusive.

As noted at the end of Chapter 4, other reasonable options are sometimes referred to as **counterplans**. Counterplans are typically offered by negative advocates. Affirmative advocates, accused of not sufficiently considering alternatives, might then subject counterplans to the same critical questions posed in response to any policy proposal. Thus, the affirmative/negative burdens are reversed for a period of time, as both sides consider the alternative option. In general, however, counterplans are rarely presented as full considerations of the problem, as they rely on the work of affirmative advocates to outline an insufficient status quo. Negative advocates, as a result, often simply offer an alternative plan, since affirmative advocates already made the fuller case for the *need* for such a plan.

Ideally, negative advocates offering counterplans would clearly explain them and try to demonstrate that they solve the problem *better* than the policy proposal offered at the conclusion of a disjunctive argument. By "better" we mean to point out that audiences will generally expect that a counterplan will *both* offer advantages that would be lost if the counterplan is not adopted *and* avoid disadvantages associated with the affirmative advocates' proposed solution. In the realm of public policy advocacy, the term "opportunity losses" is sometimes used to describe the benefits lost when an alternative is not pursued (*If C is pursued, what will be lost by not choosing A, B, D, or E?*). Offering a counterplan as a negative advocacy strategy may have the unintended effect of agreeing that a significant problem warrants a solution. It's a tricky position for negative advocates to say, in effect, "We don't believe there's a problem, but if *you* do, then we think our solution is better." Audiences may be inclined to favor the side that originally sought to solve a serious societal problem. You might think of this dynamic as it played out, for instance, in the debate over the Affordable Care Act. After Democrats achieved this signature legislative victory in 2010, Republicans sought to "repeal *and replace*" the ACA, essentially granting that some significant healthcare policy reform was needed.

In terms of the second critical question, another common error in disjunctive reasoning occurs when advocates determine certain options cannot be pursued. Advocates may not have a sensible reason to reject one or more options. The dismissal of policy options should be justified in accordance with the stock issues we have discussed and principles of sound reasoning encouraged by the six critical questions associated with causal reasoning, with the most obvious being, *Will the proposed solution solve the problem?*

The third critical question raises the issue of whether an alternative option might be salvaged if it is combined in some productive way with another option. Just as you may not have a sensible reason to reject an option, you may not have a good reason to reject options that could be pursued *with* your favored option. The assumption of "mutual exclusivity"—the idea that A cannot be combined with B, C, or D—often drives the dismissal of options that combine policies. Rather, A *and* B might be pursued *simultaneously* to achieve the desired advantage or an alternative advantage that is desired by more stakeholders. In classroom debate, the adjoining of two policy options is often referred to as a "permutation." Permutations are essentially a call for *both*–or *multiple*–solutions.

Reasoning by Induction

Reasoning by induction is reasoning by way of examples or data that considers multiple instances of something happening. A conclusion is drawn through reference to factual occurrences, which can range from a single anecdote to a collection of statistical data, which, to the satisfaction of advocates citing the example(s), proves the conclusion true. In most cases, advocates will cite more than one example to establish the validity of a claim. This is done because the greater the instances of something occurring, the greater the reliability that, given similar circumstances, something will occur again. In public policy advocacy, examples function as evidence that enable advocates to make what Huber and Snider refer to as "an inductive leap," or the conclusion that "what is true for the sample will be true for all cases."[4] Data is collected according to standards and rules that enable the researcher to discern causality with greater confidence. The conclusion of experts that cigarette smoking causes cancer, for instance, is inductively derived from numerous studies examining cases showing higher incidents of cancer when the studied subjects smoked. In the absence of strong competing theories, the evidence is reliable enough that health officials and other authorities predict outcomes based on the data with regularity.

You will find inductive reasoning used throughout public policy advocacy. It is used to establish how widespread or significant a problem is, to demonstrate links between a problem and its cause, and between a solution and its advantages. Returning to the minimum wage example from Chapter 4, you can observe that inductive reasoning can also be used to support the assertions of cause—that minimum wage increases cause reduced labor demand. Recall the quotation from *Forbes Magazine*:

"... a comprehensive survey research on minimum wages by David Neumark and William Wascher finds that minimum wages do, in fact, reduce employment."[5]

Negative advocates cite such research to establish that raising the minimum wage will have negative consequences. Several instances prove, argue the opponents of a wage increase, that minimum wage increases reduce labor demand, before deductively concluding that it will have the same effect in a specific instance. This conclusion is drawn from economic data; others might need to (or choose to) rely on a single or handful of representative instances to induce a conclusion. Sometimes single instances of something occurring is all that is available to advocates. Single examples of a policy working in one situation is a common way affirmative advocates establish the likelihood their solution will lead to their claimed advantage. Likewise, to refute the solvency of a proposed solution, negative advocates may raise instances when similar solutions failed to produce advantages claimed by affirmative advocates.

Considering inductive argument generally, it is difficult to isolate the types of objections inductive reasoning will generate. Cited examples may exist in the form of testimony, studies, surveys, experiments, polls, and other forms of information that are subject to the tests appropriate for each respective type of evidence. Again, we recommend that you isolate the policy proposal and pose the critical questions concerning causal reasoning as a first step. Still, you may find it necessary to target a specific inductive claim with the following critical questions:

(1) Are the instances cited real occurrences as far as can be determined through reliable evidence?
(2) Are the instances representative of the practices, behaviors, activities, or phenomena under consideration?
(3) Is a single or limited occurrence compelling enough to indicate a problem?

In terms of the first critical question, cited instances are best if they *actually* occurred, because it is too easy for an advocate to construct an ideal set of hypothetical examples that seem realistic. The demand that cited examples be real is common within debates over proposed anti-discrimination laws, for example. Advocates of additional anti-discrimination measures within their communities point to similar anti-discrimination laws adopted by other communities. Municipal leaders often ask for real examples of discrimination against community residents that involve the specific discrimination scenarios addressed by the proposed amendments.

The second critical question concerns *quality* rather than *quantity*. In the above example concerning amendments proposed to a community's anti-discrimination provisions, the audience might ask, *Are the instances representative or characteristic of the practices, behaviors, activities, or phenomena advocates seek to address with their proposal?* Instances of violence against transgender individuals might be cited to establish the need for human rights protections, for instance. In response, a municipal leader might argue that the instances cited are representative of situations when law enforcement failed to protect individuals against violent criminals *but not* instances when transgender individuals were unable to receive relief because there was no anti-discrimination provision specific to transgender individuals. Advocates can prepare for such a challenge by diligently researching and collecting a record of representative instances. Many advocates build a repository of instances that they can later draw upon when reasoning inductively (sometimes referred to as a "pattern or practice"). You might also benefit from organizations whose researchers might maintain such a record and publish reports that can be cited in support of your inductive claims.

In terms of the third critical question, we believe it is wise to accept that there are plenty of instances of single examples being used to draw generalizations that achieve widespread adherence among a public. In 2003, then Chicago Mayor Richard M. Daley ordered the city's crews to bulldoze Meigs Field, a single strip airport built on a human-made peninsula just east of Soldier Field in downtown Chicago. Daley's decision to demolish the airport in the middle of the night reflected, for many, his disregard for democratic process. In an editorial written at the time, the *Chicago Tribune* describes it as an instance of "Daley's increasingly authoritarian style that brooks no disagreements, legal challenges, negotiations, compromise or any of that messy give-and-take normally associated with democratic government."[6] "The signature act of Richard Daley's 22 years in office was the midnight bulldozing of Meigs Field," writes *Chicago Tribune* columnist Eric Zorn.[7] Ed Bachrach and Austin Berg's highly critical book, *The New Chicago Way*, begins with a preface titled, "The Field," calling the demolition "a microcosm of the political culture that has brought Chicago to its knees."[8] Daley surely would challenge the notion that, during the entirety of his term in office, he permitted no disagreements, legal challenges, negotiations, or compromises; nevertheless, this single example was significant enough to engender wide acceptance as representative of Daley's anti-democratic approach to most decisions. Stories or narratives of hardship, injustice, or inhumane treatment may also be enough to produce consensus that a problem is significant enough to warrant change. These narratives can be hypothetical or fictional—think of the impact of the novels *Uncle Tom's Cabin* and *The Jungle*, for example—but are more often instances of real tragedy. Instances of school shootings, deportations, human trafficking, mass transit accidents, oil spills, and so forth, may be cited with significant potency for public audiences. These instances are often highlighted through personal narratives told by real people, sometimes in public testimony at hearings and public comment periods at meetings of government bodies. In the field of communication, much has been written on the compelling nature of these narratives.[9]

Reasoning by Analogy

The final form of reasoning we discuss is reasoning by analogy. When advocates reason by analogy, Martha Cooper writes, "the audience is asked to grasp a similarity between two apparently different phenomena in order to conclude that the characteristics common to one are also common to the other."[10] While on its face the use of a single comparison may seem a relatively poor way to reason about policy outcomes, in the public policy arena there are times when analogies are very effective. Consider a commonly referenced analogy in the realm of American foreign policy, the "Vietnam analogy." "Vietnam" in the Vietnam analogy has come to represent a conflict initially justified with appeals to protect a people from aggression and repression that spirals into a protracted conflict that is unwinnable and results in needless casualties. In just about every conflict involving U.S. military intervention following the Vietnam War, those opposed to U.S. involvement have used the Vietnam analogy to argue that what occurred in the actual Vietnam conflict will occur again in the new conflict, resulting in substantial loss of life, with no end in sight, and likely a "loss" for the United States. The Vietnam analogy might emerge in the following form:

> U.S. involvement in the Vietnam War (A) was unwise (B).
>
> U.S. involvement in Conflict X (C) is just like U.S. involvement in Vietnam (A) in all relevant respects.
>
> Therefore, U.S. involvement in Conflict X (C) would be unwise (B).

The key to dealing with this analogical reasoning is to evaluate the comparison in the minor premise–*U.S. involvement in Conflict X is just like U.S. involvement in Vietnam in all relevant respects*. But, like the other types of reasoning considered above, we recommend that you first thoroughly evaluate the policy position supported by the analogy. In the above case, the advocate is opposed to a proposal to intervene in a conflict and claims the impacts of intervention would be disastrous (as bad as the impacts of the Vietnam War). If you support intervention, you would be wise to start by considering the causal connection the negative advocate is making between intervention and the alleged disadvantages.

There are two types of analogies: literal and figurative.

Literal Analogies. When you compare things of the same class, such as, in the above example of two foreign policy conflicts, you are using *literal analogies*. We advise you to pose the following critical questions when evaluating a literal analogy:

(1) Are the practices, behaviors, activities, or phenomena being compared similar enough to warrant the policy position being advocated?
(2) Can the comparison be characterized as fundamentally flawed or socially offensive?

In terms of the first question, literal analogies should be practically useful, and you should not underestimate their potential as appealing arguments. They function much like examples in inductive claims, as if to argue, *Because it was so in that case, it will be so in this case.* As such, it is practically useful for you to ask whether the instances are similar in all important respects and whether the comparison provides support for the goals of the advocate. The effort to invalidate an analogy, Huber and Snider write, may be aided by a consideration of the inductive and causal nature of analogies. If an analogy, for instance, cites examples that are not factual, objections pertaining to examples or inductive reasoning may be a profitable means of refuting the analogy. Huber and Snider note also that "[r]easoning by analogy is useful in supporting propositions when a policy has been tried only in a few cases—so few that induction is impossible."[11] Barbara Warnick and Edward S. Inch make a distinction between "quality" versus "quantity," concluding that a "quality comparison includes both that the comparison is of two things from the same class," and the similarities cited should be "relevant" to the claim the analogy allegedly supports.[12] In terms of quantity, they argue simply: "[t]he larger the number of relevant similarities, the more probable the conclusion."[13]

In terms of the second critical question, we observe that analogies can be rejected on two grounds: (1) they are fundamentally flawed or false, or (2) they are socially offensive. An analogy you use may be deemed flawed when the differences between the compared subjects outweigh the similarities. Thus, as a practical matter, you might argue that an analogy is flawed when the practices, behaviors, activities, or phenomena being compared are not similar enough to warrant the policy position being advocated. A common way to refer to a flawed analogy is to refer to it as a "false analogy."

Analogies may also be rejected on social grounds. S. Morris Engel considers the matter of an analogy that, while it may be "sound" according to the tests of logic, might be rejected because it is in bad taste. While he advises the advocate to argue, if possible, that "the fallacy lies, however, in the comparison drawn rather than in its lack of taste,"[14] we have encountered instances when an analogy's socially inappropriate nature is the basis on which it is deemed unworkable. In July of 1993, during the confirmation hearing for Supreme Court Justice Ruth Bader Ginsburg, Senator Orrin Hatch (R-Utah) made an analogy between what he characterized as "judicial activism" in the opinion of the U.S. Supreme Court in *Roe v. Wade* (the 1973 case that held that a woman had a right to seek an abortion because there was a constitutional right to privacy) and an earlier—allegedly comparable—moment of "judicial activism" in *Dred Scott v. Sanford* (a 1857 case that held that slaves were personal property and the Fifth Amendment of the Constitution protects property owners against deprivation of their property without due process of law). Both cases, Hatch claimed, were moments when the Supreme Court created a right that did not exist in the Constitution, and thus each was a moment of judicial activism. Hatch questioned whether Justice Ginsburg agreed. Seated alongside Hatch was a newly elected African American female Senator named Carol Moseley-Braun (D-Illinois). Moseley-Braun ardently objected to the analogy on the grounds that it was offensive to her as a woman and an African American. Hatch apologized and considered an alternative means of conveying the same concerns about judicial activism, even while the same analogy has been at the center of many intellectual debates over the right of judges to interpret the intent of the Constitution beyond a reading of only the words on the page.[15]

Offensive literal analogies are not always as complex as Hatch's; often they are simply exaggerated comparisons intended to criticize leadership styles and practices. Offense is often taken when leaders want to draw attention to anti-democratic or authoritarian practices of other policymakers. We advise you to use extreme caution before making comparisons between contemporary decision makers grappling with routine societal problems and, for instance, the oppressive leadership practices of dictators, such as Adolph Hitler and the Nazi Party. You only need to perform a brief online search to learn that most analogies related to the Third Reich are highly problematic.

Figurative Analogies. When you compare things belonging to different classes, such as comparing the service you have performed on your car to regular physical exams from your physician, you are using *figurative analogies*.[16] We advise you to pose the following critical questions when contemplating figurative analogies:

(1) Is the comparison offered likely to assist the advocate in their effort to gain the support of the audience?
(2) Can the comparison be characterized as fundamentally flawed or socially offensive?

In terms of the first question, we note that figurative analogies are typically marshaled to encourage understanding of complex subjects relevant to the actual issues involved in a controversy. Warnick and Inch are very practical when discussing the potential persuasive power of figurative analogies. Of the figurative analogy, they write, "the comparison is metaphorical and illustrative rather than concrete and literal" and will "function primarily to make what is remote or poorly understood, immediate and comprehensible."[17] Thus, the primary test of a figurative analogy is one of "rhetorical effectiveness," whether the analogy causes an audience to reshape its attitudes in the direction desired by the advocate.[18]

In terms of the second critical question, we observe that figurative analogies, similar to literal analogies, can be rejected because they are fundamentally flawed, or false—when the differences between the compared subjects outweigh the similarities—or because they are socially offensive. Thus, you can determine a figurative analogy is a false analogy in the same manner in which you argue that *the practices, behaviors, activities, or phenomena being compared are not similar enough to warrant the policy position being advocated.* It is easy to imagine socially inappropriate analogies coming in figurative forms. Engel provides an example of a particularly offensive figurative analogy comparing the slaughter of Native Americans during the settlement of the American frontier to the adage, "you can't make an omelet without breaking a few eggs."[19] In the realm of public policy advocacy, political leaders often stray into offensive territory when they compare individuals to animals—"he's a snake in the grass" or "she's a wolf in sheep's clothing"—or make other comparisons that suggest a loss of capacity—"she's a little long in the tooth" or "you can't teach an old dog new tricks." We advise you to carefully consider figurative analogies you plan to use in your advocacy. Spend some time consulting reputable sources to determine if they have complex historical origins.

In the next chapter, we consider the role of evidence in public policy advocacy, beginning with a theoretical discussion that focuses on how and why evidence is used in practical advocacy situations.

Birtherism and Categorical Deduction

In considering examples of contemporary public issues that illustrate a form of reasoning we discuss in this chapter, one that comes to mind is the assertion that U.S. President Barack Obama was born in Kenya. This case also illustrates how imbalances within the democratic system can sometimes make it challenging to focus on the stock issues. The "birther debate," as it's become known, is hinged to a categorical deductive argument: most simply, *whether or not Obama belongs to a category of persons who are eligible to serve as U.S. president.* Suffice it to say, there is nothing ordinary about challenging the birthright citizenship of a presidential candidate, or seated president. Critics of birtherism, both then and regarding its resurgence in the 2020 campaign concerning Democratic vice-presidential candidate Kamala Harris, consider the charge to be motivated by, and intended to exploit, racism and anti-immigrant sentiment.[20]

One way to illustrate the argument is how it might be voiced by those accusing Obama of not being a natural born citizen:

General Rule: Only natural born citizens (A) are eligible to be president of the United States (B).

Specific Case: Barak Obama (C) is not a natural born citizen (A).

Therefore: Barak Obama (C) is not eligible to be president of the United States (B).

The three critical questions concerning categorial deduction compel us to ask a simple question: *is Barak Obama a natural born citizen?* If he is, then the specific case or instance under consideration is not true, and thus not affected by the general rule. In this wording, the meanings of the terms used throughout the argument are consistent; however, it is easy to imagine this argument appearing in alternative forms with different terms or intended meanings for what constitutes a "natural born citizen." In fact, more recent makers of this argument claim that what constitutes "birthright citizenship" may be different depending on the citizenship status of one's parents. The claim that Kamala Harris is not a natural born citizen, and thus not able to ever assume the office of president, is based *not* on the allegation that she was born outside of the United States (she was born in California), but that she was born to two parents who were not citizens of the United States.[21]

The persistence of the birther argument might also be fairly viewed as a case of those defending the status quo pivoting and shifting attention away from the policy goals to which they are opposed. Challenges to Obama's citizenship status is arguably an instance when arguments are introduced as distractions, producing what we called in Chapter 3 an "unfair fight." Assertions about Obama's alleged Kenyan birth were made prior to 2008,[22] when one might think of his election bid as an overarching call for reform of the status quo. Obama's election, however, put in motion specific policy proposals (to name just a few, what became: the Lilly Ledbetter Fair Pay Act of 2009, the first bill signed into law by Obama on January 29, 2009; the $787 billion American Recovery and Reinvestment Act of 2009; the Dodd-Frank Wall Street Reform and Consumer Protection Act of 2010; the Affordable Care Act of 2010; and the appointment of two Supreme Court justices in 2009 and 2010) and other significant reforms (for instance, Obama's decision in 2011 that the federal government would no longer defend the Defense of Marriage Act and his Executive Order establishing the Deferred Action for Childhood Arrivals [DACA] program in June of 2012).[23]

While candidate Obama was outlining his policy priorities, questions about where he was born continued to gain momentum as a public issue. In a column in the *National Review* on June 9, 2008, Jim Geraghty argued that rumors of Obama's Kenyan birth would go away if Obama released his birth certificate.[24] Just three days later, Obama—who had consistently asserted that he was born in Hawaii—released his short-form birth certificate. Suggestions were made that the short-form was a fake, that it was the wrong color, that it was missing the state seal, and that it wasn't creased during mailing.[25] A critical mass of vocal online doubters existed, and, in 2009, more than 400,000 people purportedly signed a petition created by conservative news site World Net Daily demanding the release of the president's long form birth certificate.[26] Before his re-election for a second term, in 2011, he publicly disclosed his so-called "long form" birth certificate establishing his Hawaiian birth.

The question of where Obama was born, or whether he was willing to provide proof of his Hawaiian birth, addressed in no way the merits of the public policies he was introducing and supporting; however, birtherism operated in the realm of public policy and compelled multiple official responses. Providing proof of his natural born citizenship likely injected more energy into the birther conspiracy theory than was necessary. Indeed, according to *Politico*, "the birther movement really didn't take off . . . until the Obama team tried to debunk it."[27]

Exercise: Using Knowledge of Reasoning in a Critique of a Newspaper Opinion Piece

Select a letter to the editor, column, or editorial wherein the writer is addressing a public controversy. Identify the controversy and which side of the issue the writer is on, if that can be clearly determined. Identify an instance of reasoning by deduction (categorical or disjunctive), induction, or analogy (literal or figurative). Then ask and answer the critical questions that apply to the form of reasoning.

Notes

1 Martha Cooper, *Analyzing Public Discourse* (Long Grove, IL: Waveland Press, Inc., 1989).
2 Anthony Weston, *A Rulebook for Arguments* (Indianapolis: Hacket Publishing Co., 2009), 76. The bracket, second instance of "equal" was added to assist the point.
3 Ibid., 76–77.
4 Robert B. Huber and Alfred C. Snider, *Influencing Through Argument* (Updated Edition) (New York: International Debate Education Association, 2006), 93.
5 Art Carden, "Should We Care About the Minimum Wage?" *Forbes Magazine*, May 13, 2011, https://www.forbes.com/sites/artcarden/2011/05/13/should-we-care-about-the-minimum-wage/#134c60ee78de.
6 "A Pre-emptive Strike on Meigs," *Chicago Tribune*, April 1, 2003, http://articles.chicagotribune.com/2003-04-01/news/0304010283_1_meigs-field-mayor-richard-daley-soldier-field.
7 Eric Zorn, "When the Mayor Bulldozed an Airport: Daley's Action Inspired Admiration, Outrage and Amusement," *Chicago Tribune*, April 30, 2011, https://www.chicagotribune.com/news/ct-met-zorn-daley-moments-0501-20110430-column.html.
8 Ed Bachrach and Austin Berg, *The New Chicago Way: Lessons from Other Big Cities* (Carbondale: Southern Illinois University Press, 2019), 3.

9 See Walter R. Fisher, "Narration as a Human Communication Paradigm: The Case of Public Moral Argument," *Communication Monographs* 51, no. 1 (1984): 1–22.

10 Cooper, *Analyzing Public Discourse*, 76.

11 Huber and Snider, *Influencing Through Argument*, 151.

12 Barbara Warnick and Edward S. Inch, *Critical Thinking and Communication: The Use of Reason in Argument*, 6th ed. (Boston: Allyn & Bacon, 2009), 116–117.

13 Ibid., 117.

14 S. Morris Engel, *With Good Reason: An Introduction to Informal Fallacies*, 2nd ed. (Boston: St. Martin's Press, 1982), 129.

15 See John R. Butler, "Carol Moseley-Braun's Day to Talk About Race," *Argument and Advocacy* 32, no. 2 (1995): 62–74.

16 Weston, *A Rulebook for Arguments*, 19.

17 Warnick and Inch, *Critical Thinking and Communication*, 117.

18 Ibid., 117.

19 Engel, *With Good Reason*, 129.

20 Ian Millhiser and Aaron Rupar, "The Trump Campaign Attack on Kamala Harris's Citizenship is Right Out of the Birther Playbook," *Vox*, August 13, 2020, https://www.vox.com/2020/8/13/21366668/trump-campaign-birtherism-kamala-harris-born-in-oakland.

21 Millhiser and Rupar refer to this as "a fringe legal theory holding that children of temporary visitors to the country are not conferred citizenship even if they are born here," noting that it derives from a *dissenting* opinion in a U.S. Supreme Court case from 1898.

22 Loren Collins, "The Secret Origins of Birtherism," *Bullspotting*, September 2016, http://www.bullspotting.com/articles/the-secret-origins-of-birtherism/.

23 For a brief list of key policies implemented by Obama, see Paul Glastris and Nancy LeTourneau, "Obama's Top 50 Accomplishments, Revisited: The Comprehensive Legacy of the 44th President," *Washington Monthly*, January/February 2017, https://washingtonmonthly.com/magazine/januaryfebruary-2017/obamas-top-50-accomplishments-revisited/.

24 Jim Geraghty, "Obama Could Debunk Some Rumors by Releasing His Birth Certificate," *National Review*, June 9, 2008, https://www.nationalreview.com/the-campaign-spot/obama-could-debunk-some-rumors-releasing-his-birth-certificate-jim-geraghty/.

25 "White House Spokesman Robert Gibbs 'Lied' When He Said President Obama's Birth Certificate is Posted on the Internet," Politifact, June 17, 2009, 2020, https://www.politifact.com/truth-o-meter/statements/2009/jul/28/worldnetdaily/birthers-claim-gibbs-lied-when-he-said-obamas-birt/.

26 "Rage Grows in America: Anti-American Conspiracies," Anti-Defamation League, November 2009, https://www.adl.org/sites/default/files/documents/assets/pdf/combating-hate/Rage-Grows-In-America.pdf.

27 Ben Smith and Byron Tau, "Birtherism: Where It All Began," Politico, April 22, 2011, https://www.politico.com/story/2011/04/birtherism-where-it-all-began-053563.

6

EVIDENCE I: THEORIES AND USES

Takeaways

(1) The subject of evidence often arises explicitly as an issue in public policy advocacy.

(2) Building a sophisticated practice of using and evaluating evidence begins with asking, *what do you need evidence to say?*

(3) You will typically use evidence to support your assessment of the status quo, to describe or outline the proposed solution, and to support predictions.

(4) In describing and assessing the status quo, you will typically use evidence to characterize the status quo as either insufficient (if you are an affirmative advocate) or sufficient (if you are a negative advocate).

(5) To describe or outline proposed solutions, you will typically use evidence to establish the facts supporting the goal, the consistency of the goal with solutions proposed in similar cases, and a forthright consideration of costs.

(6) To support predictions (such as that solutions will lead to advantages or disadvantages), you will typically find yourself using and evaluating correlations, theories, authorities, and analogies.

Imagine you are involved in a long-term relationship with a person who accuses you of secretly seeing another person. You will likely first ask, "What causes you to think that?" (or, more formally, "What evidence points to this suspicion?"). Imagine the accuser then tells you that you (1) "have been distant lately," (2) "have been hiding your phone whenever a text message is received," and (3) "have been defensive whenever you are asked about your whereabouts." Moreover, you are told that (4) "a mutual friend noticed that you appear attracted to another person." Take a moment to consider how you would respond.

Assuming your partner is wrong, you might argue there is no concrete evidence to support the accusation and lots of evidence to support that you have been a faithful partner. You might also argue your mutual friend's suspicion is caused by their well-known belief that no one can be completely faithful to another person. As for being distant, protecting your phone, and being defensive, you might argue that these are highly subjective observations that, even if they were true, could point to a number of other issues that have nothing to do with whether you are being an honest and faithful partner. The way evidence is used and evaluated in the realm of public policy will follow a course similar to this hypothetical exchange.

In this chapter and the next, our goal is to provide you with a framework for a rigorous and practically useful approach to using and evaluating evidence. We begin that process by locating the places within public policy advocacy where good evidence is most crucial; more simply, we consider when, why, and how evidence is used. Aspiring advocates might also think of this as a consideration of *what do you need evidence to say?* Our discussion of the role of evidence is organized according to locations within the stock issue structure where evidence is most typically used. You need evidence to help you establish the problem and its cause, to help you describe and explain the solution, and to substantiate the causal links between proposed solutions and advantages or disadvantages.

By focusing on these central lessons, we leave many standard lessons about evidence for others to provide. Other frameworks and advice are available to assist you in such objectives as gathering evidence and learning more about evidence from specific formats such as scholarly articles, books, newspapers, online sources, position papers, blogs, and so forth. We also do not discuss the tools and techniques used to locate such resources (the internet, search engines, indexes, and so on), except later as they relate to the changing nature of news as an authority. In the digital age, dramatic changes have occurred that have altered the way you locate, package, and present evidence in public policy settings. Depending on the depth of your involvement in public policy advocacy, you may wish to consider the subject of evidence beyond the guidance provided by this and other argumentation and debate textbooks. The field of public administration, for example, has produced guidance on the way advocates generate interest in an issue, set the agenda for policymaking bodies, determine the legislative history of an issue, and consider the appropriate format for communication (position papers, petitions and proposals, briefing memos and opinion statements, talking points, testimony within public hearings, and written public comment).[1] Many disciplines, fields, and professions have specialized standards for what is expected of practitioners attempting to justify a desired course of action. We have briefly discussed such matters as advocacy that occurs in technical spheres. For most advocates, experience in these spheres and fields is often required before they develop a clear sense of what they need evidence to say and what forms of evidence are best suited for such purposes. We suspect you have encountered, or will soon encounter, a variety of data types and indicators, some with particular names, such as "levies," "millage rates," "shrinkage," "teacher-to-student-ratio," "consumer price index," "adherence rates," "housing starts," and so forth. Extended advocacy campaigns will expose you to the unique language, modes of reasoning, and standards of evidence preferred by advocates operating in certain technical environments.[2]

Putting Evidence to Work in Public Policy Advocacy

You have already learned that evidence (or "data") is linked to a claim through reasoning, but evidence may function provocatively on its own; its purpose, therefore, will evolve as claims are made by stakeholders. Evidence may produce immediate claims or reveal the policy objectives of the person deploying the evidence, whereas the infrastructure of reasoning may be virtually undetectable. Consider a video of the brutal execution of a hostage by terrorists widely viewed on the internet (evidence that causes millions to conclude military force against the captors is necessary), images of children locked behind cages in U.S. detention facilities on the U.S. southern border (evidence that causes an immediate widespread rejection of hardline immigration policies of the Trump Administration), a study posted online that finds that African American women are experiencing high rates of new HIV infections (evidence that more needs to be done to address the problem), or video footage of a Minneapolis police officer using his knee to press an arrested man's head against the ground (evidence that causes a national movement for police reform). It is not always clear how advocates link evidence to claims, but it is almost always possible to determine the evidence on which advocates base their positions (or definitively determine they have failed to do so). Moreover, evidence often brings a controversy into existence where one may not already exist.

We discussed stock issues in Chapter 3. In this chapter, we consider the manner in which evidence functions to support an advocate's establishment of—in the case of the affirmative—or challenge of—in the case of the negative—the problem and cause, the solution, and the causal links that support a proposed solution's advantages or disadvantages. Robert Newman and Dale Newman, in their foundational text, *Evidence*, describe three primary ways evidence is used in the practice of policy advocacy in terms that help illustrate why evidence is critical to these objectives: to support approving or disapproving assessments of the status quo, to support policy goals, and to support predictions.[3] Consistent with the structure of stock issues, they note that approving or disapproving assessments of the status quo will often occur first, and so we shall consider first the use of evidence to support descriptions of what we refer to as an *insufficient* or *sufficient status quo*.[4]

Before we begin a closer consideration of the places in your advocacy that require the use and evaluation of evidence, we will make an overarching observation—your task when considering how best to support your claims is to ask *what do you need evidence to say* and then *look for high quality evidence that says it*. That evidence will come in many forms, and may not be precisely on point. In the first instance regarding the status quo, it might be a leading expert in the phenomenon that concerns you, someone describing the problem within the status quo, statistical evidence found in a study that quantifies instances of some phenomenon, evidence of a trend, evidence that ideologies are either driving or preventing meaningful policymaking, evidence pointing to a variable that makes an alleged cause and effect relationship sensible or not, and more. Asking *what do you need evidence to say* can guide your reading of source content and identification of useful evidence to support your claims. To make this point really clear, imagine yourself reading something and saying out loud, "Yes, I need this, because it says something that will help me illustrate why the status quo is not working well."

Evidence Used to Support the Problem and Cause

Affirmative advocates maintain that a significant problem, worth correcting, is caused by something in the status quo. Negative advocates claim that the status quo is not causing a problem or that the problem is not significant enough to warrant a change. Newman and Newman refer to such descriptions of the status quo as "positional statements," which they note answer the question, *Where are we now?*[5] We recommend describing the status quo as either *insufficient* or *sufficient*. When affirmative advocates use evidence to establish *where are we now*, they describe a status quo that requires adjustment in order to prevent a continuation of some relationship between the problem and its cause (an insufficient status quo). If you are an affirmative advocate, you will thus describe how the status quo (a cause) produces some type of injustice, unfairness, preventable suffering, and so forth (an effect, or problem). In response, if you are a negative advocate, you will use evidence to describe a status quo that either produces no harms or produces the fewest harms possible under the circumstances (a sufficient status quo).

Disagreement over evidence in determining *where are we now* is common in public policy, particularly in areas of government where policymaking is generally expected, such as U.S. foreign policy. Few expect the United States to do nothing or engage in no policy debate over an impending foreign conflict or humanitarian crisis. In late 2013, at the center of the debate over whether the United States should intervene in the civil war in Syria, advocates on both sides debated the reliability of evidence concerning the status quo. *Were chemical weapons used to kill civilians? How many civilians died? Was the Syrian government led by Bashar al-Assad responsible?* The Obama Administration's answers to these questions described an insufficient status quo—a system that permitted the use of chemical weapons by governments against their own people and an international system that may lack the resolve to address such atrocities. Those opposed to a U.S. strike against the Syrian regime offered different answers to these questions, such as the claim by Russia's President Vladimir Putin that evidence pointed to the possibility that the Syrian opposition forces fired chemical weapons on innocent civilians in order to encourage U.S. intervention against the Syrian regime. Some opposed to a U.S. strike also agreed with part of the Obama Administration's description of the status quo. Following Barack Obama's speech on September 5, 2013, regarding the alleged use of chemical weapons by the Syrian government (wherein Obama laid out certain conditions that might warrant U.S. intervention), economist and political commentator Robert Reich wrote an intentionally abbreviated assessment of the Syrian conflict, offering an example of an advocate describing the status quo:

> Cliff notes on a potentially disastrous decision. (1) Were Syrian civilians killed by chemical weapons? Yes. (2) How many? Estimates vary. (3) Was Assad responsible? Probably but not definitely.[6]

Reich's description of the status quo was designed to suggest it was *sufficient* to the extent that it offered a viable option short of a U.S. military strike (economic sanctions and a freeze on Syrian assets). While Reich does not provide any evidence in the above summary, we can imagine a variety of information he might have used. Available evidence is central to the establishment of an insufficient or sufficient status quo.

The importance of evidence in the establishment of an insufficient or sufficient status quo, however, may not always be as central to the public's deliberation. In the realm of domestic policy, for instance, there are often issues of great national importance about which the public struggles to coalesce around clear policy proposals. Affirmative advocates may need to convince the public that *where we are now* is unacceptable. Doing so is not only a burden affirmative advocates should fulfill to test the logical soundness of their advocacy; it is also a persuasive move, psychologically preparing the audience to move from complacency and comfort with the status quo to desire a remedy. In Chapter 3, we introduced you to Leon Festinger's notion of "cognitive dissonance," a theory maintaining that the human mind seeks psychological comfort by reconciling new knowledge with existing knowledge and beliefs.[7] What this means for public advocacy is that target audiences may be psychologically inclined to preserve their current comfort level by filtering information that establishes the existence of problems in ways that avoid reckoning with those problems (selective exposure, selective reception, selective retention, and so on). Depending on the audience's knowledge and attitudes about the causes and consequences of problems, affirmative advocates may need an information strategy to move the target audience to desire change.

Consider the injustices that concern Black Lives Matter activists and their allies. While there have been a number of protests before and after the 2014 killing of Michael Brown in Ferguson, Missouri (Philando Castile, Laquan McDonald, Freddie Gray, and more followed), little actual policy action has been taken to address the way the status quo may be contributing to this problem. *Why is so little policy adopted to address these recurring events?* Focusing

on the stock issues of problem and cause, you might assume that the public
(and policymakers paying close attention to the public) do not believe the
problem is significant *enough* to warrant policy action. They may accept that
each police shooting is troubling, and may be supportive of fair investigations,
prosecution of responsible officers, or civil lawsuits initiated by the grieving
families. Yet, they may not view such shootings as a trend that evidences a
flawed *system* of policing in their communities. Even if they did recognize a
disturbing trend, there is a considerable difference between people willing to
respond affirmatively to a poll or media inquiry asking whether the killing of
unarmed Black individuals by police is problem that must be fixed, and people
willing to call public servants, to contribute personal funds to organizations,
or to join protests. And, there are additional differences between those willing to take personal actions in favor of legal justice (i.e., initiating lawsuits
and supporting settlements), and those pursuing changes in the way policing occurs in their communities (i.e., proposing new policies). There may
also be members of the public who resist the idea that there is a problem.
Some may be preserving their psychological comfort through the operations
of cognitive dissonance, selecting only information that supports their existing attitude (for instance, that those who find themselves engaged in conflict
with the police must have done something wrong, or that policing is so complicated that loss of life is bound to occur). Some may be steeped in implicit
bias, perhaps combined with the impressions formed from consuming years of
news narratives that presuppose the shooting victim's guilt, regardless of any
contrary or new information they encounter. Others may hold tightly to the
assumption that police are not capable of murder and always deserve the benefit of the doubt, or dismiss critical news about police as "fake."

These examples illuminate the nuanced evidentiary challenges advocates
deal with when they set out to establish the existence of a problem significant enough to warrant policy action. Advocates on different sides of the
issue must consider "where" the audience is. *Do they already accept that a significant problem exists? If not, are they ignorant of the problem, or unmoved by
it? If unmoved by the problem, is it because of ideological inclinations?* Nothing
changed between 2019 and 2020 as far as the problem with police violence
was concerned. The regular news drip of police killings continued. The nature
of the available evidence, however, changed on May 25, 2020, when a video
of George Floyd's killing at the hands of four Minneapolis police officers went
viral on social media. The video recordings more than functioned to factu-
ally evidence George Floyd's killing, but it also implicitly functioned as a call

to action. It moved many from awareness of the problem to being utterly convinced of the status quo's insufficiency and the need to shift public funding away from supporting armed policing toward other strategies that might de-escalate situations that lead to the use of deadly force (a policy solution, among many). It appears to us that video of the death of George Floyd while under the control of the Minneapolis police render counter-arguments about the problem almost implausible. Floyd was handcuffed and under the full control of the arresting officers. There's little room for arguing that Floyd's killing isn't indicative of a problem, part of a trend of unacceptable events that warrants a public policy solution.

Evidence Used to Describe or Outline the Solution

If the stock issues of problem and cause answer *where are we now*, the solution answers the question, *what do we want to accomplish?* Affirmative advocates use evidence to describe or outline the specifics of a proposed solution or policy. Negative advocates use evidence to counter the idea that the solution consists of the necessary components to reduce or eliminate the problem described by affirmative advocates. In either case, evidence will generally be used to describe *what policy is being pursued*, or, as Newman and Newman write, "[o]nly when the policy goal is clearly defined can the goal itself be criticized."[8] To that end, they advise advocates to focus on (1) the facts supporting the goal, (2) whether the goal can be sought consistently, and (3) what costs are associated with achieving the goal.[9] We admit it might be somewhat idealistic to expect affirmative advocates to proactively offer more information than necessary to detail a policy goal; however, we find that affirmative advocates often have a keen sense of what those opposed to their solutions will argue, and choose to address those concerns up front. Ideally, this leads them to offer evidence supporting the fit of their solution to the particular problem, that their solution is consistent with their prior advocacy (theirs and other's), and that the costs of their solutions do not outweigh the benefits. Some of this evidence will be offered as the solution is offered; at other times it will be offered in defense of a solution.

Facts Supporting the Goal. In referring to "facts supporting the goal," there is a wide variety of facts that might be offered to establish that a goal is *grounded* in something.[10] To be grounded in something means to give something abstract a firm theoretical or practical basis.[11] For example, if the goal is to meet the obligations of the United States to stand up to dictators who use weapons of mass destruction against innocent civilians, some facts must be cited to establish that such obligations exist, that the targeted regime is a dictatorship, that the regime is indeed responsible for an alleged act of aggression, and/or that international laws have been violated. For this purpose, an obligation to intervene would be grounded in treaties or international law, a United Nations resolution, and so forth, in which case the relevant clauses of such documents would be the evidence. Reports of neutral agencies based on eye-witness accounts and surveillance or highly credible documentation of war crimes would likely also be required.

Consistency. Advocates are often criticized for their use of evidence in support of inconsistent policy goals. We find consistency tends to be more important when the stakes are highest, such as when U.S. leaders evaluate information in relation to a proposed use of military force.[12] For instance, consider President Barack Obama's argument in late August 2013, when he called on Congress to authorize a strike against government facilities in Syria, claiming the use of chemical weapons by the Syrian regime constituted the crossing of a "red line" that could not be ignored by the international community. Obama's justification was questioned by many, particularly by Iranians, who recalled the U.S. government's lack of action in the 1980s, when then-U.S. ally Saddam Hussein used chemical weapons against Iranians and Kurds.[13] But, consistency can also be the central issue in criticizing evidence cited in defense of domestic policy goals. Shortly after the death of U.S. Supreme Court Justice Ruth Bader Ginsburg, and just six weeks before the 2020 Presidential Election, U.S. Senator John Barrasso (R-WY), Chair of the Senate Republican Conference, appeared on NBC's *Meet the Press* to defend the Republicans' reversal of position on whether a Supreme Court nomination should be considered so close to the outcome of an election.[14] Despite Republicans' refusal to consider Obama's nominee in March of 2016 (nine months before the 2016 Presidential Election) on the grounds that it was too close to the election, Barrasso cited what he called "the Joe Biden rule," claiming that "if we did something different now we would be breaking with the precedent that has long been established that when the president and the Senate are of the same party you move along with confirmation."

In both instances, evidence purportedly being used to justify inconsistent positions was criticized. In the instance involving use of force against the Syrian regime, critics questioned the factual basis for Obama's assertion that a "red line" is (or has ever been) recognized by the United States or the international community. Evidence of U.S. complacency in response to Hussein's use of chemical weapons when he was an ally of the United States certainly suggests otherwise (Iraq's use of mustard gas in Halabja in 1988, wherein more than 3,000 Kurds died, was met with no counteraction by the United States, nor were several instances of chemical weapons use by Iraq in the Iran-Iraq War in the 1980s). As for the precedent Barrasso claims backs the Republicans' rush to confirm a justice before the 2020 election, *Meet the Press* host Chuck Todd pushed back, saying, "I've scoured all of these 2016 notes looking for these footnotes that have been added now, this new explanation. Not once did you say [in 2016], 'oh, it depends on what party the Senate holds vs. the party of the president.' This just sounds like a power grab pure and simple."

Costs. "Costs" concern consequences of a proposed solution, which may include actual monetary costs and/or undesirable consequences of policy goals. In Chapter 3, we discussed funding as one of four planks of a solution offered by affirmative advocates. We note that, if a problem is worth solving and the solution is likely to be effective, affirmative advocates should not hesitate to defend what is required to fund their proposals. Evidence would thus be used to establish those costs and their feasibility. As Newman and Newman make clear, "[t]he achievement of any goal will cost something, and the calculation of costs is clearly an evidential matter."[15] We have noted in several examples how claims about costs were and continue to be central to the public debate over the Affordable Care Act (ACA). Supporters of the ACA cannot avoid (and, in our view have not avoided) presenting evidence to substantiate their claims that the costs to Americans to purchase health insurance are outweighed by the benefits (the Act is, after all, titled the *Affordable* Care Act). Just as affirmative advocates should be expected to support their assessment of costs with evidence, negative advocates should also be expected to substantiate their claims about costs. Indeed, a main claim of those opposed to the ACA was that it would make healthcare "unaffordable."

Costs are not always unintended or considered undesirable among advocates who acknowledge them as a consequence of their policy goals. Advocates are often aware of the impact of one policy goal on another policy goal. Consider, for instance, what is referred to as the "SALT Cap." The Tax Cuts and Jobs Act of 2017 (TCJA) limited the amount of money taxpayers could deduct from their federal income tax liabilities in recognition of property taxes they paid to state and local governments (the TCJA capped this benefit at $10,000 a year). It may first appear to some that the cap prevents wealthier people from insulating their incomes from federal taxation by purchasing expensive homes (which have much higher property tax assessments and deductions). Democrats have used evidence to point out, however, that the SALT Cap functions as a tax increase on middle-class earners in higher-tax states where Democrats hold a majority in state government, or so-called "Blue States." Republicans, for their part, don't appear to care about this disadvantage. Democrats have suggested this is due to the way the cap may motivate middle-class earners in Blue States to advocate for smaller state government. Democratic leaders in Congress have made known their desire to repeal the SALT Cap (thus allowing for higher deductions); however, some progressives aligned with Democrats have also argued that the more equitable and responsible policy goal would be to eliminate the deduction altogether.[16] These different policy goals come with costs that can be introduced as relevant evidence.

Costs may also include the effects of disadvantages, which we have already discussed in Chapter 4 in relation to the fifth critical question associated with causal reasoning (*Will the proposed solution cause additional problems or disadvantages not already occurring in the status quo?*). Disadvantages *are* a type of cost; however, considering how evidence is used to support disadvantages is more aptly addressed as a matter of supporting predictions.

Evidence Used to Support Predictions

In the prior chapters, we noted that public policy advocacy relies significantly on establishing causal relationships. Newman and Newman devote an entire chapter of their text to "Supporting Predictions," isolating forms of policy prediction commonly supported with evidence.[17] Evidence, they write, is "indispensable" to whether society is reaching the goals it sets for itself in policymaking, noting "the greatest cash value of evidence in deliberation is its use in predicting the consequences of present or proposed policies."[18] Within the system we have been laying out for you, such evidence will typically first appear in the form of support for a proposed solution's likelihood to result in advantages. Negative advocates, then, will likely provide evidence either to prove that a solution will fail to realize claimed advantages or will lead to undesirable consequences, or disadvantages. In each case, we have provided critical questions that will assist you in challenging the potentially fallible inferential leaps.

Here we will discuss four ways the quality of evidence becomes especially relevant to the soundness of these causal relationships: when evidence asserts a correlation, when evidence comes in the form of a theory, when evidence consists of observations and conclusions of an authority, and when evidence is an analogy.

Correlations. Evidence of correlations is often considered "the gold standard" for establishing causal relationships used in advocacy. This is likely because many believe correlations are derived from scientific and/or statistic processes that render predicted outcomes valid. A correlation is a mutual relationship between two phenomena that appear to behave in relation to one another—a co-relation. The term "correlation" is both a technical term and a term used less formally. Technically, it is a statistical term describing the strength of relationship between two phenomena, like height and weight across a population. Of this use, advocates often use the term "empirical" to describe phenomena based on measurements and observations that others can verify. You might find that data points predictably track with each other—as average height goes up, so does average weight; as sugar intake is reduced, weight loss occurs; as weight loss occurs, fewer heart attacks occur. Less formally, you might learn of observations about correlations (when minimum wages increase, some might observe that people in their neighborhood have been losing their jobs, for instance). They might react to this relationship by asserting that the two are correlated, even though they are only really recognizing that, after one phenomenon happened (a minimum wage increase), another phenomenon happened (some people they know lost their jobs). In other cases, even when a correlation can be statistically demonstrated, it may not prove causality. For instance, as per capita gun ownership increases, so too does gun violence. As one goes up, so does the other. They can be said to correlate, but *is that relationship necessarily causal?* What if, for example, the increased gun violence occurs only at certain times of the day, involves generally certain age groups, and/or might be tied to certain types of events? If you rely on correlations in establishing a causal relationship, your evidence should plausibly explain the relationship and rule out alternative explanations.

Evidence used to support and challenge correlations will come in a variety of forms. Statistical analysis will often appear to be the strongest type of evidence used in the contemplation of correlations. However, as we note in the next chapter, you should by no means assume statistical evidence is free of errors, both in terms of how the data is developed and how it is used by advocates. As we noted in Chapter 4, claims of causality are first brought under the microscope when you ask critical questions about the alleged cause of a problem (all five critical questions for causal claims apply here, but particularly *Are there other probable causes that might reasonably produce the problem?*). Such questions will focus your attention on the evidence used to support a correlation. From that point, you will likely find that claimed correlations come in the form of claims made by authorities, backed by some kind of statistical analysis, or the statistics themselves.

Theories. In trying to explain how one phenomenon is related to another, advocates will cite theories. That minimum wage increases cause reductions in labor demand is an economic theory. That carbon pollution causes global warming is a theory coming from science. Theories are explanations on which predictions are often based. Like "correlation," the term "theory" can be used either technically or less formally. Used technically, theories are scientific explanations of phenomena that have (a) been shown to have explanatory and predictive ability, and (b) have withstood the scrutiny of scholars who have tested them. Used less formally, a theory is little more than an explanation offered by an observant person. Along these lines, think of an explanation offered by your uncle at Thanksgiving dinner for why the U.S. Centers for Disease Control recommended social distancing and mask wearing during the COVID-19 pandemic, one that suggested the "deep state's" goal all along was to erode support for the incumbent president and assure the challenger in 2020 would win. While your uncle may be generally aware of current events, just as in science, his theory is only good to the extent that it is grounded in reliable factual information. In public advocacy, predictions are almost always based on a theory, whether the theory is explicitly or implicitly stated. Moreover, all explanations of correlations are theoretical. Consider that AR-15s are correlated with more death and injury when used in mass shootings. That the two are co-related is a fact. The reason most often cited explaining this correlation—that the ease of use and rapid firing ability of AR-15s causes the correlation—is a theory. Public policy advocates will both explicitly and implicitly use theories. Sometimes they will explicitly cite them, such as when politicians cite Keynesian economic theory to justify deficit spending. Doing so might give the public confidence in knowing that a familiar theory is informing policy, thus making desired outcome (advantages) more likely. Implicitly, an advocate might merely reference what they believe is a well-known principle, such as the notion that tax cuts help the economy. Theory is not always cited. In some cases, the relationship between the phenomena might be so widely accepted that it is treated like a natural law.

As we will discuss more in the next chapter, theories are often grounded in ideology, which is not to suggest they are flawed. Ideological analysis is inevitable and can be the basis upon which sound decisions are made.[19] You are wise, however, to consider the impact ideology may have on a causal explanation. Likewise, well-established theory can also be relied on for decades, to a point when it becomes accepted truth and emerges as foundational to public policy solutions in certain realms, even if there is evidence from other sources that point to plausible alternative causal explanations.[20]

Authorities. Quite often, even arguably most often, advocates will rely on the statements of respected or well-known authorities to help build confidence in their predictions. Evidence that asserts correlations, theories, or analogies may come from authorities. Authorities may also offer more general observations that support components of a causal claim. To generate support for a causal claim, you may turn to authorities who are widely respected sources of information on a particular issue. Dr. Anthony Fauci, the director of the National Institute of Allergy and Infectious Disease, for instance, is an authority on infectious diseases. The world has never dealt with COVID-19, so it was initially very challenging to predict what approach would help or harm people facing the threat of COVID-19 infection, and thus help the nation overcome the virus. The world has dealt with a variety of other infectious diseases, however, and Fauci played a significant role addressing these public health crises over the course of his decades-long career, including personally leading aspects of the U.S. response to HIV/AIDS.

We suggest considering the root of the term "authority"—"author"—in considering who might be considered an authority versus just someone with credentials or a title who has an opinion. An authority, then, is the person who *authored* the knowledge (conducted the research or experienced the phenomena firsthand). Perhaps they conducted the research establishing the existence of correlations, or a theory that helped predict the consequences of policy in some particular policy realm (John Keynes, after whom Keynesian economic theory was named, for instance, authored the theory being used to render predictions that deficit spending during recessions will stabilize the economy and lead to growth). Some authorities have directly relevant *credentials*, but many who are cited in public policy advocacy do not. What makes the vast majority of authorities credible is presumption given to them because of their credentials. Maybe they have an advanced degree, are publicly known because of their publications, or are affiliated with a trusted entity (a major research university or respected bi-partisan think tank). Affirmative and negative advocates should be aware of the credentials of the authorities they cite.

In addition to the critical questions we pose in the next chapter regarding authorities, when considering the use of authorities in supporting predictions another useful measure is to determine the extent to which their observations make evidence *relevant* to a prediction. Data may not be available to precisely support a prediction, in which case authorities help you determine what is and is not relevant to a prediction.[21] During the summer and fall of 2020, for instance, Anthony Fauci might have been asked by a news anchor or lawmaker to evaluate the impact of a specific COVID-19 treatment protocol on the likelihood that schools will be able to open sooner than previously expected. The relevance of the new treatment to the predictions is where Fauci's expertise is most useful.

Analogies. Sometimes a change in public policy is strongly desired, but the best evidence advocates can rely on to make predictions is analogical. Analogies in this regard are comparisons made between two allegedly similar cases in order to predict the outcome of a policy's adoption. In the aftermath of the George Floyd killing at the hands of Minneapolis police officers, some cities and states normally resistant to change in policing approaches and policies were suddenly looking for police reform models applied successfully in other cities and states. Analogies were and will continue to be used in public discussions about these policies as public officials and activists debate the efficacy of one or more proposals. If you are affirmative advocates in this public debate, you will argue that adoption of a policing approach in one city will produce similar outcomes in other cities. If you are negative advocates, you might counter that the instances are too different to warrant comparison. As we noted already in our discussion of reasoning by analogy, analogies tend to be most useful when they support ideas that have been tried only in a few instances. Regarding healthcare policy, for instance, the Obama Administration often cited the case of Massachusetts in proving the ACA would achieve its objective of universal coverage. A mandated market-based health insurance program had never been adopted before, except in Massachusetts. It was very difficult for the Obama Administration to marshal evidence predicting the ACA's success on a nationwide basis, other than to quote speculation by authorities and to rely on this one analogy. ACA advocates also found themselves constantly on the defensive against counter-analogies that claimed government-provided healthcare in Canada and England restricted choice and access, and produced undesirable health outcomes. Based on the comparison with Massachusetts, in particular, Obama predicted that problems with the national health insurance enrollment website would track the way Massachusetts's enrollment did. That is, enrollment in Massachusetts' so-called "Romneycare" was very slow, but they eventually approached universal coverage.

We have already provided critical questions to address reasoning by analogy. In terms of evidence use and evaluation, analogies marshalled by advocates in support of predictions must meet the same tests; particularly in the case of historical analogies upon which predictions are based, your emphasis should be on whether the analogy addresses *variables* that are probative for or against the prediction.[22] Authorities might prove helpful to this effort as well, given that they can point to especially relevant issues or questions that should be considered in the assessment of particular analogies.

In the next chapter, we focus on the types of evidence used to establish the need for policy action or to oppose such action, offer critical questions for addressing these types of evidence, consider some source-specific issues that accompany evidence drawn from such sources, and contemplate how evidence often reveals the ideology of advocates.

The Voucher Debate

The debate over school vouchers demonstrates the way evidence is used to frame the cause of a problem. Betsy DeVos, the U.S. Secretary of Education under the administration of Donald Trump, a member of one of the nation's richest families,[23] has been a consistent advocate for school vouchers. Depending on the proposal, school vouchers take various shapes. Generally, however, they involve directing money in the form of a voucher or certificate parents can use to cover costs associated with sending their child to a private school. In most formulations, voucher advocates hope to allow families to spend school property tax dollars on private schools. The goal of vouchers, at least for the parents, is to improve their child's academic performance. Quite often, the outcome objectives of vouchers are packaged rhetorically in ways to provide educational "choices" and "options" for low-income parents. Parents may be displeased with their local public school option and wish they could send their child to a better performing school, but they lack the financial resources to do so. To address this problem, say voucher advocates, parents need vouchers and the "school choice" that comes with them. In a speech delivered to the Brookings Institute, DeVos stated, "I'm opposed to any parents feeling trapped."[24] She continued, emphasizing the value of school choice; "Alternatives," she said, "are constructive, not destructive, for students, parents and teachers." The exercise of choice, she claims, allows resource-strapped parents to pursue better options.

We have discussed how identifying the cause of a problem is an essential step in advocating for a solution. DeVos' logic defines the cause of poor education outcomes as the poverty of some parents, and the resulting lack of choice. Her solution removes the barrier of poverty that stands in the way of low-income parents sending their children to higher-performing schools. Without choice between schools, she claims, parents and their children can't escape a bad school. However, in her talk at the Brookings Institute, DeVos presents no evidence supporting the claim that lack of school choice causes poor academic performance.

There is plenty of evidence that DeVos' solution—vouchers—has a troubled history and aggravates the very inequities she claims they solve. The school choice mantra emerged after the Supreme Court's *Brown vs. Board of Education of Topeka* decision in 1954, a decision that desegregated the nation's public schools. Soon after the decision, public school systems in the South attempted to convert tax dollars devoted to newly-desegregated public schools into vouchers to be used at segregated private schools.[25] If successful, parents would have been able to segregate their children in private schools with public dollars. Beyond its racist origin, school choice inflicts harmful consequences upon already poorly funded public schools. An alternative cause of poor academic performance (in conjunction with many other factors), firmly established by empirical research, is low socioeconomic status. That is, poverty (of the household and the community) was the more likely cause of poor academic performance. The American Psychological Association cites multiple peer reviewed studies establishing the deleterious effects of low socioeconomic status on students.[26] If true, that means that school vouchers would allow students to leave their local public school systems and redirect their local community's tax dollars to already well-funded and adequately performing schools. This would leave poor performing public schools in low-income areas with even fewer resources.

The consequences were put to DeVos by Leslie Stahl on the CBS News program *60 Minutes* in 2018. Stahl asked, "what about the kids who are back at the school that's not working? What about those kids?" DeVos replied that improvements had been experienced in Florida, but conceded that Michigan had seen harms from vouchers overall. In fact, even Florida's popular voucher program has been shown to have "mostly no effects or negative effects on student learning."[27] Championing solutions that are based on thin evidence or untested theory can exacerbate problems or create new ones. If vouchers are the solution to poor performing schools, moreover, DeVos appears to be suggesting that what was needed all along was someone to threaten poorer school districts with fewer resources (removal of tax dollars as vouchers). That is, of course, absurd. Wealthier school districts, argue those opposed to vouchers, perform better because they and their students have an abundance of resources (both in school and at home, among other things). Consequently, vouchers that siphon resources away from schools already in socially and economically stressed communities will predictably exacerbate school performance problems and related inequities.

Exercise: Evidence Used to Support Predictions

Identify a contemporary example in which evidence is used to support an overarching policy goal. Identify the predictions cited as justifications for the policy proposal and describe how evidence is used to support those predictions. Identify what alternative plans for addressing the problem exist (either your own ideas or ideas being discussed within the controversy). What would advocates need evidence to say to support such alternative plans for addressing the problem?

Notes

1 See Catherine F. Smith, *Writing Public Policy: A Practical Guide to Communicating in the Policy Making Process* (New York: Oxford University Press, 2010); see also Sandra M. Nutley, Isabel Walter, and Huw T.O. Davies, *Using Evidence: How Research Can Inform Public Services* (Bristol, UK: Policy Press, 2012); Karen Bogenschneider and Thomas J. Corbett, *Evidence-Based Policymaking: Insights from Policy-Minded Researchers and Research-Minded Policymakers* (New York: Routledge, 2010).

2 Advocates who frequently engage school districts, for instance, might consult Robert Asen's study of deliberations of school district boards and community members (*Democracy, Deliberation, and Education* [University Park: The Pennsylvania State University Press, 2015]). See also Paul Gary Wyckoff, *Policy and Evidence in a Partisan Age: The Great Disconnect* (Washington, D.C.: Urban Institute Press, 2009). Wyckoff considers evidence used to support claims related to fiscal policy, long-term growth policy, education, state and local economic development, and welfare.

3 Robert P. Newman and Dale R. Newman, *Evidence* (Boston: Houghton Mifflin Company, 1969).

4 Ibid., 16.

5 Ibid., 16.

6 Robert Reich(@RBReich), "Cliff notes on a potentially disastrous decision," Facebook, September 5, 2013, https://www.facebook.com/ RBReich/posts/660416167304316.

7 Leon Festinger, *A Theory of Cognitive Dissonance* (Stanford, CA: Stanford University Press, 1957).

8 Newman and Newman, *Evidence*, 6.

9 Ibid., 6.

10 Ibid., 6.

11 *The New Oxford American Dictionary*, 2001, s.v. "grounded."

12 All examples used by Newman and Newman when discussing this category of "rational goal criticism" concern foreign policy decisions (*Evidence*, 11–12).

13 See Marco Werman, "How Iran Might Respond to a Military Strike on Syria," *The World*, PRI, September 3,2013, https://www.pri.org/stories/2013-09-03/how-iran-might-respond-us-military-strike-syria.

14 Meet the Press, NBC News, September 20, 2020.

15 Newman and Newman, *Evidence*, 14.

16 Christopher Pulliam and Richard V. Reeves, "The SALT Tax Deduction is a Handout to the Rich. It Should be Eliminated Not Expanded," Brookings Institute, September 4, 2020, https://www.brookings.edu/blog/up-front/2020/09/04/the-salt-tax-deduction-is-a-handout-to-the-rich-it-should-be-eliminated-not-expanded/.

17 Newman and Newman, *Evidence*, 33.

18 Ibid., 33.

19 Ibid., 38.

20 See Wyckoff (*Policy and Evidence*), who seeks to demonstrate the fallibility of even some of the most accepted theories upon which public policies are based.

21 Newman and Newman, *Evidence*, 47.

22 Ibid., 40.

23 "#351 Richard DeVos and Family," *Forbes Magazine*, March 6, 2018, https://www.forbes. com/profile/richard-devos/?list=forbes-400%20-%203e3f2d5eff44#2da9ff0ff44e.

24 "U.S. Secretary of Education Betsy DeVos' Prepared Remarks to the Brookings Institution," U.S. Department of Education, March 29, 2017, https://www.ed.gov/news/speeches/ us-secretary-education-betsy-devos-prepared-remarks-brookings-institution.

25 Chris Ford, "The Racist Origins of Private School Vouchers," Center for American Progress, July 12, 2017, https://www.americanprogress.org/issues/education-k-12/reports/ 2017/07/12/435629/racist-origins-private-school-vouchers/.

26 "Education and Socioeconomic Status," American Psychological Association, July 2017, https://www.apa.org/pi/ses/resources/publications/education.

27 Christopher Lubienski and Joel Malin, "Do School Vouchers Lead to Better Education? New Research Raises Questions," *Miami Herald*, August 1, 2019, https://www.miamiherald. com/news/local/education/article232847252.html.

7

EVIDENCE II: EVALUATION

Takeaways

(1) Instead of basing your assessment of evidence on personal trust in the source or on the amount of evidence used, you should focus on the purpose and quality of evidence, and whether it withstands objections.

(2) Focusing on the capacity, potential bias, or accuracy of an authority is not the same as the unproductive practice of ad hominem attack.

(3) A relatively short list of critical questions can be marshaled to consider evidence used in public policy advocacy, particularly by authorities and in the form of statistics.

(4) Beyond the general applicability of the critical questions, several source-specific considerations are useful in evaluating evidence derived from the news media and scholarship, and concerns about "fake news."

(5) Evidence used in support of claims might reveal the interests and ideologies advanced by advocates and their appeals.

Imagine you are attending a local planning commission meeting considering whether to allow your organization to erect a large digital sign that displays video outside of your headquarters. A resident opposed to the sign testifies to the commission that several drivers recently involved in accidents claimed they were distracted by large video signs. *What would be your response?* After reading this chapter, you might claim that neither the drivers nor the resident possess the expertise to determine whether large video signs cause accidents. You might also offer a study indicating that no findings support that traffic accidents can be linked to digital signs. The resident might then counter that you are not citing a study but a newspaper article that discusses the position of a sign manufacturers' association, and the data is not specific to your city or any city of comparable size. The resident might also argue that the manufacturers' association has a substantial material bias in the data they have developed—therefore, that data can't be trusted. The resident might go further to argue that the authors of the report cited in the newspaper article did not perform a study or that their study was unscientific and unrepresentative.

Weaved into this dispute are a wide range of claims made about evidence. Determining whether evidence is reliable begins with considering *who the source is* and *what is being offered*, which leads us to a discussion of authorities and statistics as categories of evidence. We refer to the *who* as "authorities." In terms of *what*, we have in mind a wide variety of types or forms of evidence (testimony, statistics, examples, scholarship, documents, news, secondary sources, and so on). As a practical matter, your vantage point is also important. *Are you evaluating your own use of evidence or another's use of evidence?* Consideration of who offers evidence, what specifically they offer, and from which vantage point you are considering the evidence, focuses attention, ideally, in a productive manner.

In this chapter, we address three topics related to the evaluation of evidence: elements of evidence reliability, a framework for the evaluation of evidence provided by authorities and in statistical form, and advice about the role of ideology in the development and use of evidence. We also provide a relatively short list of critical questions to address the most common general categories under which a variety of evidence is considered in public policy advocacy—authorities and statistics. Our intention is to spark your thinking about these issues, not to offer a complete framework for evaluating all information. In discussing evidence from authorities, we also provide source-specific considerations for the evaluation of news media and scholarship, and reflect on the concept of "fake news." We begin by considering elements of reliable evidence.

Elements of Reliable Evidence

As with evaluating reasoning, it is useful to begin with some semblance of an ideal notion of evidence use. This will encourage you to contemplate assumptions you have about evidence. The result, we hope, will be a framework for considering evidence that maintains high standards for its use.

Ideally, Evidence Has a Clear Purpose

Generally, the purpose of evidence is to support advocates' claims. Many argumentation and debate textbooks will refer to evidence as "facts," but data comes in many forms, such as findings of studies, statistics, examples, and analogies, and not all of this information is "factual" in the purest sense of the term.[1] In the realm of public policy, it is best to assume that no evidence is perfect, that it can always be critiqued. Whether considering global warming, Iran's pursuit of nuclear weapons, or claims about the current state of the U.S. economy—to name a few familiar examples—public policy controversies over evidence are common even when some believe the facts are indisputable.

Evidence occupies a critical role in the performance of effective advocacy. The Toulmin model described in Chapter 4 refers to evidence as "data," as noted below:[2]

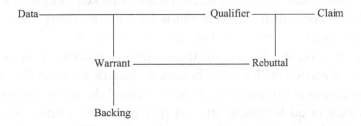

"Although anything that an audience will accept as evidence or support for a claim may act as data," writes Martha Cooper, "communication scholars have long recognized three prominent types of data: *testimony*, *statistics*, and *examples*."[3] You have already learned that data/evidence is linked to a claim through reasoning, and that evidence may function persuasively on its own. Its purpose, therefore, will evolve as claims are made by concerned stakeholders. If you wish to improve your advocacy, you should understand the purpose of evidence deployed on either side of a policy issue and engage in a healthy level of scrutiny.

Ideally, Evidence is of High Quality

Students of public speaking often learn that information provided by sources with high credibility—also referred to as a matter of "ethos"—is considered reliable by those who trust the source. A bad habit we have observed, and hope to counter in this chapter, however, is an over-reliance on personal trust in advocates or the sources on which advocates rely. If you trust an advocate, you might accept their arguments without considering the quality of their evidence. Likewise, if you trust the sources of evidence (the author or researcher who published the evidence), you might agree with advocacy backed by such sources without much consideration of the quality of the evidence. But even well-trusted sources of information may have it wrong. In scrutinizing evidence, ideally, you will look beyond your personal trust in sources of information—advocates and/or the authorities they rely on to support their claims—and focus on the quality of evidence.

For reasons we will explore more in this chapter, there are legitimate and helpful concerns you might bring to your assessment of evidence, and some of these concerns may center on issues of capacity and bias. However, objections based on *who* is making an argument or who is responsible for the information cited by an advocate (and not the quality of the observations, conclusions, and data they offer) often breaks down the quality of policy deliberation. Criticism of a source's character might prompt attacked sources to assert that their critic is committing an *ad hominem* fallacy—attacking the source and not the argument. The term "probative" is useful here. If criticism of evidence is to be probative, it will focus on the usefulness of evidence in proving, or disproving, a particular claim. We believe an intense focus on the credibility of an advocate or persons and organizations behind the information they offer (or relevancy of ad hominem attacks) may move you further away from a systematic and probative consideration of evidence. What's needed are more pointed critical questions that can assist you in determining the quality of evidence and thus keep your scrutiny within productive boundaries.

Another bad habit we have observed is the assumption many make that the *more* evidence advocates provide, the stronger their argument becomes. It is likely within public policy advocacy that fewer sources of support, properly selected and qualified, are sufficient to establish the reasonableness of an argument. This reality results in both "good" and "bad" decisions, but it does not necessarily mean more or less evidence is better or worse. As noted in our discussion of inductive reasoning (Chapter 5), a single instance of something occurring, properly applied, might be probative in the realm of public policymaking. Sometimes a preponderance of evidence is not available, and advocates work with what they have. Sometimes advocates have no evidence, or very little, but move forward nonetheless with confidence. The decision of the U.S. federal government to invade Iraq was based on a relatively small amount of evidence, which turned out to be significantly flawed. Scrutinizing evidence through the application of critical questions focuses attention on the quality of evidence.

Ideally, Evidence Withstands Objections

In considering the reliability of evidence in the realm of public policy advocacy, we believe the best test for whether evidence is reliable is *whether evidence withstands objections* (recalling Martha Cooper's simple rule, "good reasons withstand objections"[4]). There is, in our view, value for you to adopt this practical guideline and to expect that others may be comfortable with much less rigorous standards—such as those that focus on the trustworthiness of the source or the amount of evidence used to support a claim. This is not to say that trustworthiness and quantity have no value in the assessment of evidence. Critical questions can focus specifically on the credibility of the source and the number of instances cited to establish a point. Your goal should be to cultivate a rigorous and practically useful approach to evaluating evidence, a comprehensive framework.

There are many useful rubrics for scrutinizing evidence.[5] Our approach first seeks to orient you to when, why, and how evidence is used (Chapter 6) and then to narrow your attention to two categories under which we sort the most common uses of evidence: authorities and statistics. In this chapter, we are concerned with the evaluation of evidence offered by either side (in support of, or in opposition to, a policy proposal). Like we offered in Chapters 4 and 5, we provide *critical questions* that can be easily configured into objections that evidence will or will not withstand. We also offer more focused guidance concerning the news media, including brief consideration of "fake news" and scholarship.

Authorities

Authorities are *who* said or wrote what is being used to support a claim. To determine what type of authority is offering information and to begin to evaluate the information as evidence, we recommend you pose the following initial general question: *To what particular profession or community does the authority belong that causes the authority to offer information?* The phrase "causes the authority to offer information" is packed with meaning. The idea of an authority having *cause* to offer information should trigger a critical disposition whereby you are considering a variety of factors that led to both the generation of the knowledge and the willingness/desire to share it. You are, in effect, asking whether the authority can justifiably claim to possess some level of expertise, deeper understanding, or experience relevant to the information offered. Through this initial question, your close evaluation of evidence provided by authorities begins.

Similar to the analysis of reasoning, we recommend that you pose critical questions that should permit you to exercise more control over the manner in which evidence is used in public policy advocacy. Those evaluating the reliability of authorities should ask the following five critical questions:

(1) Is the authority known?
(2) Does the information offered by the authority support the claim?
(3) Is the authority capable of observing the phenomenon they claim to understand?
(4) Is the information offered by the authority likely to be affected by bias?
(5) Is the information offered by the authority accurate?

The first critical question concerns the clear identification of the authority. While an authority is often a person, it might also be an organization such as the Centers for Disease Control or the Cato Institute. For such authorities to influence an audience's thinking, it must be clearly identified. "Scientists say . . .," or even the more commonly used "They say . . .," are *always* insufficient references. In everyday communication, it may be appropriate to indicate that you heard a report on NBC News, but in public policy advocacy you would be expected to provide additional details of the report so that an authority is identified and can be evaluated.

The second critical question is one of the most basic in the practice of argumentation and debate: *whether the information provided by the authority supports the claim.* While this is a very basic question, the answer provided is not. If you are challenging the authority on this level, you must indicate how the claim and the information offered by the authority differ. Typically, this is done in tandem with the third critical question, because you would ideally focus on what is being observed by the authority and note that it is not the same as, or differs in significant ways from, the subject matter of the claim.

You may also need to focus on the terms used by the advocate versus the terms used by the authority. Whereas the advocate's claim is, "Russia will initiate a nuclear attack," for example, you would surely be correct to protest if the authority offers only that "Russia, a nuclear power, has reacted with hostility when states along its border are on the brink of independence." If you are selecting an authority to support your claim, our recommendation is to let the authority's particular claims and language guide your writing of the claims you are constructing.

The third critical question concerns *whether the authority is capable of observing the phenomenon they claim to understand*. This is a question of *capacity*, or more precisely labeled by Newman and Newman as "perceptual capacity."[6] Capacity is most often a matter of training in research methods that produce bias-free or objective conclusions. A molecular biologist is trained to observe phenomena others cannot observe. While noting that all areas of expertise are unique, Newman and Newman generally conclude that experts:

(1) should have training and expertise in the area under study
(2) know relevant languages and technical jargon
(3) have a genuine intellectual curiosity about what they are observing[7]

Capacity is relatively easy to determine within areas of expertise that are associated with collegiate disciplines and professional fields. It is more challenging to address disagreement among peers of relatively equal capacity, a subject taken up by philosophers Richard Feldman and Ted A. Warfeld, who write about "revealed peer disagreement."[8] Capacity in general is made more complex by the wide range of credentials available in an abundance of fields and professions. Many areas of expertise are less recognized or unregulated. One can become certified in a variety of fields by purchasing accreditation through professional associations or after relatively short online curricula, tutorials, and exams. For instance, a person can become a certified essential oil practitioner at the Essential Oil Academy (https://essentialoilacademy.com). Many of these programs are accredited by third parties and lead participants to satisfying careers; many are not and do not. Credentialling can occur in several ways resulting in a wide range of titles and indicators of specialized knowledge. Authorities may also derive their capacity through many years of work within occupations or organizations where no credentialing process occurs. Joseph Needham, for instance, was an accomplished biochemist who, without training, became known as an expert in the history of Chinese scientific advancements later in his career. We would be remiss not to add here that scholars are tracking a more general contemporary decline in public faith in expertise. For instance, Tom Nichols cites the impact of easier access to information via the internet, the notion that all knowledge is equal in its trustworthiness, and a cultural aversion to elitism as causal forces leading to the widespread view "that each person's opinion about anything must be accepted as equal to any-one else's"— what he characterizes as "the death of expertise."[9]

The fourth critical question concerns bias. The question of bias is cap-tured in a concept explored by Newman and Newman, labeled "perceptual distortion," which they define as "a bias, belief system, or perspective" that acts as "a set of lenses which focuses the attention of an observer" so that he or she "perceives certain phenomena and disregards others, thus distorting reality."[10] Accordingly, to identify bias begins by classifying a bias as caused by such things as ideology, national interest, self-interest, unconscious parti-sanship, or power. Robert James Branham simplifies these categories further, explaining that there are three basic sources of bias:

(1) Having a *material stake* in the outcome of a dispute
(2) Having an *ego investment* in the matter
(3) Having an *ideological stake* or perspective sufficient to distort one's judgment or expression[11]

Perceptual distortions that might be caused by economic or material interests may not always be visible. *Who is being paid to write (or say) what by whom?* is a useful question to begin an effort to determine whether an authority has an economic interest sufficient enough to render their perception unreliable. Bias of a material nature would include employment and career considerations as well—*How might an authority's conclusions be affected by how the authority derives revenue or income?* Naomi Oreskes and Erik Conway, for instance, trace the origins of research funding in their book *Merchants of Doubt*, in order to demonstrate links between studies minimizing environmental harms and industries benefitting from the status quo.[12] Somewhat related to such eco-nomic concerns, Newman and Newman argue that scholars and others who originate ideas and steward theories through the development and publication process can be affected by "a parental affection" for their work.[13] Branham refers to this form of bias as an "ego investment," a desire to receive credit or praise for an achievement.[14] Advocates evaluating evidence affected by this form of bias tend to exaggerate moments when their conclusions are con-firmed and minimize or ignore moments when their conclusions are proven to be unreliable.[15] Within the critical question framework we recommend in this chapter, ideology (discussed at greater length at the end of this chapter) figures as a matter of bias. Newman and Newman cite ideology as the most potent factor that distorts perceptions.[16] Contemporary examples of the types of identifications that signal bias might include free market advocates, "Tea Partiers," "Greens," "Neo-Conservatives," "Jihadists," "Fiscal Conservatives," "Never Trumpers," "Globalists," "Creationists," and so forth.

In all forms of bias, two additional observations are useful. First, it is important to remember that an authority's mere association to persons, institutions, and organizations does not by itself constitute a bias sufficient to distort a judgment or perspective. You may find it useful to further determine whether a recognizable or suspected bias is (1) relevant to the subject matter under consideration by the authority (the subject the authority is addressing) and (2) evident in the specific material (the specific information offered by the authority). The case study we feature in this chapter concerns an accusation of material bias that deserves more scrutiny. Second, biases may contribute to a strengthening of evidence. Newman and Newman introduce a basic evidence standard, or indicator of credibility, which holds "[t]he greater the damage of his [or her] own testimony to a witness, the more credible it is."[17] On a practical level, the assessment that an authority is reluctant can boost the credibility of information provided by that authority. Typically, that the authority is reluctant is a matter of conjecture on the part of advocates using the authority to support a claim. Rarely do authorities admit that their latest conclusions on a matter they have previously addressed represent a reversal in their thinking. Where authorities do experience shifts in thinking or findings, however, their revised position might offer significant support for courses of action that are highly controversial. For example, during 2012 and 2013, several conservative Republican political figures announced publicly that they could no longer support the denial of marriage equality to same-sex couples. As converts, their positions on such issues as same-sex adoption and the fundamental right of all Americans to marry the one they love surfaced as support for the marriage equality platform and legal argument.

The fifth critical question concerns the accuracy of the information provided. First, authorities may "get it wrong" because of limited perceptual capacity, but this is not the same as *intentionally* misleading or offering information they know to be untrue, as has been shown to be the case in Florida, where Governor Ron DeSantis intentionally hid information from the public about the spread of COVID-19,[18] and nationally, where Donald Trump admitted he intentionally misled the American public early in the pandemic's spread.[19]

There are times, such as in these examples, when authorities can be said to deliberately report something they know to be untrue, what might be labeled a "willful distortion."[20] A willful distortion is a lie, and the assumption behind the use of this label is always that the authority is aware of the lie. Willful distortions are most often motivated by the same biases discussed above, and they are more common, according to Newman and Newman, when tensions are high. Such distortions are likely to be repeated by the same authority over time—causing what may sometimes emerge as an irreparable loss of trust in the authority. Regardless of the reason behind or frequency of willful distortions, for the student of evidence, willful distortions are no different than false information generated due to a perceptual distortion—both must be rejected as unreliable. The fifth critical question might also identify a "nonauthentic" or "fraudulent" document.[21] An inauthentic document is essentially one that does not really come from the attributed source, which might include a "fake" document falsely credited to a source that does not really exist, or a source that did not create, or is unaware of, the document. An inauthentic document might also include a fully or partially plagiarized document.

Source-Specific Considerations and Fake News

Authorities belonging to professions or sectors of society are more or less prone to certain flaws concerning evidence use. In their 1969 text, Newman and Newman provide a comprehensive review of the government, the press, pressure groups, and professional scholars, arguing that the conclusions of these sources require particular scrutiny and deserve more or less respect according to several source-specific standards.[22] We wish to offer some updated guidance concerning the news media, including a brief consideration of "fake news" and scholarship.

News Media

Much has been written about the news media and the reliability of information offered by news sources. Internet sources of news have increasingly replaced printed news outlets and altered the character of broadcast news significantly. The consolidation of American news corporations into large publicly traded corporations seeking to reduce costs (and maximize profits) has had a direct impact on the amount of time reporters can spend within the proximity of the activity about which they are expected to report. Alex S. Jones documents the precipitous decline of the news media's capacity to hold those with power accountable.[23] What this means for those evaluating the use of evidence derived from news media sources is an open question for scholars, students, and practitioners of public policy advocacy.

For the most part, the critical questions are useful tools for evaluating the reliability of news. The question of bias is perhaps the most important critical test you should apply to news media, whether it is traditional print news, television news, or news found online. Asking *whether the information you acquire is even intended to be news* may serve as a starting point in assessing perceptual distortion. A search for the latest news on the "causes of obesity" will instantly offer links to a myriad of websites owned and operated by manufacturers of weight loss products and providers of weight loss services, some that will take on the look of news programming, in some cases highlighting a recent scientific discovery related to weight loss. Posing the critical questions to challenge evidence from authorities, however, should cause serious concerns about the reliability of such information, depending on the claims you are considering. And, of course, other forms of "fake news" have come into closer focus as that term has emerged as a popular label for both genuinely artificial news and accurate news that those in power believe the public will doubt if they label it "fake." We address that phenomenon more below.

While the news media continues to generate a significant amount of information, carefully assessing the quality of that information is challenging in several respects. First, as noted by Jones, many who have always gone online for information have not developed the "news habit."[24] Young Americans do not generally engage in a routine effort to acquire the news.[25] If you are one who rarely consults news in any form, you will find the evaluation of evidence used in news, or news used as evidence, regardless of the means used to find it, to be particularly challenging. You may be attracted to blog or Facebook posts that provide information on topics that concern you personally, but you may not regularly consult a mainstream news service to learn what is occurring in terms of domestic and foreign affairs (subjects of public policy). Imagine you are personally concerned about the progress of immigration reform, for instance, and you read a post written by a pro-reform advocate you are following on Facebook who alleges that the Obama-era DACA program is in jeopardy because of activities in the U.S. Congress. You may view this information as reliable, even if you have little to no idea what Congressional action has occurred or know little about the advocate making the claim. After some inquiry, you may find that such concern was prompted by a single represen-tative or senator introducing an amendment that has no chance of passing—a common occurrence in the legislative branches of the United States. We suggest imagining that a hierarchy of periodical news sources exists, and that the reputations, experience, and investment in news production (number of funded news bureaus and dedicated reporters, for instance) actually affects the confidence you should place in the reliability of its reporting.

Second, the authority is not always clear. In evaluating news, you must first determine the authority to which you will apply the critical questions. *Is it the author of the information you are evaluating? Or, is it an authority referred to in the article or post?* Once you have determined who the authority is, the standard critical questions would apply. Most likely, news sources will not clearly answer those questions for you; you will need to consider the news content carefully.

Third, it is often difficult to distinguish between authentic news and infor-mation produced for other reasons. Today, in the era of inexpensive means of video production and ample opportunities to post information online, it is easier for institutions, individuals, and organizations to release information as fully packaged stories that are reposted and linked in accordance with social affiliations and political perspectives. We have personally encountered family members and friends who were excited to share with us provocative conspir-acy theories offered online in attractive documentary formats. Whether such material relied on authentic information, or could itself be considered authen-tic, information is a highly relevant question for the student of evidence.

Finally, the common notion that primary sources are more credible than secondary sources is complicated when applied to online news. The value of a primary source lies in your ability to evaluate it more closely than a second-ary source. Yet, so much of online news aggregates and consolidates the expe-riences, observations, and opinions of those who have generally come to be viewed as primary sources. It is reasonable to favor news reports that rely on pri-mary sources; however, according primary sources more respect may cause you to apply insufficient scrutiny to the plentiful primary sources available online. Almost anyone can function like a journalist online, what is sometimes referred to as "citizen journalism."[26] You will need to be especially cautious when select-ing information offered by ordinary people claiming to know something about subjects that are complex and technical, and/or tied to a specialized field.

While you should apply scrutiny to online citizen journalism, internet and social media platforms have developed into complex and multifaceted marketplaces of ideas, including the perspectives of skilled and seasoned journalists disconnected from mainstream news media outlets. Consider, for instance, veteran journalist Dan Rather, who, since his departure as the anchor of CBS Evening News in 2005, has developed a highly regarded online and social media presence. No stranger to the precarious standing of truth and accuracy in public communication and news,[27] in 2006, he began to produce and host "Dan Rather Reports," on HDNet, high-definition television network, which became AXS.tv. Later, Rather began to host "The Big Interview." He has his own multimedia production company ("News and Guts") with an online presence (https://www.newsandguts.com/), and he regularly uses social media as a platform to practice his craft. When asked by Ryan D'Agostino of *Esquire*, "Can social media be a form of journalism?," Rather had this to say:

> I know people get tired of hearing this, but . . . like every other journalist who's worthy of the name, the purpose is: to gather facts, and analyze the facts, in order to get as close to the truth as is humanly possible. Recognizing that sometimes you can get reeeally [sic] close to it . . . and other times, even with your best efforts, you don't get very close.[28]

Fake News

The critical questions for evaluating information from authorities, and the added skepticism driven by the considerations above concerning the news media, should serve as adequate protection against what is widely referred to as "fake news." Still, we believe the concept is sufficiently obscure to warrant separate consideration. "Fake news," or what Claire Wardle and Hossein Derakhshan prefer to call "information pollution,"[29] appears in different forms. They outline three:

(1) Mis-information is when false information is shared, but no harm is meant.
(2) Dis-information is when false information is knowingly shared to cause harm.
(3) Mal-information is when genuine information is shared to cause harm, often by moving information designed to stay private into the public sphere.[30]

Journalist Brian Stelter notes how the concept of fake news went from a term "coined by reporters and researchers to describe made up stories on social media" to when Donald Trump began to use it to describe "news you shouldn't believe."[31] Similarly, Nolan Higdon recounts the uses and consequences of fake news throughout American political history;[32] but he also notices a significant shift in the meaning of the term in January of 2017, when Trump, enraged at CNN's coverage concerning Russian efforts to compromise him, accused the entire network of being "fake news."[33]

Up to that moment, the fake news that concerned most Americans was *real* fake news. The most significant body of recent artificial news stories of concern was created by Russian government agents through "hacking and insinuating substantial amounts of content into our social media stream with an intent, during the post-convention period at least, of defeating Hillary Clinton and electing Donald Trump," according to Kathleen Hall Jamieson, who studied whether such attacks and subsequent exploitation of false information was effective in aiding Trump's victory.[34] Jamieson examines how social media platforms, the press, citizenry, candidates, and "polarizers," "unwittingly helped the Russians achieve their ends in 2016."[35] Efforts to protect the United States from similar cyberattacks are a must, but so too is the need to focus on the susceptibility among the U.S. public to fake news, claims that *real* news is fake news, and conspiracy theories.

Conspiracies also require diligent information scrutiny. One significant dimension of this scrutiny, argue some, must be to attend to the tendency of Trump to position himself as a primary source of news and arbiter of the legitimacy of news for his political base. That the "news" Donald Trump offers comes in the form of unsupported claims and conspiracy is the subject of Russell Muirhead and Nancy L. Rosenblum's work, as well as countless efforts by journalists to fact check and counter misinformation.[36] "No president—indeed, no national official—has resorted to accusations of conspiracy so instinctively, so frequently, and with such brio as Donald Trump," write Muirhead and Rosenblum.[37] While acknowledging the existence of conspiracy theory on both sides of the political aisle, they conclude that "conspiracy *without theory* comes more often and with greater impact from the political right."[38] To that end, some have focused on the complacency and propagandistic nature of some news networks in contemplating the ongoing challenge of overcoming Trump's precarious relationship with the truth, the most notable being Fox News.[39]

Toward this same end, Higdon offers a comprehensive approach to detecting and addressing fake news. He starts with the premise that "to focus on Trump is to miss a larger problem: most Americans are unable to distinguish objective journalism from fake news."[40] He goes on to cite some stunning data that establishes the problem across age groups, from middle schoolers to senior citizens.[41] Calling for a critical media literacy approach, he outlines a 10-part process—a "Fake News Detection Kit"—that includes questions, similar to those we outline above, to determine "Does the evidence hold up under scrutiny?" as well as unique tests to determine "Does the content qualify as journalism."[42] We strongly recommend these and other approaches to assessing content you believe may be inaccurate.[43]

Scholarship

By most standards, scholars are considered the most reliable sources of evidence. Scholars are expected to follow *scholarly methods* to validate their claims within their fields of expertise. Historians are expected to use the *historical method* and scientists the *scientific method*, for example. Such methods are conventional practices for accruing knowledge within a discipline and permitting verification, so that other scholars can confirm the findings if they follow the same method. Due to their training and commitment to these methods, the conclusions scholars draw are generally viewed as superior to those of non-scholars. Concerning the problem we have just discussed, for instance, we note economist Bruce Bartlett's recommendation to consult academic sources in his simple but lucid guide to combatting fake news.[44] In our view, Newman and Newman's assessment of "independent scholars" as highly credible holds true today, as do their various reservations, particularly their view that scholars who get especially close to government, or enter government service, can lose their capacity to be "professionally critical and objective."[45] Certainly academics are susceptible to bias and capable of becoming ideologues, apologists, and even propagandists. However, scholarly methods continue to imbue academic research with a high measure of validity. Within the realm of public policymaking, particularly in dealing with intractable social problems and priorities, we have observed a steady call for "evidence-based policymaking," which essentially means linking knowledge producers (what some call "policy-minded researchers") to the policy process (where they link up with "research-minded policy-makers"), including efforts by policymakers to assure that academic research is consulted in drafting legislation and budgeting at the U.S. federal level.[46]

The nature of *shared* research is a key characteristic of evidence drawn from scholars. Scholars formally share the findings of their research through specialized journals (referred to as scholarly journals) affiliated with their disciplines or in the form of book-length works published by academic or university presses. In either case, the work is typically *peer reviewed* by an editor and several reviewers who, to avoid bias, do not know the identities of the author(s). This is the first step in sharing research. The second step occurs when the scholarship is accepted for publication, which is typically contingent on the approval of these "blind" reviewers, and often comes only after substantial revisions have occurred so that the final product conforms to the highest standards of excellence in the discipline to which the scholar belongs. Here too, you might imagine a hierarchy of scholarly journals in each discipline, based upon a ranking that recognizes the prestige and quality of the scholarship they publish. The standards of scholarship, however, are not always followed in each instance a scholar writes something and shares it with others. Scholars, like anyone, can post an opinion in a journalistic format or online. Increasingly, scholars have developed blogs to post their views and cultivate professional associations with other scholars. Such writings are rarely subject to the same peer review that precedes the formal publishing of scholarship intended for an academic audience.

While scholarship can be highly reliable as evidence, it presents you with several unique challenges. First, you may find scholarship difficult to comprehend and require a general introduction to research processes before properly discerning what portions of a scholarly work should be cited as evidence. Most scholarship commences with either a *research question* or *hypothesis*. Some form of review of what others have written on the subject (*literature review*) may appear before or after the research question or hypothesis, which may be brief but linked to citations in the form of footnotes or endnotes, with which the scholar may agree or disagree. A *methodology* for answering the research question or testing the hypothesis is almost always explained, in some instances in a very formal, complex section. The "meat" of scholarship for you is typically the *findings*, which are offered in some form of a *discussion*. For large research reports, an *executive summary* may also be provided at the beginning, which summarizes the findings. Some scholars end their writing with *implications*, concluding remarks about what the findings may suggest about related matters and the direction in which the research might be expanded. You will find the most useful material to cite as evidence within the findings or discussion, whereas the other material is written principally to explain the technical steps the scholar took to perform the research.

Second, it is difficult to disqualify scholarship. Typically, scholarship is discounted with alternative conclusions offered by other scholars with expertise in the same areas. Scholarship often exists for this very reason, as generations of scholars rethink prior conclusions and exploit the potential of innovations and new technologies to generate new knowledge.[47] In most advocacy situations when scholarship is used as evidence by your opposition, you will find yourself offering alternative scholarship and leaving the audience to sort out the relative value of either side's evidence. It is far more challenging for non-scholars to effectively discredit the complex conclusions of scholars. Non-scholars wishing to do so might attempt to claim scholars are biased, such as by highlighting particular material/economic or ideological commitments of the scholars they wish to discredit (the case study below examines such a situation). Otherwise, non-scholars must assume the burdens associated with the methodologies used to produce the scholarship. Discrediting a conclusion by a historian, for example, might require bringing to the surface archival documents the historian ignored or failed to discover in assembling his or her conclusions, which would require extensive research.

Third, you often must distinguish between scholarship and opinion that is buoyed by the strength of a scholar's authority and reputation. The question you should ask is not whether the source is a scholar, per se, but *whether the evidence is, indeed, scholarship produced through a scholarly method and peer review* or whether it is more appropriately considered journalism, blogging, or simply an individual's perspective. For example, the opinion of Robert Reich we considered in Chapter 5 concerning the prospect of a U.S. military strike on government facilities in Syria is not scholarship, even though Reich would be considered by most to be a scholar. Reich is a lawyer by trade who became a government official during the administration of Jimmy Carter, then a professor at the John F. Kennedy School of Government at Harvard University, and then the Secretary of Labor under Bill Clinton. Today, as a professor of public policy at the University of California, Berkeley, Reich's areas of expertise can be found listed on his faculty webpage, but among the listed areas you will *not* find American foreign policy, international relations, American national security, or the politics of the Middle East. Asking whether a scholar's work is scholarship is tantamount to registering objections concerning *whether the authority possesses the perceptual capacity to accurately observe a phenomenon under consideration.*

Finally, it is challenging to present scholarship to decision makers. Scholarship is written for other scholars, rarely for policymakers. Karen

Bogenschneider and Thomas J. Corbett, in their book-length consideration of the subject of evidence-based policymaking, note that policymakers almost always prefer presentations that provide an opportunity to discuss research rather than written material,[48] suggesting that it is better to have a scholar present his or her own findings or translate the finding of another scholar than to provide written materials and expect a decision maker to review them. If that is not possible, research presented to policymakers must pass what they refer to as an "accessibility test," which amounts to brief summaries, understandably written.[49]

Statistics

In our experience as teachers of argument, debate coaches, and practitioners of public policy advocacy, if statistics appear related to the subject being discussed they are afforded a level of respect above whatever else may be offered. The most important point to make about statistics is that such numbers, as a type of evidence, should be subject to the same level of scrutiny as evidence offered by authorities. You do not need to be an expert in mathematics to use or effectively evaluate statistics. You merely need to be observant. *Quantitative literacy* should be the goal of any person with a serious interest in public policy, but it is an evolving skill that comes with study and experience with data in the workplace and/or through public service. In considering statistical data, Newman and Newman advise you to ask three critical questions:

(1) Who wants to prove what?
(2) What do the figures really represent?
(3) What conclusions do the figures support?[50]

This is one of several useful rubrics.[51] We like it because it is relatively simple to recall and apply, and because the questions are likely to uncover bias or the influence of ideology on the data.

The first question overlaps with our discussion of evidence offered by authorities, and we have explored extensively the critical questions you should pose in that regard.

The second question—*What do the figures really represent?*—is a matter of understanding how the statistical data is produced. Statistics may be simple numbers, percentages, averages, high scores, low scores, and so forth, or it may be the conclusion of a formula or several formulas. Asking *what do the figures represent?* begins with asking, *what is being counted or measured?* Once you have determined what is being counted or measured, your next objective is to determine *if* what is being counted or measured is relevant to, or representative of, the phenomenon you are considering in the context of your advocacy. Only through determining what the figures represent can you begin to assess the potential impact of the statistics being offered and determine the extent to which they help or harm your cause. The most common objection that results from asking this question is that the statistics measure something different than what is under consideration in the public policy debate (i.e., they are "not representative").

To highlight the importance of determining what statistics *really* represent, you might note the different value of using alternative measures of "central tendency" (mean, median, and mode) in public controversies, such as, for example, the state of the U.S. economy. If you wish to gauge the health of the economy based on average household incomes, you have three averages from which to choose. If you want to make the U.S. economy appear worse, you might use the median as your measure of central tendency—or the value that falls in the center of the available data. According to the U.S. Census Bureau, the median household income in 2018 was $63,179.[52] If you want to paint a sunnier picture of the economy, you might use the mean instead—the sum of a set of numbers divided by the quantity of numbers added. In this case, the mean household income was $106,045[53]—more than 1/3 greater than the median! Neither one of these averages is, by its nature, more or less accurate, but each may tell a different story.

The third question—*What conclusions do the figures support?*—bears on whether the statistics serve any effective purpose. If you are marshaling statistics to support your claims, you can assess whether they do indeed strengthen your argument, and, if they do not, what statistical data might. If you are evaluating the statistics used by another to support a conclusion with which you disagree, you can determine the extent to which you need to invalidate them through objections—the most common being that *the figures do not support the claim*. It is unlikely in the realm of public policy advocacy that you will have at your reach statistics that support your precise position. One of the reasons statistics are so well-regarded is that, at their best, they are objective facts that are not intended to support any position. Statistics are commonly used by advocates to piece together a picture, to establish the existence and extent of a problem, support causal relationships, and measure the likelihood of advantages and disadvantages. As we recommend in Chapter 6, asking *what do you need evidence to say?* is an important question for you to ask when gathering and encountering statistics.

When statistics are used to prove that a proposal will be effective, we urge you to recall the uncertainty that accompanies predictions and observe the way advocates infer from statistics a conclusion. For example, it is common for many universities to require that first-year students live in the residence halls, but some universities have contemplated a second-year residency requirement for sophomores. Often, statistics are used by proponents of such a proposal to illustrate that students who live in the residence halls a second year are more likely to continue into their junior year and to graduate (as reflected in sophomore-to-junior "retention rates"). *Do such figures support the conclusion that retention rates will increase if there is a second-year residency requirement?* Opponents argue they do not, because there are so many other factors that could have caused the returning students to stay enrolled (their household income or the enhanced quality of the particular residence halls the returning students lived in, for instance). They note too that the students included in the statistics elected to remain in the residence halls—they were not required to do so. Moreover, such statistics do not factor into the equation the potential decline in enrollment that might occur if first-year students, wishing to avoid a mandatory second-year requirement, choose to enroll in another university.

The Role of Ideology in the Evaluation of Evidence

Beyond the function of evidence in relation to the stock issues of policy advocacy, advocates' use of evidence may reveal their values, or what also might be called their ideology. In his early work and beyond, Robert Newman devoted his scholarly career to the consideration of ideology in policy decision making.[54] As noted above, in *Evidence*, Newman and his co-author Dale Newman explain the functions of bias,[55] identifying both strong biases that render the generator, user, or consumer of evidence either incapable of perceiving something that is plainly evident or perceiving something that is not supported by the evidence[56] *and* bias that is so strong that the generator or user of evidence aims to intentionally mislead or lie.[57] In a later analysis of foreign policy decision-making, Newman argues that, "[w]hat primarily distinguishes policy argument is the necessary factoring into all policy arguments of human goals and values."[58]

Something of a model begins to take shape in Newman's work, as he directs us to consider both a "value premise" and corresponding prediction advanced by advocates as a means of unmasking their ideological interests. To illustrate, he cites arguments made by those opposed to an air strike against Soviet missile installations in Cuba when the issue was discussed among President John F. Kennedy and his advisors on October 17, 1962:

Value premise: The United States should uphold its traditions.

Prediction: A surprise air strike would be, and would be perceived to be, in conflict with those traditions.[59]

It is not difficult to imagine how advocates' values may have influenced the prediction, and the type of evidence introduced in opposition to such a strike. Advocates' ideologies may surface in the examples, theories, analogies, authorities, and/or statistics they introduce to support their positions.

Ideologies behind claims are often difficult to detect and may be intentionally concealed. For many years before the U.S. Supreme Court legalized same-sex marriage, advocates sought the same employment benefits for same-sex couples that were provided to opposite-sex married couples (i.e., "equitable coverage"). Public and private employers who did not want to appear discriminatory asserted that their denial of such coverage was—simply— *consistent* with the policies of similar employers. For some employers, *other* values influenced their position, which emerged in support for the status quo that heralded the importance of supporting marriage and family (recall marriage was not available to same-sex partners). In defending the status quo, employers might assert that "family is important," and other such general claims. More determined opponents of equitable coverage might draw on research that highlighted the value of traditional family structures or was more directly critical of same-sex relationships. The resulting value premise and prediction might have been something like the following:

Value premise: The most effective and healthy family structure involves a marriage [between a man and woman]; encouraging marriage through the provision of benefits allows us to attract employees with good values.

Prediction: Changing our benefits structure will upset a longstanding effective means of attracting good employees, which is consistent with other employers in our industry.

Even when some employers offered equitable coverage for same-sex domestic partners, the requirements for such benefits—justified by referring to examples (inductive proof) of other employers' policies—revealed expectations rooted in ideological notions of what constitutes a legitimate marriage-like relationship.[60] Ideological evidence is ubiquitous within public policy advocacy in the area of LGBT rights, as with most political "wedge" issues, as are efforts by advocates to appear unbiased in grappling with such issues. The widespread effort to regulate transgender individuals' participation in sports and limit medical care provided to transgender youth is one contemporary example.[61] In situations in which you determine public policy advocacy is grounded in an ideology, your focus may have to shift to exposing the bias of the evidence being used and the way advocacy is affected by such bias.

Values and ideologies are also often revealed through the words advocates or their sources use (rhetorical scholar Michael Calvin McGee refers to such terms as "ideographs"[62]) or through the personal and professional organizations and scholars with which they are associated. Consider in this regard the controversy generated when Supreme Court nominee Amy Coney Barrett used the term "sexual preference" in her response to questions posed to her during her 2020 confirmation hearing.[63] For many veteran LGBT rights activists, the prospect of this term—signaling that she believed sexual orientation was a choice—appearing within a future opinion written by Coney Barrett (or within evidence she might cite in a future opinion), was very concerning. To the extent you are capable of deducing such dynamics, assessing an advocate's values in relation to their predictions and evidence can be a highly probative endeavor.

In the next chapter, we consider the practical and ethical issues raised when you contemplate the audience of your advocacy.

Ad Hominem and a Science Educator

Kevin Folta, Ph.D. is considered an expert in the field of genetic plant modification (GMOs). His program of study is directed at increasing farmed vegetable production to feed the planet's growing population. As a professor and chair of the Horticultural Sciences Department at the University of Florida, he is considered a top authority by many and has become an influential science educator. Thus, he has training and expertise in the area under study, understands the relevant technical jargon, and has a genuine intellectual curiosity about what he is observing.[64] He is also a highly effective public speaker, well regarded for his capacity as a science educator who champions reliance on scientific evidence in public discussions at public libraries and universities.

Over the last decade, Folta has been in the cross hairs of science skeptics, including opponents of biotechnology, vaccines, and anthropogenic climate change. These individuals do not accept the validity of scientific evidence used to support, in Folta's case, the safe use of genetic modification techniques in food production. Some of his critics, however, do not limit their attention to the scientific knowledge he provides in his public addresses and writings. They attack *him*. Students of argumentation and debate learn that such attacks are often referred to as *ad hominem*, or criticism of an advocate's character. Activists specifically charge that his public education efforts are propaganda campaigns funded by corporations that profit from products and technologies he claims are safe.[65] Folta asserts he is an independent scholar, and he vigorously rebuts reporters and activists who claim otherwise. The attacks have resulted in an accumulation of information available online, which include allegations unrelated to the science. Folta tells us this of the ad hominem-oriented attacks:

> It is all they have. I can gently and kindly point out simple inaccuracies or outright false statements, and there rarely is a discussion about the veracity of my comment. The immediate defense is to go after me personally, leveraging the false information scattered all over the web.[66]

Ad hominem is considered a logical fallacy because it diverts audience attention away from the veracity of claims (including evidence used to support those claims), redirecting such criticism to the source of claims. Source criticism is an appropriate technique used in any argument, which is why it straddles a fine line between source bias and a diversionary tactic. It does not, however, substitute for the evaluation of factual claims. Criticism of this kind has become more effective in the age of the internet and social media. Critics can project accusations on issue-based websites that are not subject to fact checking and other conventions of professional journalism. Additionally, Wikipedia-like pages like SourceWatch and TruthWiki collect accusations against Folta. In some cases, the bias is obvious, such as TruthWiki's use of the label "Dr. Quack Folta" to refer to him.

In one high-profile instance, Folta was one of several scientists whose emails were secured through Freedom of Information laws, which exposed personal communication between him and a Monsanto executive. Folta was apparently seeking to secure a grant to fund his science education efforts at schools and libraries, and in one instance promised the executive a "solid return on investment."[67] Using the terms considered above regarding bias, anti-GMO activists might argue Folta has a "material bias"; however, a financial relationship of this kind, whereby industry provides support for science education activities, would not stand *on its own* as sufficient reason to reject the scientific knowledge about which Folta is speaking. As noted above, activists would need to establish that the bias is significant enough to compromise the integrity of Folta's research or cause him to engage in perceptual or willful distortion.

But Folta is a well-respected and accomplished scientist. Moreover, whether Monsanto's grant compromises Folta's objectivity as a scientist has no bearing on the question of whether science can safely expand a farmer's yield. However, the point of ad hominem is often to distract the audience's attention from advocacy. Describing the technique, Folta says:

> If I make a reasonably good point, someone will post the 9/6/2015 *New York Times* article [that accused him of personally enriching himself by advocating for large biotech companies]. Because of its implicit credibility, it immediately destroys the trust in my message, even though it is 100% consistent with scientific literature.

Whether anti-GMO activists can generate enough skepticism or doubt in Folta and like-minded scientists through such tactics is an open question. Most people don't have the time, ability, or resources to evaluate the evidence, which often makes ad hominem attacks effective when they might otherwise not be.

Exercise: Evaluating Evidence in a Scenario

Consider a current public policy controversy, such as gun control, defense spending, stimulus spending, and so on, and identify the status quo and the general proposition under which both sides are engaged. From there, consider one instance or example of evidence used by each side that comes from an authority and one instance or example of statistics used by each side (for a total of four pieces of evidence). Apply the critical questions to both sets of evidence and assess its overall quality—strengths and weaknesses.

Notes

1 We discuss under "Authorities" some criteria you might reliably use to determine if an expert has the "perceptual capacity" to offer "facts" (borrowing the tests found in Robert P. Newman and Dale R. Newman, *Evidence* [Boston: Houghton Mifflin Company, 1969], 54–58).

2 Stephen Toulmin, *The Uses of Argument* (New York: Cambridge University Press, 2008).

3 Martha Cooper, *Analyzing Public Discourse* (Long Grove, IL: Waveland Press, Inc.: 1989), 56 (italics in original).

4 Ibid., 117.

5 Robert B. Huber outlines several lines of argument to validate and invalidate evidence from authorities, statistics, and what he refers to as "ordinary witnesses" (*Influencing through Argument* [New York: David McKay Company, 1963]: beginning on 92); Newman and Newman (*Evidence*) offer a more elaborate system of concerns, tests, and indices, and devote more nuanced attention to certain sources of evidence; Cooper offers eight "typical objections" (*Analyzing Public Discourse*, beginning on 121); Robert James Branham poses several "preliminary questions," requirements, and tests, and provides further guidance on weighing evidence and ethical considerations (*Debate and Critical Analysis: The Harmony of Conflict* [Hillsdale, NJ: Lawrence Erlbaum Associates, 1991]: beginning on 76); Paul Gary Wyckoff proposes a "Hierarchy for Policy Evidence" heavily focused on statistical evidence (*Policy & Evidence in a Partisan Age: The Great Disconnect* [Washington, D.C.: Urban Institute Press, 2009]: beginning on 15); and Jeffrey P. Mehltretter Drury offers three general "tests of support" and several specific tests tailored to different support types, and he rates the quality of information found through several common debate research websites (*Argumentation in Everyday Life* [Los Angeles: SAGE, 2020]: beginning on 93).

6 Newman and Newman, *Evidence*, 54.

7 Ibid., 55–56.

8 Richard Feldman and Ted A. Warfield, Eds., *Disagreement* (United Kingdom: Oxford University Press, 2013), 3 (this is a collection of essays on the subject of peer disagreement and the epistemology of disagreement).

9 Thomas M. Nichols, *The Death of Expertise: The Campaign Against Established Knowledge and Why it Matters* (New York: Oxford University Press, 2017), 5.

10 Newman and Newman, *Evidence*, 58.

11 Branham, *Debate and Critical Analysis*, 80.

12 Naomi Oreskes and Erik M. Conway, *Merchants of Doubt* (New York: Bloomsbury Press, 2011).

13 Newman and Newman, *Evidence*, 62.

14 Branham, *Debate and Critical Analysis*, 81.

15 Newman and Newman, *Evidence*, 62.

16 Ibid., 60.

17 Ibid., 79.

18 "Stop Hiding True Covid-19 Stats, Gov. DeSantis. Our Lives are Still at Risk," *Miami Herald*, May 7, 2020, https://www.miamiherald.com/opinion/editorials/article242557271. html.

19 David Smith, "Trump Knew Covid Was Deadly but Wanted to 'Play it Down', Woodward Book Says," *The Guardian*, September 9, 2020, https://www.theguardian.com/us-news/ 2020/sep/09/trump-bob-woodward-book-rage-coronavirus; and Maggie Haberman, "Trump Admits Downplaying the Virus Knowing it Was 'Deadly Stuff,'" *New York Times*, September 9, 2020, https://www.nytimes.com/2020/09/09/us/politics/woodward-trump-book-virus.html.

20 Newman and Newman, *Evidence*, 66.

21 Ibid., 68.

22 Ibid., 89–203.

23 Alex S. Jones, *Losing the News: The Future of the News that Feeds Democracy* (New York: Oxford University Press, 2009), 2–3.

24 Ibid., 180.

25 Ibid., 180. For more on the "news habit," see Thomas E. Patterson, "Creative Destruction: An Exploratory Look at News on the Internet", report from the Joan Shorenstein Center on the Press, Politics and Public Policy, August 2007, http://shorensteincenter.org/wp-content/ uploads/2012/03/creative_destruction_2007.pdf.

26 Ibid., 190.

27 Mary Mapes, *Truth and Duty: The Press, The President, and The Privilege of Power* (New York: St. Martin's Press, 2005). See also the motion picture based on Mapes' book: *Truth*, directed by James Vanderbilt (2015; Sony Pictures Classics).

28 Ryan D'Agostino, "'One of The Low Points in American History': Dan Rather Goes Long on Our Defining Moment," *Esquire*, September 24, 2020, https://www.esquire.com/news-politics/a34125163/dan-rather-interview-trump-journalism-election-2020/.

29 Claire Wardle and Hossein Derakhshan, Information Disorder: Toward an Interdisciplinary Framework for Research and Policymaking, a report of the Council of Europe, September 27, 2017, https://firstdraftnews.org/wp-content/uploads/2017/11/ PREMS-162317-GBR-2018-Report-de%CC%81sinformation-1.pdf?x25881.

30 Ibid., 20. Wardle and Derakhshan encourage a move away from the term "fake news," due to the way that term is "becoming a mechanism by which the powerful can clamp down upon, restrict, undermine and circumvent the free press" (16). See also Francesca Giuliani-Hoffman, "'F*** News' Should Be Replaced by These Words, Claire Wardle Says," CNN Business, November 3, 2017, https://money.cnn.com/2017/11/03/media/claire-wardle-fake-news-reliable-sources-podcast/index.html. We will use the term to make certain our readers follow what concerns us, and seek to appropriately distinguish between the original meaning of the term and its later appropriation by leaders to circumvent the truth and achieve partisan political ends.

31 Brian Stelter, *Hoax: Donald Trump, Fox News, and the Dangerous Distortion of Truth* (New York: One Signal Publishers, 2020), 94–95. Stelter writes that this reappropriation of

the term "was probably the most important thing he did during the presidential transition," noting the enduring effectiveness of Trump's claims that every report critical of him and his administration's activities could be a hoax.

32 Nolan Higdon, *The Anatomy of Fake News: A Critical News Literacy Education* (Oakland, CA: University of California Press, 2020), 27 and 4.

33 Ibid., 1; Stelter, *Hoax*, 96. The news story that prompted Trump's outrage was Evan Perez, Jim Sciutto, Jake Tapper and Carl Bernstein, "Intel Chiefs Presented Trump with Claims of Russian Efforts to Compromise Him," CNN, January 12, 2017, https://www.cnn.com/2017/01/10/politics/donald-trump-intelligence-report-russia/index.html (originally posted January 10, 2017). The briefing between President-Elect Trump and intelligence officials concerned the discovery of the "Steele Dossier," a research report written by Christopher Steele (a former head of the Russia Desk for British intelligence then working for a private opposition research firm) that documented a collection of embarrassing information the Russian government had developed that might be used to blackmail Trump.

34 Kathleen Hall Jamieson, *Cyberwar: How Russian Hackers and Trolls Helped Elect a President. What We Don't, Can't, and Do Know* (New York: Oxford University Press, 2018), 35. Jamieson applies theories of interpersonal and media influence to troll posts, polling data, and analysis of how the press used hacked content to determine it is probable that Russian cyber tactics helped elect Donald Trump.

35 Ibid., 216 and 222.

36 Nancy L. Rosenblum and Russell Muirhead, *A Lot of People Are Saying: The New Conspiracism and the Assault on Democracy* (Princeton: Princeton University Press, 2020).

37 Ibid., 1.

38 Ibid., X (italics added). Of the left, they write: "the left has not been prone to the bare assertion that marks conspiracy without the theory" (X).

39 See Stelter, *Hoax*; Reece Peck, *Fox Populism* (United Kingdom/New York: Cambridge University Press, 2019); and Jane Mayer, "The Making of the Fox News White House," *New Yorker*, March 4, 2019.

40 Higdon, *Anatomy of Fake News*, 5.

41 Ibid., 5–6.

42 Higdon (*Anatomy of Fake News*) names his methodology a "Critical Media Ecology Approach" (8) and later refers to a "Critical News Literacy Education" (139); his "Fake News Detection Kit" begins on page 144; question 7 ("Does the evidence hold up under scrutiny?") begins on page 150; question 10 ("Does the content qualify as journalism?") begins on page 155. For another rubric for addressing fake news, see Bruce Bartlett's stream-lined guide, *The Truth Matters: A Citizen's Guide to Separating Facts from Lies and Stopping Fake News in its Tracks* (New York: Ten Speed Press, 2017).

43 We note also there is significant interest in the subject of processing inaccurate information among scholars who study argumentation in the context of cognitive science, literacy, and education. See, for instance, the studies collected in David N. Rapp and Jason L. G. Braasch, Eds., *Processing Inaccurate Information: Theoretical and Applied Perspectives from Cognitive Science and the Educational Sciences* (Cambridge, MA: MIT Press, 2014); consider particularly Pater Afflerbach, Byeong-Young Cho, and Jong-Yun Kim, "Inaccuracy and Reading in Multiple Text and Internet/Hypertext Environments," 403–424. For more

current scholarship of this type, see: M. Anne Britt, Jean-Francois Rouet, Dylan Blaum, and Keith Millis, "A Reasoned Approach to Dealing with Fake News," *Policy Insights from the Behavior and Brain Sciences*, 6, no.1 (2019): 94–101 (the authors conclude with specific policy recommendations for mitigating the "several ways that cognitive biases leave people susceptible to misinformation and exploitation" [98]).

44 Bartlett, *The Truth Matters*, 45 (see his entire chapter six, titled, "Trusting Academic Sources").

45 Newman and Newman, *Evidence*, 202 (see their entire chapter nine, titled, "Professional Scholars").

46 These are the terms used by Karen Bogenschneider and Thomas J. Corbett, in their *Evidence-Based Policymaking: Insight from Policy-Minded Researchers and Research-Minded Policymakers* (New York: Routledge, 2010); see also Sandra M. Nutley, Isabel Walter, and Huw T. O. Davies, *Using Evidence: How Research Can Inform Public Services* (Bristol, UK: Policy Press, 2012); and consider the work of the Commission on Evidence-Based Policymaking (CEP), established by the bipartisan Evidence-Based Policymaking Commission Act of 2016 (https://cep.gov/about.html).

47 For more on this phenomenon, and how it relates to argumentation, see Feldman and Warfield, *Disagreement*.

48 Bogenschneider and Corbett, *Evidence-Based Policymaking*, 44–45.

49 Ibid., 34.

50 Newman and Newman, *Evidence*, 206.

51 See Wyckoff's "Hierarchy for Policy Evidence," which is heavily focused on statistical evidence, beginning on 15 (his consideration of "sampling errors" and "confounding factors" is excellent); see also Cooper's objections for "unrepresentative sample" and "lack of proportion" (*Policy & Evidence*, 123–125).

52 Gloria Guzman, "U.S. Median Household Income Up in 2018 from 2017," United States Census Bureau, September 26, 2019, https://www.census.gov/library/stories/2019/09/us-median-household-income-up-in-2018-from-2017.html.

53 "Real Mean Family Income in the United States," Federal Reserve Bank of Saint Louis, September 10, 2019, https://fred.stlouisfed.org/series/MAFAINUSA672N.

54 Beginning with Robert P. Newman, *Recognition of Communist China: A Study in Argument* (New York: Macmillan, 1961), then with the subsequent *Evidence*, Robert devoted his entire career to, in the words of David Deifell, "acclaiming the available evidence that should have held sway and decrying the ideologies that compelled people to ignore it" (Robert P. Newman and David Deifell, *Invincible Ignorance in American Foreign Policy* [New York: Peter Lang, 2013], 166).

55 Newman and Newman, *Evidence*, 58.

56 Ibid., 58.

57 Ibid., 66.

58 Robert P. Newman, "Foreign Policy: Decision and Argument," in *Advances in Argumentation Theory and Research*, ed. J. Robert Cox and Charles Arthur Willard (Carbondale: Southern Illinois University Press, 1982), 320.

59 Ibid., 328.

60 Partners might have to prove they lived in the same residence (often for a minimum of a year), even though an opposite-sex married employee could cover their spousal dependent the moment they were married and offer continual coverage regardless of who lived with whom. In doing so, employers were expressing a bias for a particular kind of traditional relationship rooted in ideals that might not be realistic for all modern couples—regardless of sexual orientation or gender identity; also, they may have been revealing an underlying belief that LGBT employees could not be trusted when they claimed they were involved in a "real" domestic partnership.

61 See: "A Wave of Anti-Transgender Legislation," *The Daily* (podcast), April 20, 2021, https://www.nytimes.com/2021/04/20/podcasts/the-daily/transgender-girls-sports-republicans.html.

62 Michael Calvin McGee, "The 'Ideograph': A Link between Rhetoric and Ideology," *Quarterly Journal of Speech* 66, no. 1 (1980): 1–16.

63 Harmeet Kaur, "Why Amy Coney Barrett's Use of the Term 'Sexual Preference' at Her Hearing Alarmed So Many," CNN, October 14, 2020, https://www.cnn.com/2020/10/14/us/sexual-preference-amy-coney-barrett-offensive-trnd/index.html.

64 Learn more about Folta at: https://hos.ifas.ufl.edu/people/on-campus-faculty/kevin-m-folta/.

65 Alan Levinovitz, "Anti-GMO Activist Seeks to Expose Scientists' Emails With Big Ag," *Wired*, February 23, 2015, https://www.wired.com/2015/02/anti-gmo-activist-seeks-expose-emails-food-scientists/.

66 This and subsequent quotes from Folta are from email and phone conversations between Philip Dalton and Kevin Folta on or about September 20, 2019.

67 Eric Lipton, "Food Industry Enlisted Academics in G.M.O. Lobbying War, Emails Show," *New York Times*, September 5, 2015, https://www.nytimes.com/2015/09/06/us/food-industry-enlisted-academics-in-gmo-lobbying-war-emails-show.html.

Part III
REASONABLE GOALS

8

TARGETING YOUR AUDIENCE

Takeaways

(1) Targeting your audience is a matter of setting reasonable goals for your advocacy, which you can achieve initially and over a longer period of time.

(2) Often, your target audience must be called into existence through your advocacy. Public policy advocacy generates awareness of a public issue and calls for interested parties to support action related to the issue.

(3) Targeting your audience raises certain ethical considerations for public policy advocates. Issues analysis focuses your attention on what your audience thinks about a public issue and raises healthy and productive questions about who makes up your audience.

(4) Depending on the nature of your policy goal, some communication theories related to how audiences are influenced might be useful in forming your strategy.

It is a general rule of thumb in politics that candidates should not target the entire voting public with their message, and with good reason. Many will not vote for a candidate regardless of how compelling the candidate may be.

So why target the opposition with robocalls or mailers? It's not just a waste of resources (time and money); some believe such outreach might even activate voters who support an opponent. Just as in politics, your public policy advocacy efforts will likely be limited by your resources. Understanding what segments of the public believe about the issue that concerns you is a process that begins with some assumptions you might make about your community and expands to consider different levels of understanding that might assist you in crafting messages.

This is the first of two chapters that make up the third and final part of this book, which we title "Reasonable Goals." Within these two chapters, we consider two aspects of controversies over which you can have more control if you choose to consciously consider them: *who is your target audience and what might they think about your policy goals,* and *how might you thoughtfully respond to what are varied and complex dynamics of your advocacy settings.* We have already noted that good public policy advocacy benefits from advocates' respect for, and understanding of, their audience. Advocates belong to a community experiencing the effects of the status quo, people who are more or less inclined to want the present system to change or remain the same. As advocates on either side of that equation (affirmative or negative), you might start off with a general sense of what appeals will be effective in your community, but you will soon need to strategically define your target audience and set reasonable advocacy goals.

We recognize this goal setting is also where you might be tempted to use information about your audience to craft messages that are motivated more by the desire to "win" than to develop (or maintain) effective solutions to societal problems. You have surely encountered people who appear to tell different audiences just what they believe will get those audiences on their side, even if the messages conflict with other statements they've made or are inaccurate. When these shifts negatively affect matters that are important to you, you likely assess such instances as unethical. Many of the lessons we have already provided—about reasoning and evidence use and evaluation—should help you address these moments. For your own advocacy, however, it is important you set goals for what you can reasonably achieve with your advocacy based on an analysis of *who* your audience is and *where* they are in relation to your policy goal. This process raises questions such as: *Who is likely to care about the issue? How much do they know about it? What opinions might they have formed about it already? How close are they to agreeing with you?*

If you are new to public policy advocacy, asking and answering these types of questions will likely push you beyond your existing knowledge base—what you generally know about your audience and what will or will not be mean-ingful to them—and into a more thoughtful issues analysis and identifica-tion of reasonable goals. That analysis is often aided by techniques that give you a more precise profile of an audience and assist you in crafting messages that appeal to them. We begin this chapter by discussing a general ethical orientation that acknowledges the value of crafting persuasive messages for specific audiences without compromising the pursuit of good policy. We then introduce a system of *issues analysis* that recognizes the way advocates bring audiences into existence with their advocacy, set particular goals for those audiences, and form a basic but sophisticated understanding of their target audience. Professional audience analysis techniques are often unnecessary and outside of the time and financial wherewithal of ordinary advocates. Increasingly, however, we find that analytical tools are becoming easier to access and use in the pursuit of targeted advocacy campaigns, a trend that makes ethical considerations more relevant to the enterprise of public policy advocacy. In the final section of the chapter, we underscore the point that audiences are dynamic and active. They think, they process, they resist. We briefly review various theories from the sub-disciplines of persuasion and mass communication that have complicated ideas about audiences being passive receptacles of information.[1] Advocacy is not as simple as transferring new information to an audience. Instead, to be successful, advocates consider audi-ence tendencies as opportunities to craft effective messages.

Audiences and Public Policy Advocacy

You will learn often that you should adapt your messages to your audience, but here we advise you to remember the essential role of argument in shaping good public policy. Advocacy you encounter within public policy controver-sies will be situated along a continuum with verbal coercion on one end *and* advocacy that seeks the best policy outcome, respecting the autonomy and agency of the audience, on the other. "[A]nonymous public relations apparat-chiks" and "barracuda tacticians of modern politics," as they are described by rhetorical scholar Thomas B. Farrell, inhabit the verbal coercion end; on the other end are scholars and other "reform-minded individuals and groups who still hope for more responsive and participatory civic institutions."[2] Coercive public communicators use knowledge about their audience and communica-tion strategies with the exclusive goal of gaining compliance. In many cases, that's what they're paid to do. The coercive approach exhibits less concern for good policy, can erode a community's democratic framework, and casts the entire advocacy enterprise in shades of cynicism. Advocates should aspire to pursue the best policy outcomes because, as Thomas Goodnight explains, deliberative argument "is a form of argumentation through which citizens test and create social knowledge in order to uncover, assess, and resolve shared problems."[3] Long-term, society suffers if bad policy is adopted, so there is no value in short-circuiting an audience's willingness and ability to scrutinize either your claims or the claims of those who oppose your ideas.

Convincing audiences involves crafting arguments that are sensible and will be well received. As a starting point for distinguishing between good arguments and bad arguments, we have already noted—in our discussion of critical questions in Chapter 4—that you should consider yourself part of the community you are seeking to convince, and expect that those who are part of this community will share with you an affinity for common patterns of thinking or ways of constructing claims that are rational. We draw here from Martha Cooper, who advises advocates and analysts to think not only of particular people they know are directly consuming their advocacy, but also of a larger audience made up of people trying to act sensibly, or what rhetorical scholars Chaim Perelman and Lucie Olbrechts-Tyteca refer to as a "universal audience."[4] Perelman and Olbrechts-Tyteca's universal audience is an assumed larger society that can be convinced "that the reasons adduced are of a compelling character, that they are self-evident, and possess an absolute and timeless validity, independent of local or historical contingencies."[5] This "ideal image of the most reasonable audience imaginable," according to Cooper, will not match in all respects the real audience you are addressing, but your ability to develop messages with some degree of confidence is significantly aided by this conception of "an audience that [is] trying to be reasonable and respond to the message with reasoned skepticism."[6] Moreover, given the frequency by which advocates articulate incomplete arguments, hoping their audience will assume certain premises and fill in missing information, it is likely consistent with how most already view their audiences.

A Balanced Approach

The notion that you can develop strong evidence-based, well-reasoned arguments for a community that shares a common rationality gives you something stable to consider when developing your message. Our interest in this notion is not intended to suggest we believe you can perfectly align your logic with that of your audience. It is more constructive, we believe, to accept that targeting one group of people may cause you to be less effective with another. There is something to be said about trying your best to present your ideas to as many people as you can and hoping that the quality of your appeals, if constructed with the best of intentions to solve real problems (that have real consequences for real people), is a worthy pursuit. The impulse to engage in good policymaking versus the temptation to develop messages that effectively persuade your target audience is a tension often discussed among communication scholars. We recommend a thoughtfully balanced approach.

Thomas B. Farrell addresses this tension as one between *ethics* and *aesthetics*, examining the manner in which Aristotle sought to encourage a public rhetoric that is "ethically significant *and* a practice that is an art."[7] By "ethically significant," Farrell has in mind public advocacy that conforms to "standards of excellence that, if achieved, yield conduct that is ethical" (this assumes advocates and their audience share a common appreciation of rational problem solving and responsible conduct).[8] But audiences can also be moved to take actions that are rational and responsible through appeals that affect them emotionally, provided such appeals are not used to distort or deceive (this is what concerned Aristotle's teacher Plato).[9] If advocates view their relationship with their audience as a kind of "civic friendship, in which each party is accountable to one another and to the common good," persuading by way of aesthetic adaptation (adapting your message to address in some manner audience dispositions, passions, fears, appreciation for learning, and other emotional needs) might be both practically useful and widely appreciated.[10]

Convinced you are right, should you stop at nothing to convince an audience? That's an important ethical question, and one that is considered from a number of perspectives.[11] As we noted already, you may find yourself up against entrenched opposition, a situation in which any sort of "victory" is possible only over the course of a sustained advocacy effort, during which you develop a better understanding of the origin of a public issue and build support for your position over time. In the words of business coach John C. Maxwell, "sometimes you win, sometimes you learn."[12] Beyond such life lessons, there are harms associated with executing a scorched earth strategy that seeks policy success at all costs. You might erode relationships that may someday be useful to you along the course of another advocacy campaign (it is tempting to think only about the issue that concerns you today). Scaling up from there, failing to respect or facilitate the audience's capacity to understand and evaluate your advocacy can be destructive to the quality of public deliberation. Efforts to circumvent reason, frighten, distract, or overwhelm an audience can have lasting impacts on the norms and practices of a community when they seek to solve problems.[13]

To complicate this further, however, adherence to popular norms of civility can also function to silence or discredit communities as they fight to raise awareness about lesser-known or lesser-felt issues. As we noted in our earlier discussion of "counterpublics," disruptive argumentation is often necessary for people living on society's margins to address their grievances. Consider the protests following the killing of George Floyd by Minneapolis police officers in 2020. Public awareness of extrajudicial killings of African Americans by police across the United States existed before, as we have noted in prior chapters, but little changed. In fact, the presidential election of Donald Trump resulted in the rollback of various reforms enacted by the Obama Administration to help solve the problem. Increased knowledge and awareness, in this case, was not enough to generate continuous progress. Evidently, neither was agreeing it was bad.[14] Regardless of public support for reforms, state and local governments either were not budging, or were moving in reverse. *Under such circumstances, does one remain "civil" and hope the public comes around?* Following Floyd's killing, protests broke out across the United States, prompting many to suggest his death would lead to meaningful reform. In the words of one protester at the time (Tracey Edwards, Long Island regional director of the NAACP), "Peaceful protesting has historically led to substantive change . . . and I believe that this will also have the same effect, if we focus on policy and reforms."[15] Some don't consider protests civil, but protests remain an essential tool of advocacy. Adapting messages to the passions, dispositions, and fears among members of historically marginalized communities and their progressive allies—persuading by way of aesthetic adaptation—might produce rational outcomes while at the same time inspiring respect for forms of resistance that are, for whatever reason, "alternative" to the prevailing idea of what is "civil" in a democratic society.

Issues Analysis

Because advocates and their audiences usually share some basic community ties, your own rationale for supporting a policy is a useful starting point for developing your message; however, your personal investment in the issue may inhibit your ability to anticipate how others will react to your advocacy. In calling for *issues analysis*, we draw from the work of Robert L. Heath and his co-authors who write about issues management as a responsibility of an ethical and comprehensive public relations practice.[16] Issues analysis, according to Heath and W. Timothy Coombs, "asks whether there is a problem, whether stakeholders think there is a problem, and whether they see it as affecting them."[17] This approach is preferable to audience analysis protocols that, in our view, run the risk of inviting notions of message receivers as objects to be understood and efficiently persuaded. An audience is not a passive, moldable collective whose compliance is achievable with little regard for whether the policy outcome is good for it. Issues analysis assumes advocates and their audiences (stakeholders) share a concern for the wellbeing of their community. Methods of understanding audiences through issues analysis avoid underestimating the agency of audiences and, as such, frustrate coercive communication practices.

We advise advocates to consider three matters as a general framework for issues analysis. First, determine the extent to which your target audience already exists or needs to be called into existence. Second, once the target audience is imaginable, determine starting points for your advocacy. Finally, consider audience divisions, or segments, that can be understood using common research methods.

Calling Your Audience into Existence. For the sake of clarity, we will now make a distinction between the aggregate group of people that will encounter your message (the audience) *and* the group of people for whom your message is primarily tailored (the "target audience"). Skilled advocates possess the ability to call their audience into existence by increasing knowledge and generating interest in an issue. We have already touched on this subject briefly in Chapter 1, ways to think about how audiences, publics, or "the people," are constituted, and how such phenomena are considered by observers of public controversies and political eras.[18] Philosopher John Dewey's description of "publics" (similar in many ways to target audiences) in his book, *The Public and its Problems*, is instructive. He describes publics as diffuse and transitory groups of people that coalesce around problems.[19] Target audiences often consist of people who share an interest in an issue but do not know each other well or may have never met each other. Dewey attributes public awareness to journalists, though we also recognize the role public policy advocates can play in this process. Critical analyses of this process acknowledge the challenges brought on by contemplating a body of people that is at once real and the product of advocates' imagination. We believe this is aptly described by

Michael Calvin McGee, one of the earliest rhetorical scholars to call for more attention to how "the people" are formed by advocates of their era. McGee writes that "[the people] are conjured into objective reality, remain so long as the rhetoric which defined them has force, and in the end wilt away, becoming once again merely a collective of individuals."[20]

Because of this impermanence, your task might include activating, building, and maintaining your target audience. Imagine that you are one of the first people to argue that bisphenol A (BPA) can be harmful to the human body. BPA is commonly found in plastics and on metals and papers. It has been linked to cancer, diabetes, and a host of other hormonal imbalances in lab animals. Imagine that you reserve time to speak about this harmful substance at the local library and find yourself dismayed when no one shows up. Why? Because no one knows what BPA is. And if it is so alarming, some might ask, Why isn't everyone talking about it? Many are silent about BPA because a public of concerned people has not yet been built. Building a public over time is a very challenging task for advocates. Your description of the problem functions to convince others that there is a problem worth fixing, that it is significant, and that it is something about which others should be concerned. You generate awareness and concern about a public issue, and in so doing, create a community of people connected by that shared concern. While it will not always be your task to form a target audience, at times the possible need to do so expands the undertaking of advocacy.

Gauging Different Starting Points. Careful consideration of your target audience involves determining if it possesses developed attitudes, specifically about the public issue or controversy. To better understand those attitudes, we suggest advocates consider three general types of audiences: *nascent, familiar,* and *established.* What you will likely be capable of achieving with each type of audience will vary. You should think in terms of the metaphorical "distance" you can cover with each audience in a given instance—the distance between what the target audience accepts (what we call "starting points") and the "destination," or what you wish the audience to accept.

When a target audience has *little or no familiarity* with an issue, it is a *nascent audience.* What this audience is willing to accept may be further from your end point than if an audience has more familiarity. Picture yourself as an advocate for student loan reform invited to speak at a university. Because the effects of the student loan industry have drawn so little public discussion, you may be safe in assuming that there are few grounds from which to launch a convincing argument for a specific policy. *Will the audience accept that student loans can be harmful? Do audience members perceive such loans as having the capacity to negatively affect their quality of life? Do they even know how much debt they have? Are they familiar with key language like "subsidized," "unsubsidized," "default," "forbearance," or "deferment?"* Faced with a nascent audience, you may need to be less ambitious when attempting to get it to agree with your conclusion. Instead of attempting to persuade the audience to accept your specific proposal, aiming for a less distant destination may be more achievable. Teaching a nascent audience about the nature of the student loan industry, how it works, or what its material effects are on students may be a more meaningful and useful objective. Doing so could get it to accept the existence of a problem caused by student loans.

The *familiar audience* possesses knowledge of the public issue that concerns you, though it may have formed no opinion or possess no significant attitude concerning your proposal. Using the student loan example, the familiar audience may be aware that student loan debts are rising, that the availability is driving up the cost of higher education, and that the burden of paying back loans is making life miserable for many. Regardless of this knowledge, this audience might reasonably assume student loans would not exist if they could do so much harm; after all, these loans ostensibly exist to help, not hurt. Some may feel hypocritical condemning a program on which they themselves rely or have relied. Under these circumstances, it becomes your task to build on the accepted facts that both you and the audience share. You should help this audience find a way to reason from these facts to your conclusion.

Your task changes when the audience has more firmly formed opinions about the public issue, when it is an *established audience.* Audiences with established opinions may fall into one of three categories: *convinced, opposed,* and *inclined.*

There is little need for you to work to convince *those already in agreement with you,* unless it is to motivate or equip them to act. There is a difference between agreeing with someone and possessing the motivation to act in concert with them. The world is filled with people who behave in ways they know are self-destructive, and so your task when faced with a target audience convinced you are correct is to motivate it to act.

Whether to work to convince *those opposed to your position* depends on your circumstances and needs. *Who (how many people?; which different constituencies?) do you need to convince in order to accomplish your policy goal, and what resources do you need?* No person or group has unlimited resources, and so decisions about target audiences must be made with resources in mind. The challenge in convincing those who are opposed to your position is that you need to dislodge them from their position, which involves challenging accepted facts and values.

There will also be *those inclined to agree with you*, but they may be unaware of the specifics of your proposal. You might assume the grounds for supporting your claim are, for the most part, understood and accepted by your target audience. As such, your task is to convincingly reason with the inclined audience, working from shared grounds to the specific solution. The stock issues of solution and advantages exist, in large part, for this purpose. They are the standard means of convincing a target audience that a policy is desirable. An agreeable audience may be called into existence once it has accepted the problem's existence and significance. Target audience members may be convinced to support your specific policy proposal once you explain the policy goals and merits, reasons to believe the policy is both workable and effective, and the advantages.

The final matter of audience type deals with the *salience* of policy issues. While your target audiences may agree or disagree with your position for different reasons, they might also differ according to how salient your matters of concern are to them. To illustrate, consider an audience that is convinced you are right. Audiences that agree with you will vary by issue salience. Though a group may believe you are right and that your proposal is strong, it may find little reason to care. For example, some may believe food deserts (neighborhoods where healthy food is not sold) exist and contribute to poor nutrition. However, they may also have done nothing to solve the problem. On this matter, they belong to a familiar audience. They accept many facts that point to the problem's existence and are inclined to support efforts to remedy it. They are committed to no specific solution to the problem but would like it solved. However, this is—overall—an issue of low salience to them. It may be "down-list" of other pressing and prominent problems. You would therefore need to find ways to explain not just how reasonable it is to accept your conclusion; you will also need to explain why it matters enough to warrant immediate action.

Understanding Audiences. Audience attitudes depend on what members of an audience know about an issue and how salient that issue is for them. Considering again the hypothetical student loan address, people who have college loans are likely to find the issue to be salient because of the relevance and immediacy of student loans to their lives. On the other hand, this subject may be much less salient for senior citizens, who may be opposed or indifferent to such appeals. Audience variations in terms of issue salience, acceptance of grounds, shared values, or inclination toward change make understanding the nature of the audience an integral part of developing compelling advocacy.

Advocates have many excellent sources to assist them in what is generally referred to as audience research. We recommend sources that are focused on issues analysis and monitoring as a function of public relations or issues management (methods used in political campaigns and marketing are similar but are informed by what we consider to be more coercive motives). Heath and Coombs, for example, distinguish between "primary research" (research you or your organization develops) and "secondary research" (research that is available because it was developed by someone else for another purpose).[21] Common forms of primary research pursued by aspiring advocates tend to be informal or qualitative in nature, such as interviews, focus groups, informal surveys, and the close examination of terms used in written feedback or opinions. Secondary research is likely to be more formal, gathered and analyzed through quantitative techniques, such as scientific sampling in public opinion surveys or more formal content analyses. We assume you would apply the same degree of scrutiny to audience research that you would to any other evidence you encounter (as outlined in Chapter 7) in order to form reliable impressions of your target audiences.

Two common forms of secondary audience research are of special interest to us: analyses of *demographics* (descriptions of audience subdivisions) and *psychographics* (descriptions of audience attitudes).

Demographics are statistical descriptions of an audience's subdivisions. These subdivisions might be important to you because they help delineate different sectors of a target audience. *Who is convinced? Who is inclined to support? Who is opposed? Demographically, do these groups share characteristics, and do these commonalities shed light on matters of issue awareness, salience, and attitude?* Demographics are particularly valuable when they unexpectedly inform us of communities who do not share the same grounds associated with an issue. For instance, people who have a general understanding of Democrats might assume that all Democrats support teachers' unions and public schools. A more nuanced look at party demographics reveals that, contrary to the assumptions of many, a majority of African Americans appear to support vouchers or the transfer of public school money to private schools.[22] Awareness of this demographic fact indicates that some African Americans generally proceed from different grounds (or starting points), compared to Democrats overall, when considering this issue, a factor that perhaps explains why Donald Trump has made vouchers a central feature in his appeals to African American voters.[23]

In the above example, the demographic of race appears to be related to the attitude about vouchers, though race is only sometimes a factor in determining knowledge, attitudes, or perspectives on matters of public policy. Exposure to this issue-specific information helps you determine who fits within the various segments of the target audience you are analyzing. Returning to the matter of school vouchers, a closer look at demographics reveals that vouchers are more likely to be supported by low-income households, suggesting that audience understanding of the voucher issue is likely less a matter of race than one of socioeconomic status and the related issue of private school affordability.

Primary formal research sometimes looks beyond age, gender, ethnicity, and other commonly considered group characteristics. For well-funded advocacy campaigns, a broader net is cast, often with professionally conducted polls and surveys seeking to find unexpected audience configurations. Polls may consider age, gender, ethnicity, regionality, religion, income, profession, hobbies, marriage status, political affiliation, and education. The point of such information is not necessarily to learn if a respondent is Catholic, for instance. Instead, professionals will statistically analyze these responses to find out which demographic characteristics correlate. Doing so helps identify unique audiences characterized by various shared demographic qualities. This gives advocates an opportunity to understand the perspective they may share and thus determine starting points for advocacy.

It may be possible for you to conduct a far less complex demographic analysis by acquiring a demographic breakdown of the group to which you plan to speak. If you are the student loan advocate, you may ask your host about the university's demographics. If visiting a town library to give a talk on an issue, you may look up demographic statistics at Census.gov (information about the age distribution, number of high school graduates, median income, race and ethnicity, rates of home ownership, among other information that may relate to your issue). Political information in many states is available through a state or county board of elections. Of course, if your advocacy effort is well-funded, you may also turn to a private consulting firm that studies demographics.

Psychographics provide descriptions of attitudes and values shared by a demographic group. Today, technology can enable advocates to identify alignments of demographic factors that predict an individual's attitude with a high degree of validity. By finding demographic qualities shared by people with certain attitudes, social scientists believe that these conclusions can be reasoned in reverse. For purposes of illustrating, imagine that being a white male homeowner with an annual income of under $75,000 per year is highly associated with strong support of the Second Amendment. This won't be right in every instance, but statistics show that it is more often right than wrong, and truer for this group than other known groups. A pro-Second Amendment message, then, can be more narrowly tailored to this group with an increased likelihood of encountering a sympathetic audience. Such a message can be less generic, which may also be more resource-effective.

In popular discussion, the compilation of citizen and consumer demographic information is pejoratively referred to as "data mining," and it has been made famous by the Netflix documentary *The Great Hack* that documented the role that the consulting firm Cambridge Analytica played in using Facebook-gathered data to execute Donald Trump's successful presidential campaign in 2016. Data mining is defined by Statistical Analytical Systems as "the process of finding anomalies, patterns, and correlations within large data sets to predict outcomes."[24] By finding patterns in data about populations, experts can predict who is more likely to possess an attitude or be inclined to act.

Today's political parties rely heavily on psychographics. Democrats use a system termed the NGP VAN that collects voter information and combines it with other demographic information to draw conclusions about voters. Most important is whether individuals fit the profile of a likely voter. The NGP VAN will also give scores to individual voters on the assumed strength of adherence to specific issues. One of the authors of this textbook was ranked a .74 (on a scale from 0 to 1) on the issue of gun control, meaning that he is a likely supporter of gun control, but not a very strong supporter. His pro-choice position was ranked above .90. He was never surveyed about these topics; he just shares demographic qualities with others who support these positions— obviously sharing more qualities with pro-choice voters than pro-gun voters. Republicans use a similar system named i360. The managers of the i360 website describe their methods this way:

> Our team of data scientists build and refine proven, sophisticated models that enable us to predict behaviors and actions, such as the likelihood to support or oppose an issue, redeem a coupon, subscribe to an email list, or even purchase a particular brand or product. This knowledge is powerful, informing messaging and enhancing your ability to target and reach the right customer to achieve success at scale.[25]

Both parties use this psychographic data to target their messages efficiently and precisely to audiences with the greater likelihood to respond.

Returning to the student loan example, the information you've gathered, combined with the general knowledge of who will be attending, will leave you with questions to answer before you prepare your talk. You will likely be without psychographic information, but you may glean some demographic information, and form related impressions, about the university's student population from its website. Some of your audience will be interested in your topic. Others will reluctantly attend in order, perhaps, to earn extra credit for one of their classes. You might decide that your target audience consists of two groups: an inclined audience that is familiar with the issue and inclined to consider solutions for it, and a nascent audience that, despite little or no interest in the issue, has student loans or knows people who do. For the inclined audience, which already accepts that the student debt problem needs to be solved, your primary task would be, for instance, to convincingly describe your proposal and outline the advantages it produces. For the nascent audience, on the other hand, you would have a different starting point. You would likely decide that audience members need to both gain acceptance of facts about the existence and significance of the problem and make a case for the cause of the problem. Once you've determined where to start your message, you are significantly more prepared, aware that there is no critical mass for any specific challenge to the status quo. Your task would be to create a larger audience for your solution, as opposed to motivating those inclined to agree to support your specific solution.

A Sampling of Theories About Audience Response

Over time researchers have come to understand audiences as highly dynamic and responsive. They are not passive entities that will be triggered into action merely by a skillfully crafted message. Sustaining advocacy campaigns requires much more than breaking through the din of competing messages. Ideas from the field of persuasion help explain how audiences engage advocacy, how they have their own purposes and uses for messages,[26] and how advocates might anticipate and accommodate a variety of audience responses. There is much more to learn about how audiences respond to advocacy; this is merely a sample of theories that relate to some of the ideas in this text, including that sustained advocacy may be required to influence attitudes that reside in your target audience. One or more of these theories may also prove useful in understanding dynamics of a target audience you are considering.

First, we begin by considering two ideas that help explain why audiences tend *not* to come into existence, both of which highlight the value of sustained advocacy. The first is the Noelle-Neumann "Spiral of Silence" theory.[27] According to this theory, people are motivated by a fear of isolation, which is triggered when they believe their opinion is in the minority. If they do not encounter their opinions (in the news media, for instance) they will keep it to themselves, and this produces a spiral of silence throughout the community that shares the minority opinion. Though the attitudes of people may be aligned with an advocate, that does not guarantee they will either act on it or even voice it. You may also encounter what is referred to as the "sleeper effect," a phenomenon whereby your advocacy initially works to change people's attitudes, but those attitudes decay over time, reverting to where they started prior to your advocacy.[28] Again, the takeaway is a need for sustained advocacy, for you to build a community of vocal, willing advocates so that your target audience attains some comfort, or "cover," in realizing others share their opinions.

A second line of theory concerns members of an audience that may be inclined to agree with you, but not strongly enough to enact a desired behavioral change. Albert Bandura focuses on audience members' perceptions of self-efficacy (the belief that they can accomplish something), noting that it may be sufficiently limited to prevent them from acting.[29] They may agree with you, but elect not to act on your message. Target audience members might wonder if they can really address the issue. Seeding public discussion with the impossibility of success is a technique used often by negative advocates. During the 2019 presidential primaries, U.S. Senator Bernie Sanders argued for student loan forgiveness, universal childcare, and single-payer healthcare. His opponents asserted that such lofty goals were practically impossible. In this sense, the public may be inoculated against affirmative advocacy. In addition to perceptions that individuals may not be effective at producing change, Lynda Kaid, Mitchell McKinney, and John Tedesco introduce "political information efficacy," or PIE.[30] PIE concerns "the extent to which individuals have sufficient confidence in their level of political information or knowledge to participate in the political process."[31] Some audience members may choose not to express opinions or act on them because they feel they do not possess enough knowledge about their positions.

A third body of research concerns what is commonly referred to as "agenda setting." Maxwell McCombs and Donald Shaw write that mass media has an agenda setting effect, and the issues the media favors often determines the way issues are prioritized by audiences exposed to the coverage of such issues.[32] McCombs and Shaw's research has also supported the idea that public issue agendas can influence how political candidates are evaluated. "Priming" occurs when issues that are of higher salience to the public influence the context in which audiences evaluate office holders and candidates.[33] In light of the agenda setting phenomenon, it stands to reason that a target audience may agree with you without prioritizing the problem you seek to address because the audience may not share your priorities. Your audience may understand that Appalachian poverty is a major injustice, for instance, but be more concerned about healthcare, policing, taxes, or immigration. The audience may already know about the problem you are addressing and agree it's a significant problem, but may not rank the problem among its chief concerns. The agenda setting concept reinforces the need for sustained advocacy and an emphasis on a problem's significance to move issues up levels of public salience and concern.

Fourth, we know from research conducted by Philip Converse,[34] and later by Richard Zaller,[35] that audiences, or some components of audiences, may resist new information based on the strength of the positions they already hold, and the amount of information they have to support those positions. Imagine a person who both believes that vaccines cause autism and regularly reads columns and blogs claiming a link between vaccines and developmental disorders. If this person encounters a five-minute video from the head of the Centers for Disease Control (CDC) explaining that there is no sound research linking vaccines to autism or any other developmental disorder, public opinion theory suggests that their inclination to fear vaccines will prevent them from being influenced by the CDC's message. The takeaway is that some audience members may be immune to your advocacy, as the store of information they possess can galvanize their position against your advocacy regardless of the problem's significance or the amount of cognitive dissonance you seek to induce. On a practical level, this might mean you must cut your losses and seek to reach audiences you *can* influence, ones with less firm positions, willing to consider new information. You might also determine your goals should be to generate an awareness of the problem. For instance, advocates opposing the ubiquity of prescription opiates worked for years merely to raise awareness of their concerns. Media coverage of the stunningly high death toll made the success of advocacy in favor of new policy and legal accountability more likely.

Fifth, sometimes resistance is not issue-based. Members of your audience may understand and agree with you, but dynamics of their social environment may influence their reaction to your advocacy. According to this "social influence theory,"[36] members of a target audience might concern themselves mainly with how changing their minds or behaviors might be evaluated by their community. They might, for example, agree that a waterless eco-friendly lawn is a good idea, but may conclude that landscaping this way might cause their neighbors to judge them negatively. The influence of the inhabitants of people's social environment is the dynamic behind the "two-step flow" model of communication discussed by Paul Lazarsfeld, Bernard Berelson, and Hazel Gaudet.[37] This theory upended the idea that mass mediated messages *directly* influence people. The value of two-step flow lies in emphasizing the persuasive role of interpersonal communication with trusted members of one's social environment and within social groups. Advocacy, then, is not merely the delivery of the message to the target audience, but also involves attentiveness to persuading influential others who cohabit the audience's social environment. Awareness of this dynamic is evident in a variety of particular advocacy contexts. Jane McAlevey, for instance, emphasizes the importance of "organic leader identification" in union organizing campaigns.[38] She makes clear that the persuasive potential of a union's value proposition often depends on *who* makes the argument and how they are perceived by the recipients.

Finally, we consider a theory that might suggest some members of your target audience are moved less by rational argumentation than by how an appeal makes them *feel*. Tony Schwartz's "resonance theory" emphasizes the value of information and attitudes that already reside within the target of your message.[39] Schwartz maintains that advocates can activate latent inclinations in the hearts and minds of their audience. For instance, a partnership of advertising and public relations organizations, with connections to a progressive political action committee, created a video campaign called "Knock the Vote," intended to motivate younger people to vote.[40] Instead of outlining the reasons to vote in a logical manner, it features senior citizens criticizing younger voters for being whiners who don't act. One woman muses, "Climate change? That's your problem. I'll be dead soon." This ad is likely designed to work by activating in younger voters a refusal to accept critical assumptions made about their cohort. They've heard these criticisms before, and may not appreciate them. The ad brings these negative judgments to the forefront of the younger voter's mind, and hopefully activates a desire to disprove them. Resonance theory is one means of gauging "where" an audience is in relation to your policy goal.

In the next chapter, we conclude the text by considering the implications of the advocacy setting, including guidance on how you can adapt to *norms* associated with the setting.

Balancing Influence in Audience Research

Impact by Design is a research firm that helps nonprofit organizations affect behavior change in areas of conservation, animal welfare, and environmental advocacy. We spoke with Amielle DeWan, Ph.D., executive director of the firm, about a recent campaign. Hired by an animal welfare organization to help improve understanding of the exotic pet trade, DeWan explains the role that large data sets play in their work. The data they collected not only helped them understand the profile of people who own exotic pets, but also what factors and behaviors may lead individuals to progress from owning *legal* exotic pets to getting into the *illegal* exotic pet trade. The ultimate goal of the project, she explains, was, "to craft a campaign targeted at the audiences most likely to engage in behaviors shown to lead to illegal pet ownership."[41]

Large amounts of data are necessary to identify and understand potential target audiences. Her firm began by hiring a market research company to explore social media trends related to the exotic pet trade, and to obtain data sets from the American Veterinary Medical Association, the American Pet Products Association, and the Nielsen Company. This data directed them to conduct another, more focused round of primary, formal research in the states of Connecticut, Florida, Massachusetts, and Texas. Next, they developed plans to conduct a large scientific survey. They wanted a total of 1,600 competed surveys, and they planned to use social media influencers, targeted ads in exotic pet forums, blogs, websites, tables at exotic pet trade shows, Google ads, and a survey panel company (a company that contracts with trusted participants, for whom hundreds of demographic data points are gathered).

Impact by Design encountered a difficulty Dewan explains to us: "Exotic pet owners can be sensitive about divulging information about their behavior when it's potentially illegal." Consequently, in their efforts to understand the behavior, they needed large data sets and firms that collect them. Impact by Design discovered that many people reported awareness of friends and acquaintances who owned exotic pets, that many who participate in the exotic pet trade obtain animals from private zoos, and that *those who do* report enjoying the attention they receive from others because of the pets they own. DeWan states, "If we hadn't been able to access a large amount of data from anonymous survey-takers . . . I don't believe we would have been able to obtain a large sample of quality responses."

Aside from offering a glimpse into the practice of issues analysis, Impact by Design's efforts in this and other advocacy campaigns highlights the power dynamics that surface when social justice activists consider the role of data in advocacy campaigns. Few are surprised to learn about the use (or abuse) of data in efforts of wealthy and powerful people and corporations to persuade the public, even when such efforts concern the American electorate, such as in the case of the political consulting firm Cambridge Analytica. Impact by Design, however, focuses on conservation, animal welfare, and environmental advocacy. And, they understand that most of the non-profit organizations that seek their expertise, including specific services to target key audiences with behavior change initiatives, are resource constrained. Asked about the palpable fears many have that persuaders, armed with enormous amounts of data, can surreptitiously influence behaviors, DeWan's thoughts are complex:

> When people with resources can know vast amounts of information about everyone else, especially those without the resources to gather their own knowledge, there are important ethical issues to be considered. This inequitable access to data tips power balances in ways that can exacerbate already unfair systems. So yes, I believe that the persuasive equation benefits the monied and skilled. Along those lines, we see that corporate interests often outperform environmental causes that we work on in the nonprofit sector—another example that the monied can use information to tip the balance toward their ultimate goals.

In her own experience, DeWan experiences entities with resources and access to data outperforming her efforts. These dynamics advantage those with more resources. She adds, however, there are a number of techniques to balance influence, such as devoting research efforts to understanding policymakers, a smaller population, instead of large populations.

Exercise: Considering Audiences and Message

Demonstrate your understanding of the relationship between advocacy and a target audience by "reverse engineering" a message, or reasoning from the message, to answer the question: *what audience is likely targeted by the message?* Begin by identifying an individual, group, or organization that is advocating for a policy change. Second, find speeches, op-eds, position papers, or press releases produced by this individual, group, or organization. Third, use your chosen text to identify who, in terms of demographics, you believe the advocate is targeting and the starting point from which you believe the advocate is proceeding. If the advocate targeted an established audience, in what category do you believe the audience belonged (convinced, opposed, inclined)? Explain the reason for each determination you made.

Notes

1 For a representative example of theory that situates the audience as a passive receiver of persuasive messages, see Claude E. Shannon and Warren Weaver, *The Mathematical Theory of Communication* (Urbana: University of Illinois Press, 1949).

2 Thomas B. Farrell, *Norms of Rhetorical Culture* (New Haven, CT: Yale University Press, 1995), 9, 2.

3 G. Thomas Goodnight, "The Personal, Technical, and Public Spheres of Argument: A Speculative Inquiry into the Art of Public Deliberation," *Journal of the American Forensic Association* 18, no. 4 (1982): 214.

4 Martha Cooper, *Analyzing Public Discourse* (Long Grove, IL: Waveland Press, Inc., 1989), 119. See also: Chaim Perelman and Lucie Olbrechts-Tyteca, *The New Rhetoric: A Treatise on Argumentation* (South Bend, IN: University of Notre Dame Press, 1991).

5 Perelman and Olbrechts-Tyteca, *The New Rhetoric*, 32.

6 Cooper, *Analyzing Public Discourse*, 120.

7 Farrell, *Norms of Rhetorical Culture*, 50 (emphasis added). Farrell's project explains why this tension exists and offers a resolution to the dilemma in a defense of the potential of public advocacy that transcends the distinction.

8 Ibid., 62.

9 Ibid., 110.

10 Ibid., 132.

11 On this ethical dilemma beyond the discipline of communication studies, work on the subject of paternalism is interesting. See, for example, Jason Hanna, *In Our Best Interest: A Defense of Paternalism* (New York: Oxford University Press, 2018); for a specific focus on persuasion, see George Tsai, "Rational Persuasion as Paternalism," *Philosophy & Public Affairs* 42, no. 1 (2014): 78–112.

12 John C. Maxwell, *Sometimes You Win—Sometimes You Learn: Life's Greatest Lessons Are Gained from Our Losses* (New York: Center Street, 2013).

13 Philip Dalton and Eric Kramer, *Coarseness in U.S. Public Communication* (Madison, NJ: Fairleigh Dickinson University Press, 2012).

14 See, for example, Juliana Horowitz, Anna Brown, and Kiana Cox, "Race in America 2019," Pew Research Center, April 9, 2019, https://www.pewsocialtrends.org/2019/04/09/race-in-america-2019/#majorities-of-black-and-white-adults-say-blacks-are-treated-less-fairly-than-whites-in-dealing-with-police-and-by-the-criminal-justice-system.

15 Olivia Winslow and Carol Polsky, "Scholars, Activists Think Protests Could Lead to Change, Like in the 1960s." *Newsday*, June 6, 2020, https://www.newsday.com/long-island/protests-and-change-1.45391810.

16 Robert L. Heath and W. Timothy Coombs, *Today's Public Relations: An Introduction* (Thousand Oaks, CA: Sage, 2006), 7. See also Robert L. Heath and Michael J. Palenchar, *Strategic Issues Management: Organizations and Public Policy Challenges*, 2nd ed. (Thousand Oaks, CA: Sage, 2009). Issues management considers public policy advocacy as a management function of organizations ("the management of organizational and community resources through the public policy process to advance organizational interests and rights by striking a mutual balance with those of stakeholders" [Heath and Palenchar, *Strategic Issues Management*, 9]).

17 Heath and Coombs, *Today's Public Relations*, 278.

18 For an excellent review of scholarship in this area, see Robert Asen and Daniel C. Brouwer, eds., "Introduction: Reconfigurations of the Public Sphere," in *Counterpublics and the State* (Albany: SUNY Press, 2001). For a recent focused consideration of the role of appeals to "the people" within the realm of public policy advocacy, see Jeffrey P. Mehltretter Drury, *Speaking with the People's Voice: How Presidents Invoke Pubic Opinion* (College Station: Texas A & M University Press, 2014). Drury's project looks at how U.S. presidents, in their public rhetoric, use "invoked public opinion" to represent the will of the people, and how such conceptions of the people are constructed and contested within political controversies.

19 John Dewey, *The Public and its Problems* (Athens, OH: Swallow Press, 1954).

20 Michael C. McGee, "In Search of 'the People': A Rhetorical Alternative," *Quarterly Journal of Speech* 61, no. 3 (1975): 242.

21 Heath and Coombs, *Today's Public Relations*, 109.

22 Albert Cheng, Michael B. Henderson, Paul E. Peterson, and Martin West, "Public Support Climbs for Teacher Pay, School Expenditures, Charter Schools, and Universal Vouchers," 12th Annual Education Next Survey (Ednext Poll – 2018), Education Next, https://www.educationnext.org/public-support-climbs-teacher-pay-school-expenditures-charter-schools-universal-vouchers-2018-ednext-poll/ (see also the 2018 EdNext Poll Interactive: https://www.educationnext.org/2018-ednext-poll-interactive/). Different perspectives on the data exist. See, for example, Neal McCluskey, "African Americans Speak for Themselves: Most Want School Choice," *Cato at Liberty* (blog), Cato Institute, July 25, 2017, https://www.cato.org/blog/african-americans-speak-themselves-most-want-school-choice; and Kimberly Quick, "School Vouchers and Race: It's Complicated," The Century Foundation, July 20, 2017, https://tcf.org/content/commentary/school-vouchers-race-complicated/?agreed=1.

23 Particularly in the battleground state of Florida, school choice was thought to be key to winning the support of some African American voters. See Steve Contorno and Emily L. Mahoney, "'School Choice' is Dividing Florida Democrats Along Racial Lines. Could it Help Donald Trump?," *Tampa Bay Times*, February 14, 2020, https://www.tampabay.com/florida-politics/buzz/2020/02/13/school-choice-is-dividing-florida-democrats-along-racial-lines-could-it-help-donald-trump/; and Laura Meckler, Michael Scherer, and Josh Dawsey, "Trump Trains His Eyes on Education as He Hunts Path to Victory," *Washington Post*, July 23, 2020, https://www.washingtonpost.com/local/education/trump-trains-his-eyes-on-education-as-he-hunts-path-to-victory/2020/07/22/4bc3c9f6-c835-11ea-8ffe-372be8d82298_story.html.

24 "SAS Insights: Data Mining," SAS.com, https://www.sas.com/en_us/insights/analytics/data-mining.html.

25 See i-360.com, https://www.i-360.com.

26 Elihu Katz, Jay Blumler, and Michael Gurevitch. "Uses and Gratifications Research," *Public Opinion Quarterly* 37, no. 4 (January 1973): 509–523.

27 Elisabeth Noelle-Neumann, *The Spiral of Silence: Public Opinion – Our Social Skin*, (Chicago: University of Chicago Press, 1993).

28 Alice Eagly and Shelly Chaiken, *The Psychology of Attitudes* (Fort Worth, TX: Harcourt Brace Jovanovich, 1993).

29 Albert Bandura, *Self-efficacy: The Exercise of Control* (New York: W.H. Freeman, 1997).

30 Lynda Kaid, Mitchell S. McKinney, and John C. Tedesco. "Introduction: Political Information Efficacy and Young Voters," *American Behavioral Scientist* 50, no. 9 (May 1, 2007): 1093–1111.

31 Ibid., 1095.

32 Maxwell E. McCombs and Donald L. Shaw. "The Agenda-Setting Function of Mass Media," *The Public Opinion Quarterly* 36, no. 2 (Summer, 1972): 176–187.

33 Shanto Iyengar, Mark Peters, and Donald Kinder. "Experimental Demonstrations of the 'Not-So-Minimal' Consequences of Television News Programs," *American Political Science Review* 76, no. 4 (1982): 848–858.

34 Philip Converse, "The Nature of Belief Systems in Mass Publics," in *Ideology and Discontent*, ed. D.E. Apter, (Glencoe, IL: Free Press of Glencoe, 1964), 206–261.

35 John R. Zaller, *The Nature and Origins of Mass Opinion* (New York: Cambridge University Press, 1992).

36 For instance, see sources like Herbert C. Kelman. "Processes of Opinion Change," *Public Opinion Quarterly*, 25 no. 1 (Spring, 1961): 57–78.

37 Paul Lazarsfeld, Bernard Berelson, and Hazel Gaudet, *The People's Choice: How the Voter Makes Up His Mind in a Presidential Campaign* (New York: Columbia University Press, 1944).

38 Jane F. McAlevey, *No Shortcuts: Organizing for Power in the New Gilded Age* (New York: Oxford University Press, 2016), 34.

39 Tony Schwartz, *The Responsive Chord* (New York: Anchor Books, 1973).

40 "Don't Vote: A Knock the Vote PSA," YouTube, September 23, 2018, https://www.youtube.com/watch?v=POiqY4FIfMY. Additional information on the 60-second spot can be found at https://www.deconstructedbrief.com/knockthevote.

41 This and subsequent quotes come from Philip Dalton's conversation with Amielle DeWan, November 1, 2019.

9

ADAPTING TO THE ADVOCACY SETTING

Takeaways

(1) The advocacy setting is a rhetorical situation, involving an exigence, an audience, and constraints. It is also the product of advocates' decisions to focus on an issue and make others aware of the issue.

(2) Norms are an important part of advocacy settings, offering limitations and opportunities, including opportunities to change the norms by pushing against them.

(3) Advocacy settings may present challenging physical contexts, which advocates can strategically address.

(4) Mediated advocacy presents many challenges, including dramatically altering a message otherwise presented verbally or in writing. You should use caution when attempting to mediate your advocacy or use media instruments.

Up to this point in the text, we hope we have illustrated some of the unseen forces at play in public policy advocacy. While we are heavily invested in the potential of rational argumentation, we have warned that not all "fights" are fair, and that you should expect your opposition to introduce distractions to make the debate about something other than whether you or they support *a policy that solves a problem without causing other new problems that are more troubling than the original problem.* The capacity of audiences to reject arguments that are well supported, such as theories of evolution and global warming, despite mountains of evidence in support of both, makes clear that *more* is operating in an advocacy moment than the exchange of evidence and reasoning. We have suggested that flaws in reasoning, poor quality evidence, bias, ideological objectives, and more may frustrate good policymaking. Additionally, we have provided you with ample reasons to consider a target audience's disposition toward the issue, or reform proposals in general, as a means of setting reasonable goals for what you can achieve with your advocacy. We now take up the matter of the *advocacy setting*.

In addition to careful analysis of your target audience's disposition toward the issue, your advocacy should also accommodate various elements of the setting—where your advocacy occurs and what you make of the situation when you address your audience. Toward that end, in this chapter we consider the implications of the setting for advocates. We consider the advocacy setting as a *rhetorical situation*, draw your attention to the impact of *norms* tied to that setting that will likely influence what you can achieve with your advocacy, and note that sometimes *physical dynamics* of an advocacy setting are relevant to your goals. In addition to your assessment of the rhetorical situation, we believe you might benefit from additional considerations of mediated advocacy. This chapter is the second of two chapters we intend as guidance on setting reasonable goals for your advocacy.

The Advocacy Setting

Where your advocacy occurs and what you make of that setting (what it means to you and its impact on your message) is often referred to using the term "context." Communication Studies scholars have devoted significant attention to context, advising practitioners to consider historical, relational, cultural, emotional, and physical aspects of the context. Sometimes the setting is also referred to as the occasion. We attempt to provide both a limited and theoretically sophisticated consideration of the advocacy setting by concentrating on the concept of the *rhetorical situation*, the role of norms in determining what advocates can achieve in an advocacy setting, and the sometimes important matter of physical surroundings. It will become clearer as you read on that we view the advocacy setting as dynamic. It is at once a situation you contemplate as an occasion for advocacy, a place where rules and conventions constrain how you communicate, and a physical location.

The Rhetorical Situation

In his landmark essay titled "The Rhetorical Situation," Lloyd Bitzer maintains that "discourse comes into existence because of some specific condition or situation which invites utterance."[1] He breaks the rhetorical situation into three components: the *exigence*, the *audience*, and the *constraints*. Together, these components make up "the context in which speakers or writers create discourse."[2] Let's consider each in an effort to form a general idea of the relationship between situation and advocacy.

The *exigence* is an "imperfection marked by urgency ... [a] thing which is other than it should be."[3] Persuasive occasions emerge, argues Bitzer, when events demand that they be addressed ("it is the situation which calls the discourse into existence").[4] Consider George W. Bush's speech atop the rubble of the World Trade Center. That iconic moment has become so consistently associated with the 9/11 terrorist attacks it is difficult to imagine Bush doing anything else the day he held the bullhorn to his mouth and delivered his threat to "the people who knocked these buildings down." Even though he had no intention to speak at Ground Zero on that day, his decision to speak imbued the site with meaning and framed it as a justification for the overwhelming use of force that Bush would propose soon after. In the immediate aftermath of the attacks, Bush was eliciting the physical setting of Ground Zero to compel Americans to support his "fitting responses" to the situation.[5]

Like the distinctions we make in Chapter 8, what Bitzer means by *audience* refers to a target audience, both those present within the situation and "persons who are capable of being influenced by discourse and of being mediators of change."[6] The audience to rhetorical discourse is exceptional (different from the audience for poetry or scientific findings, for instance), according to Bitzer, because "*the rhetorical audience* must be capable of serving as mediator of the change which the discourse functions to produce."[7] It is easy to imagine an engaged, even demanding, audience in the case of an attack against the nation; as we note below, however, there may be some issues raised by advocates who struggle to find a responsive audience.

Bitzer defines *constraints* of the rhetorical situation as "persons, events, objects, and relations which are parts of the situation because they have the power to constrain decision and action needed to modify the exigence."[8]

Martha Cooper reminds us that constraints "are *both limitations and opportunities for what can be said in what ways.*"[9] In some ways, constraints have been what we have been addressing throughout this book: the "rules" of public policy advocacy—the burdens on affirmative and negative advocates, the general logical expectations we have for those making predictions, deploying sound reasoning, and using appropriate evidence. Constraints can also include limitations of the audience, physical aspects of the setting, and norms that welcome or resist certain types of appeals or advocacy tactics. They may also include constraints of the medium used to convey your advocacy.

In discussing the rhetorical situation, we acknowledge that, while advocates do from time to time find themselves compelled to respond to an exigence (such as a president responding to an attack on the nation), most of the time advocates are *making the situation into what they need it to be.* Even in the case of Bush at Ground Zero, it might be challenging to imagine any other way he could have characterized the exigence, but he had a significant range of options.[10] Advocates choose to respond and consciously assemble their advocacy to draw attention to an issue that concerns them in a way that suits their interests. This is Richard Vatz's argument, made in an important response to Bitzer's theory.[11] "Political crises ... are rarely 'found,' they are usually created," writes Vatz.[12] Advocates both make an exigence meaningful by describing it in some way that distinguishes it as an imperfection requiring urgent response, *and* they seek to elevate certain issues over others—a process of according some issues "salience."[13] As such, imperfections such as homelessness, systemic racism in policing, family separation, COVID-19, and more are made significant for the audience. Advocates, creating the rhetorical situation to fit their needs, function to define a situation.

Consider, for instance, the rhetorical situation Donald Trump might have contemplated when he prepared to offer recorded remarks from Walter Reed Medical Center when he was admitted for complications due to COVID-19. Because of his desire to downplay the severity of his illness, and of COVID-19 generally (as something that can be controlled, managed, cured), *where* the advocacy occurs in this instance is a *place* where the president is being observed out of an abundance of caution—not, as it would be for most Americans, a site of tragedy whereby advancing disease was being combatted to save the life of a vulnerable patient. Trump could have said nothing or issued a very general statement attesting to his stable health. The responsibility in this situation is on the advocate, writes Vatz, whose actions are "*decisions* to make salient or not make salient these situations."[14]

The capacity and/or tendency of advocates to generate public interest is a phenomenon we discuss throughout this text. Not all advocates are the U.S. president. Some advocates find a public disinclined to consider their policy issue. They may not have a ready audience to accept their interpretation of where they are and what it means. This is the peculiar situation we have discussed in relation to people historically denied access to deliberation and power, or "counterpublics." When advocates are presented with situations of bias, prejudice, staunch opposition, or norms that box them out of the public discussion, they may need to be disruptive. Nancy Fraser explains that counterpublics contest "exclusionary norms" and "elaborat[e] alternative styles of political behavior and alternative norms of public speech,"[15] such as protests, marches, occupying parks, parades, lunch counter sit-ins, bus boycotts, and other forms of civil disobedience.

Norms

The rhetorical situation is one way to contemplate the advocacy setting, the way an advocate constructs an occasion to be what they need it to be. Another way to contemplate the setting is to think of it as a situation characterized by *norms*. Bitzer's rubric would consider norms as "constraints," but we believe norms are such an important aspect of advocacy settings—such an ever-present, always operating phenomenon—that they require separate consideration by advocates. To assist such consideration, the work of Thomas B. Farrell is instructive. In his book *Norms of Rhetorical Culture*, Farrell refers to the advocacy setting as a "rhetorical forum," which he defines as "the encounter setting which serves as a gathering place for discourse."[16] The "encounter setting" operates according to rules or "norms" that provide "loose but recognizable admission criteria as to who may speak, what may be spoken about, and how they are to be held accountable for what they say and do."[17] We have found that "norms" is one of those words that perplexes students. Even though the term has a basic definition—"a widespread or usual practice, procedure, or custom"[18]—it refers to something that differs depending on the situation and is typically beneath the surface. Imagine in this regard more than merely a *physical setting* (city council chamber, principal's office, city plaza, union hall, etc.); think also about the *channel* for the message (Facebook post, Twitter post, an email, an in-person speech, or even a letter). When you understand these norms, you can either respect them or ignore them (to some degree or completely). Understanding them might also help you appreciate the effect of violating the norms, which may either lead to a failure to effectively convey a message or produce a cultural shift that alters the norms of the advocacy setting.

Norms of an advocacy setting might seem like a complicated, academic subject, but it really isn't. If you are an older adult, think about how, for example, millennials or their younger counterparts use social media to express a particularly serious or complex opinion or engage in activism. If you've ever expressed surprise, shock, or frustration over the "inappropriateness" of something someone said at an event or posted online, you were contemplating norms. Consider the dramatic shifts in what is considered "appropriate" or "normal" in political speech in 2020 versus just a few years before—the personal attacks, name calling, and mocking that has become a staple of the Trump rally; the tearing up of a paper copy of the State of the Union speech, unmistakably captured on camera, by the Speaker of the House; a Party's presidential nominee saying to the President of the United States in a debate, "Will you shut up man." These are just a few examples of norm violations, but also moments when you might ask, "are the norms changing?" (which is not, to be clear, the same as asking, "should the norms change?").

Moments when norms are challenged by advocates are fascinating, particularly if those challenges contribute to a shift in norms—what is permissible on more of a regular basis, or what is judged to be necessary within particular policy areas. In 1955, an African American Chicago resident, 14-year-old Emmett Till, was murdered while visiting his relatives in Mississippi. His murderers were white men who, following their acquittal, admitted to the murder and proudly told their gruesome story to the press. They were angered that Till had allegedly flirted with a white woman at a local grocery store. His murder was a brutal lynching that left his body, particularly his face, badly deformed. After his body was found in the Tallahatchie River, Till's mother, Mamie Till, shocked the nation when she held an open-casket funeral and permitted African American newspapers to publish photographs of her son's badly beaten and deteriorated face. The impact of the photos is widely credited with sparking the civil rights movement. Before Till's murder, people across all walks of life knew about Jim Crow laws, Southern racism, segregation, and extrajudicial killings—or lynchings—of African Americans. Many even agreed that these problems needed to be fixed. But the issue was low on the general public's list of priorities, in large part because African Americans were systematically excluded from the mainstream public sphere. Mamie Till's highly disruptive, some might have said "uncivil," act of displaying her son's body for all to see, was a turning point. It was also one of many images of murdered African Americans that had been reappropriated by anti-lynching activists.[19]

Depending on your investment in status quo norms, values, and traditions, you might consider norm violations to be either positive or negative. Disenfranchised advocates often benefit from norm violations that make their causes more salient to the general public. Many believe cellphone videos of African American men being killed by police, or while in the custody of police (such as the killing of George Floyd), function like images of lynching victims. Add the power of social media to disseminate video evidence of extrajudicial killings, and it is understandable that some may compare African American newspapers of the early 20th century with the use of a Twitter hashtag to circulate images and news of injustices and related public outrage, as well as to foster alliances among supporters (we interview one scholar who has focused on this phenomenon below). But norm violations that have lasting impacts (i.e., that form new norms) might also be viewed by some as destructive to civility, democratic decision-making, confidence in expertise, and so on.

Physical Context

The physical context is the actual setting in which you engage in advocacy. A skilled advocate will adapt to or alter the physical circumstances in order to meet the demands of the setting. The size of the physical space, its lighting, temperature, arrangement, attendance, density, and decoration can all help shape what your audience expects or will tolerate from you. The grandeur of some U.S. deliberative spaces, such as the House of Representatives and Senate chambers, is remarkable. The size, arrangement, and decoration of these settings seem to impose formality, generating expectations for formal dress, language, and linear argument. Consider in this regard the dramatic juxtaposition of the norms of regular parliamentary order and the arrival of a large mob of violent and destructive protesters on January 6, 2021, while legislators were attempting to undertake the formal process of affirming the presidential election results. Most spaces will not be nearly as formal as the U.S. Capital, and you might appear to a target audience to be out of place communicating in an overly formal way in relatively less formal physical settings. Consider, for example, town halls, school gyms, or community centers. Nearly any physical space can be a deliberative space. Many consequential speeches have been delivered from "soap boxes" in public spaces. These spaces hardly generate expectations of formality, as the target audience is often those passing by. In fact, the nature of such public settings necessitates some degree of informality and flamboyancy in order to attract an audience—displays that would be perceived less positively in more formal settings.

Consider again George W. Bush's bullhorn speech at Ground Zero in the immediate aftermath of the collapse of the World Trade Center. Bush's actual words were formed as a result of listeners yelling, "Can't hear you." Bob Woodward recounts the moment:

> "Thank you all," Bush began. "I want you all to know . . ." and the gigantic canyon of rubble and humanity seemed to swallow up the words from his tiny bullhorn.
>
> "Can't hear you," a rescue worker shouted.
>
> "I can't go any louder," Bush said with a laugh. "America today is on bended knee in prayer for the people whose lives were lost here . . ." Another voice emerged from the crowd: "I can't hear you." Bush paused for an instant, then with his arm around [Bob] Beckwith's shoulder [New York firefighter], shouted back: "I can hear you. The rest of the world hears you. And the people who knocked these buildings down will hear all of us soon!"[20]

Many physical settings can be altered to complement your goals. You can accomplish this most easily by adorning the space with symbols that impart a desired mood to the event or provide visual affirmation of your credibility to address the subject. A politician may want to speak from a raised dais, flanked by flags, tractors, construction workers in hard hats, for instance. Advocates may also choose to speak in a "town hall" format, surrounding themselves with an audience, thus physically reducing the barriers between themselves and the audience. While the physical setting will not ensure a desired reaction, careful attention to it can help prevent it from limiting the effectiveness of your message. In the summer and fall of 2020, policymakers, journalists, and medical experts adapted to the need to communicate remotely, often from their personal residences, as the United States grappled with the COVID-19 pandemic. The Democratic and Republican National Conventions adopted a variety of strategies to address the public health guidelines, including many pre-recorded speeches and documentary-like productions that will likely alter the way the conventions are conducted in the future.

The Wall: Exigence and Norms of Presidential Leadership

Donald Trump's advocacy for a southern border wall is an example of a public policymaker both creating an exigence (choosing to focus on something and translating its meaning through advocacy) and violating many norms of presidential-level policy communication.

According to the Pew Research Center, the top five issues during the 2016 presidential election included the economy, terrorism, foreign policy, healthcare, and guns.[21] While immigration wasn't a top concern of voters, it ranked sixth and was on the minds of many enthusiastic supporters of the president. A border wall had not previously been a policy goal of the Republican Party within the multitude of solutions discussed among policymakers determined to reduce the number of southern border crossers, but Trump made a southern border wall a centerpiece of his presidential campaign and immigration policy. He introduced the idea in his campaign announcement speech in June of 2015, stating:

> I would build a great wall, and nobody builds walls better than me, believe me, and I'll build them very inexpensively, I will build a great, great wall on our southern border. And I will have Mexico pay for that wall.[22]

Public opinion would not shift in favor of a wall,[23] but few would deny that, because of his advocacy, the merits of a southern border wall gained a certain salience, particularly among Trump's voter base. In this regard, Trump can be said to have created a rhetorical situation where one would otherwise not have existed. As such, the occasions and settings of his border wall advocacy were similarly contrived.

From this point forward, Trump would also violate a wide range of norms of presidential leadership by continuing to define the problem of immigration in a manner that defied logic and evidence, and relied on racist appeals. Moreover, he would utilize conventions of presidential leadership, such as an Oval Office speech, reserved in most presidencies for the gravest and most serious of national issues. Trump's task was to convince the American people of the threat, thus elevating the issue in the minds of his audience and the urgency to fix it, and then focus on the advantages of the wall (ability to solve the problem at little cost, or deliver benefits exceeding the cost). Following his election, he focused mostly on generating urgency. For instance, in 2017, the White House press secretary discussed the rapes of two fourteen-year-old girls at the hands, allegedly, of an undocumented Guatemalan immigrant.[24] And, in 2018, the president described groups of migrants, dubbed "caravans," headed north from Central America toward the United States as "like an invasion."[25]

President Trump's advocacy, in the absence of a genuine exigence, failed to move the public. In the absence of a catalyzing news event, he turned to an Oval Office address on January 8, 2019, devoted exclusively to this issue. He focused much of his effort on painting a picture of a human catastrophe, describing immigration as a "humanitarian and security crisis" that has resulted in sex crimes, drug-related deaths, and "violent killings."[26] As is evident from this speech, convincing the public of an imminent immigration threat was a key part of his strategy. Instead of establishing that a wall would work (perhaps through testimony from authorities, reasoning from analogous situations, or other rational appeals), the president explains that the idea came from border patrol officials. Aside from that, he provides no reason to believe a wall will work to reduce the cited problems. He merely adds that it is "common sense."

> This barrier is absolutely critical to border security. It's also what our professionals at the border want and need. This is just common sense.

Consider this astounding moment. The president is proposing a $21.6 billion public works project because border patrol agents told him it was a good idea.[27] And, of the funds needed to build the wall, Trump says this:

> The wall will always be paid for indirectly by the great new trade deal we have made with Mexico.

Aside from this assertion being met with incredulity by many (because it doesn't seriously consider where the money is coming from), discussing funding in this context is unusual. Can you imagine another president speaking from the Oval Office about an imminent national security threat—an impending invasion—suggesting the solution is to build a wall, and then stopping to discuss where the money for it will come from? Nevertheless, the public learns that Trump is anticipating economic growth from the new United States-Mexico-Canada Agreement (the

Trump Administration's replacement for the North American Free Trade Agreement) and expects related surplus funds to cover the cost—a dubious funding mechanism at best.

Moreover, his treatment of questions about the wall's efficacy is cavalier, and arguably foolish. Comments delivered at a September 2019 visit to San Diego suggest little serious treatment by the president to support claims about the wall's deterrent effect.

> We actually built prototypes and we have, I guess you could say, world-class mountain climbers. We got climbers. We had 20 mountain climbers. That's all they do; they love to climb mountains. They can have it. Me, I don't want to climb mountains. But they're very good. And some of them were champions. And we gave them different prototypes of walls, and this was the one that was hardest to climb.[28]

It is little wonder that Trump failed to convince the majority of the public that a wall was necessary, effective, or advantageous.[29]

The U.S. Congress allotted about $1.4 billion in a 2019 budget for wall construction, far short of the nearly $6 billion Trump proposed. In response, the Trump Administration used presidential emergency powers to divert $3.6 billion from defense spending in other areas to begin the wall. Legal challenges ensued, leading a federal appeals court to rule, in October 2020, that the diversion of military funds was illegal. Subsequent appeals were later withdrawn by the Biden Administration in February 2021, putting an end to the plan to divert military funds to construct a border wall.[30]

The Medium

The medium you use to address your target audience is both an important component of the advocacy setting, and, in some cases, may constitute its most significant characteristic. "Media" is used to refer to many things. Most Communication Studies scholars and professionals think of media as a reference to the mechanisms for delivering messages. Rarely is speech or written material referred to as "media," a term more commonly reserved for discussion of the press and/or popular culture productions. The distinction between spoken/written advocacy and advocacy that relies on technology, in our view, is important to your consideration of norms and how best to adapt your message to the dynamics of *mediated advocacy*. To discuss it further and provide you with useful guidance on how best to position your advocacy for consumption through a particular medium, we consider briefly in-person public address and written advocacy, and contrast these forms with mediated advocacy.

Examining mediated advocacy in this context provides only a limited consideration of the effects of the mode of communication that enhances a message, particularly when you consider the rapidly changing technology advocates have available to them. Our observations in this regard are intended to get you thinking about media as an element of the advocacy setting and encourage you to consider the implications of the particular medium through which your advocacy reaches its target audience.

Written and Spoken Advocacy

Before the widespread use of the internet, it was fair to say that most advocacy, across the life of an advocate's career, involved person-to-person speech or written formats. Today that may no longer be a fair assumption; nonetheless, a good portion of your advocacy will involve you speaking, in person, to a target audience, or addressing a target audience in the rather traditional written formats of letters, fact sheets, position papers, and so forth (even if these are sent to audiences via email or made available online).

If you are using your voice to communicate with a target audience that is physically present, the medium is what we refer to as *public address*. You might be standing at a lectern, as would be the case if you were addressing a city council. You might be at a table, seated. You might be approaching a legislator "on the rail" in a state capital or after having "called them off the floor." You might be in an office, seated or standing among several others vying for an opportunity to address a policymaker. Most of you have, at the very least, found yourself in a courtroom to address a citation. Courtrooms are structured formats with rules for who may speak and what they may speak about. In preparation for such a setting, you have no doubt found yourself nervous, even when the matter that brings you to the court is minor, because you understand the setting is constrained by rules, and you might inadvertently break them.

Advocacy through a written medium is perhaps more common than public address, as various authority figures may wish to consider your concerns in a complete fashion and reserve person-to-person meetings for questions or additional consideration. This offers you a significant advantage, provided the receiver of the communication intends to read the material carefully. In public policy advocacy, issues analyses, fact sheets, and position papers are commonly distributed to decision makers. Often these documents consolidate the advocacy of many people working toward the same outcome. Getting your arguments on paper is a somewhat risky activity given that those opposed to your policy proposal may receive the advocacy materials and respond point-by-point in written or spoken advocacy directed to decision makers. Your positions may also change as you interact with decision makers and other stakeholders, and you may find yourself explaining contradictory or inaccurate claims that you put in writing in an early stage of your advocacy. For these reasons, you might choose to reserve written advocacy for proposals and related claims that you have thoroughly reviewed and assembled in as complete a fashion as possible.

For advocates who are foreign-born and/or for whom English is a second language (ESL), their encounter with a public address advocacy setting might be daunting, as translation often becomes necessary, and/or the unique characteristics of the speakers' voice, language choices, nuances of meaning, and other stylistic features are accorded only limited consideration. In rigid public address settings, such as a courtroom, translation challenges can place the ESL speaker/advocate at a serious disadvantage. Add to this environment the anxieties that foreign-born residents may face due to their immigration status, and the public address setting—particularly legal settings or hostile political environments—can be intimidating. Often, ESL advocates will turn to written formats because they can review their written materials with native speakers and reduce translation challenges in their favor.

For different reasons, advocates with communicative disorders or for whom a public address setting is intimidating may also prefer written advocacy. To the extent advocates can do so safely, we believe they should push themselves to engage authorities and audiences directly, and not be dissuaded from public address due to disabilities or language barriers. We are optimistic about the potential of public audiences to accommodate an ever-evolving appreciation for alternative personal styles and cultural conventions of communication. One of the authors of this textbook, John Butler, has been challenged throughout his life with a persistent stuttering disability, which manifests as an absence of sound that prevents him from pronouncing certain words in some situations. The disability fluctuates and can come into existence and diminish for extended periods of time. Over many years of practice, in such situations he has learned to instantly substitute some words he cannot say with alternative words he can say—which, to most listeners, results in a hardly noticeable delay or slightly awkward phrase. His ability to adapt to, and regularly participate in, public advocacy situations is a direct result of continuing to expose himself to advocacy situations despite the disability (indeed, he has made it his expertise).[31] The presidential candidacy of Joe Biden has also led to more attention to the challenge of dysfluency and the importance of carving out room for people with communicative disorders to participate in public life.[32]

It is a common characteristic of textbooks concerning communication skills and performance to offer guidance as if the readers' encounters will be in person or in writing in what might be called "traditional" advocacy settings. This, of course, is not realistic in this age of email, smartphones, memes, Facebook, Twitter, Instagram, TikTok, and so on. For younger generations, advocacy is more likely to be mediated in some form. However, an important assumption guiding this privileging of spoken/written advocacy is that the mastery of such practical skills will offer you the widest range of adaptation capacity and that physical presence is ultimately necessary in nearly all effective public policy endeavors. That is, while certain characteristics of public address and written advocacy may not be relevant in mediated advocacy—permissibility of expositional speech or text, or regulation of volume, rate, tone, pronunciation, and cadence, for instance—the fundamentals of advocacy are often best learned when envisioned as a person-to-person, direct exchange.

Mediated Advocacy

Mediated advocacy is distinguished from public address and written advocacy, even though we have already explained that spoken and written advocacy are forms of media. We do not wish to make too fine a distinction here, though we do wish to draw attention to the implications of your use of media that enhance spoken and written messages. Mediated messages can still be written and spoken, but they are distinguished by their delivery systems and the potential size of the audience.

One way to consider this notion of a delivery system and size of a target audience is to think of the concept of *extension*. Media permits an advocate to *extend* his or her message beyond those immediately present. Written messages can be directed to a mass audience through print duplication and physical distribution (newspapers, magazines, journals) or distribution through electronic means (social media apps, blogs, email, texts). Spoken messages can appear in video form (broadcast TV, Zoom, Instagram Livestream, Facebook Live) and audio form (telephone, radio, podcasts). In this framework, an advocacy letter you write to a university administrator, for example, is not mediated advocacy. If you distribute that letter widely through email or ask that it be published in the campus newspaper, however, it becomes mediated advocacy.

In this section, we consider some of the conventions of the mass media environment, treating media as an advocacy setting with norms that will affect the quality of your messages. Conventions of mass media are common characteristics of information delivered in mass media outlets, such as newspapers and television. In changing media environments, you should be aware of and accommodate these conventions, engage in efforts to control your messages when using a media channel, and determine when media instruments can enhance your messages. The media is a very diffuse and fluid environment, and it is not our intention to systematically inventory each media form and the unique challenges these environments pose for advocates. Instead, our intention is to share some of our general observations as a means of encouraging your own consideration of what happens to your advocacy when it becomes mediated. We recommend the following general guidance:

(1) Determine what you believe can be accomplished through a particular medium based on how the audience generally uses that medium.
What causes audiences to prefer certain media over others? Many politically liberal news consumers choose not to watch Fox News, for example, because they disagree with the way the Fox network characterizes the news. Instead, they might watch MSNBC, generally considered a politically liberal source of information. In so doing, it might matter less if MSNBC commentator Rachel Maddow changed their minds about anything and more about whether Maddow's comments reinforce their attitudes. Maddow's loyal audience might tune in more out of habit than because of a specific information need. Or, they might seek a reward that the particular medium is capable of delivering, such as when, during a presidential election, politically liberal viewers tune into politically liberal media to acquire relief from the fear that a conservative will win the White House.

You should endeavor to adapt to the realities of audience consumption habits instead of hoping that your message will be compelling enough to overcome the fact that nobody is likely to encounter your message through their selected medium. For instance, if you are seeking to generate outrage against a proposal to build affordable housing in your neighborhood and are invited onto a local talk radio program favored by politically liberal listeners, you may find that the listening audience is *not* made up of the kind of residents who would support your position, no matter how rational you believe your arguments are.

(2) Respect the practical limits of the media through which audiences are encountering your advocacy.
The most significant adaptation typically concerns the length of the information you are presenting and how the media format requires reduction of your message to less complex and detailed treatments of a subject. Your assumption may be that a good argument is a thorough argument, that the more evidence you can marshal, the more influential you will be. However, when you apply that assumption to the world of print media, for example, you may be in for a rude awakening. The op-ed policy of the *New York Times* recommends 750 words. This is the equivalent of three double-spaced typewritten pages. Letters to the editor at the same publication should be no longer than 150 words—less than a page! And, these limits are not arbitrary; they reflect both the practical limits of the medium and the tolerances of the readership.

In the present media environment, advocates are always competing for attention with other media. Smartphones, tablets, and laptops make for rich forms of entertainment available at users' fingertips. Once these means are used by you, practical limitations will present themselves. Facebook allows for long posts, but it encounters challenges of limited exposure and a limited desire, on the part of many, to read long form statements. On the other hand, images and short phrases are central to Twitter messages. The same is true of Instagram and Snapchat, both of which are more photo-based. Brevity, however, neither limits their power nor their reach. On June 29, 2020, U.S. Senate Majority Leader Mitch McConnell tweeted a picture of himself wearing a personal protective mask along with the statement, "We must have no stigma, none, about wearing masks when we leave our homes and come near other people."[33] It was brief, but powerful. One of the nation's top Republican legislators advocated wearing masks to help stop the spread of COVID-19, after other public officials politicized doing so. Such a tweet can raise awareness, help call people to action, and link readers to more-developed and evidence-based treatments of the topic.

Internet news sources and blogs are outlets for relatively more-developed advocacy. You can be your own editor (producing your own blog, for instance), or you can seek to be featured in someone else's blog or news source. Self-edited blogs have the advantage of allowing you to say and do whatever you wish. Alternatively, seeking to advocate through someone else's news site or blog has the advantage of delivering your message to an already-formed audience, yet it may have the drawback of subjecting your arguments to the editorial choices of the site's editors. According to eBizMBA.com, *The Huffington Post* attracts around 110,000,000 unique monthly visitors,[34] an enormous audience for any advocate, *if* your message survives vetting by its editorial gatekeepers.

Well-funded and attractively produced advocacy on the internet is often delivered in video. Many people encounter the video "virally" through social media sites like Facebook, Twitter, and Vimeo. One instance is a video widely distributed via social media titled *Plandemic* produced by Mikki Willis. The film disseminates misinformation about the COVID-19 pandemic, and, according to the *New York Times*, "Just over a week after 'Plandemic' was released, it had been viewed more than eight million times on YouTube, Facebook, Twitter, and Instagram, and had generated countless other posts."[35] Though the video was eventually removed by many video sharing platforms, it drew a large audience, and directed traffic to its own website. Producing effective advocacy of this sort often necessitates film and editing tools as well as knowledge about filmic conventions.

(3) Structure your advocacy to accommodate editorial preferences and journalistic news conventions, the most significant being that messages be newsworthy.

Issues common to many communities often appear on broadcast news, which allows advocates to reach large audiences. However, editorial preferences and journalistic news conventions guide media decision makers, particularly on the question of *newsworthiness*. Newsworthiness is a function of both *interest* and *adaptability* to the news format. Whether what interests you will attract the interests of media decision makers often depends on its value as a spectacle or the size of audience interest. Large public crowds and disruptive protests attract news coverage, because they are provocative events that suggest widespread interest. It is important, however, to note that advocates surrender much control over the narrative journalists apply to protests. Some journalists may feel manipulated into covering manufactured news, and they may avoid covering the event or choose to frame it according to its more negative aspects.

You need to consider how you wish to have journalists cover your issue and what to do *and what to avoid* to obtain favorable coverage. Whether a protest, an interview, or a press conference, you might pose the question: *What do I want the headline of the story about my event to say?* The differences between your needs and the journalist's agenda may manifest in the way questions are asked. *Are the questions "loaded," or do they make assumptions that you do not accept?* You can rephrase the question in your answer to avoid affirming a journalist's flawed assumptions. When communicating with journalists, it is important to know that broadcasters prefer catchy phrases and rarely show tolerance for long statements. Even when U.S. presidents speak, their comments are reduced to just seconds on the evening news. Many broadcast news outlets favor short sound bites or "quotables" that are interesting, appealing, and encapsulate the cause behind an event or group's actions.

In addition to using brevity strategically, you must also accommodate the nature of the newsgathering process that may work at cross-purposes with your advocacy. For instance, many media formats do not lend themselves to lengthy spoken stories and other less-disciplined speech acts such as jokes, satire, and the defensive rebuttal of points. You should avoid the temptation to treat an opportunity to speak to a journalist in a conversational style. Even if you know certain journalists well, assume always that they will do their job even if it means revealing something you asked them not to quote or hoped they would consider irrelevant to the issue being discussed. Stories, in particular, will almost always be edited to fit a very limited time frame (as short as five seconds) or space. You should, therefore, *expect* to have your words taken out of context, often with the effect of conveying a message you did not intend and one that may be harmful to your cause. If you were, for example, interviewed by a local news channel after having spent hours standing at a rally outdoors, and, in addition to thoughtful statements about the issue that brought you out, you remarked how early you got up that morning or how much your feet hurt, these innocuous statements may be the full extent of the interview that makes it on television.

(4) Strive to consciously control your mediated advocacy, particularly its consistency throughout its mediated appearances.
Because different forms of mass media can afford you the ability to broadcast your messages, maintaining rhetorical consistency is essential. This means talking about your cause in consistent ways, both in terms of the reasoning structure and particular language of your advocacy. What mass media gives you in terms of message exposure can be limited by poor message penetration. Many people consume mass media in passive ways. Audiences encounter

messages while they are doing something else (driving, cooking, waking up, folding laundry, or consuming other media). To penetrate the attention of an audience, quite often messages must be repeated. As such, when it serves your purpose, the content and rhetorical dynamics of your messages should remain consistent. Repetition is ideal in mediated formats. Politicians often refer to the need to "stay on message" for this very reason.

You should also be aware of the potential for your messages to be "repurposed" by third parties. Today, it is best to assume that nearly anything you say or do publicly will be recorded and rebroadcast via the internet. Consequently, you should avoid off-the-cuff remarks on any issue of importance to your advocacy effort. In 2020, CNN reported that President Trump had criticized President Obama's handling of the H1N1 swine flu, reportedly calling it a "full-scale disaster." The same report contrasted the tweet with comments Trump made on Fox News in 2009 when he said of Obama's handling, "I think it is being handled fine."[36] Talking informally with like-minded thinkers can be as tempting as telling constituencies what they want to hear. Once the material is made publicly available, however, it can be edited, re-contextualized, and framed to ridicule or embarrass you.

(5) Understand the potential that media instruments have to enhance your messages, but be aware that they should be used cautiously.
Media instruments you choose to use are tools that may or may not enhance your advocacy (Microsoft PowerPoint presentations, video conferencing platforms, charts, audio). These instruments alter the quality of messages in ways similar to those described above and thus require similar consideration. Many of the conventions concerning audience attention, length of content, the relative value of certain graphics, video footage, and so on apply to the decision to enhance your advocacy with media instruments. Each of these instruments offers you a means of projecting, extending, and/or repeating your message (either physically repeated or offered to additional audience in video, webcast or webinar, or through animated means such as storyboards). Enhancing a message is typically done to increase understanding and make key elements more moving and memorable; sometimes, they become necessary to separate you physically from others, or traverse such separation, such as in the case of public health quarantines and shutdowns.

Most advocates believe media instruments will enhance presentations. Because media instruments can change the fundamental nature of messages, however, we advise using them sparingly or with caution. Visually represented material will be received *visually*, and its reception may not conform to advocates' logical strategies. Political scientist Edward Tufte is an award-winning expert in statistical evidence and information design who advises professionals in many fields about the implications of visual displays of information, particularly quantitative information. In his book, *Beautiful Evidence*, Tufte provides readers with effective methods for showing evidence and analytical tools for assessing the credibility of evidence presentations. Tufte explains that serious responsibilities accompany the visual representation of evidence:

> Making an evidence presentation is a moral act as well as an intellectual activity. To maintain standards of quality, relevance, and integrity for evidence, consumers of presentations should insist that presenters be held intellectually and ethically responsible for what they show and tell.[37]

In the realm of public policy advocacy, visual explanations are commonly used to present data advocates believe support particular policy directions. For instance, advocates of social distancing and other behaviors intended to reduce the spread of COVID-19 will often display graphs illustrating the spread of the disease, increased number of hospitalizations or infections, positivity rates by region, and so forth. Different data sets illustrate different narratives about the disease. While it would be impossible to summarize all the ways such visual presentations can mislead, either intentionally or unintentionally, we encourage you to carefully consider the power of images to consume your audiences' attention.

Because your daily lives are surrounded by mediated presentations, you may assume that your own presentations may be more credible, professional, and/or stirring when they too are mediated. What this assumption fails to take into consideration is how novel and powerful you can be as an individual public speaker and how much more powerful you can be than an audio clip or a PowerPoint presentation. There are times, however, when such instruments have tremendous potential to enhance the sensory experience of a spoken presentation, make abstractions more comprehensible, provide recorded evidence, render statistics understandable, or strike a chord with the audience. Consider that visual displays can include video, photographs, color, logos, typography, lighting, space, and data graphics. Audio can add voice and music to a presentation. Cell phone applications and laptops can add instant interactive elements.

Our advice for using media instruments in advocacy presentations is similar to the visual aid advice students get in a public speaking course—you should use media instruments only when they help make a point better than you can by vocal delivery alone. *Is recorded evidence (videotape, pictures, or audio recordings) necessary to make a point? Can you simply use a quotation or a description? Let's say you have a provocative picture; are you tempted to use the picture because it advances your argument or because it is provocative?* For example, if your objective is to explain how COVID-19 is spread as part of an effort to put in place some policy measure, *is it necessary to show an animated image of the virus and to leave it projected on a wall while you speak?* If the image neither enhances understanding of your argument nor helps advance your argument, it likely distracts from your efforts to persuade. The same is true for the use of statistics, sound, and imagery for purposes of generating emotional reactions.

Video conferencing platforms have burst on the scene rapidly in response to the COVID-19 pandemic and have arguably revolutionized the modern workplace and teaching/learning environment. Our initial assessment is that you can be highly effective speaking directly into the camera, making room in the image for hand gestures and considering carefully surroundings to achieve balance (even space on the left, right, and above your head), implementing effective lighting, always avoiding advertising or promoting some product (such as a book) while on camera, and shifting to screen sharing only when absolutely necessary to convey information (following the same practical guidelines above for PowerPoint and other visual aids). Video conferencing appears to permit close adherence to notes, which should be placed on the screen in front of you in tight, narrow formation (to limit eye movement left to right). As much as possible, people who are speaking should be able to see that you are listening to them. We do not see any downside to the movement of family behind you or the occasional appearance of curious children; these moments simply make you more relatable, producing what we suspect is increased intimacy akin to the interpersonal effect of disclosure.

Charlton McIlwain on Media Channel and Black Lives Matter

Charlton McIlwain, Ph.D. is the Vice Provost for Faculty Engagement and Development at New York University. His most recent research focuses on the effects of the Black Lives Matter movement, particularly its use of the social media channel Twitter.[38] Twitter and the Black Lives Matter hashtag allow virtually anyone with a smartphone to amplify the organization's message. McIlwain identifies two qualities that make Twitter particularly effective as an advocacy tool: images and circulation.[39] But the channel also has its limitations.

McIlwain explains that civil rights advocates have been historically dependent on their ability to reach audiences through news media. Attention, he notes, is the lifeblood of public advocacy. Activists in the 1950s and 60s "had to get the attention of journalists and media makers first, and rely on those folks to cover their actions, their messages, their leadership." Because the news media eventually became so fractured by various forces, he adds, coverage of pretty much any issue became "episodic and sporadic." Consequently, "it was difficult to catapult any issue—much less a difficult one like race and civil rights—to the forefront of public attention for any sustained period of time."

Enter social media. McIlwain describes the media environment of the late 2010s as "vastly different" compared to what civil rights advocates faced in previous eras. "The proliferation of the internet and social media provide direct access between organizers and movements and the publics whose attention they need." Twitter allows protesters, through digitally circulated images, to achieve direct access to journalists. "Twitter and other social media channels gave [protesters] the ability to amplify their own actions and directions, to garner their own attention, and it allowed them to affiliate journalists with their cause." McIlwain's network analysis (a research method allowing scholars to collect and visualize Twitter messages and who shares them) reveals "dense networks of activists, journalists (from mainstream press and race-based outlets), politicians, celebrities, and the general public." According to McIlwain, this enabled Black Lives Matter to earn public attention and sustain it.

To illustrate his point, McIlwain's research reveals the following:

> For practically the first 48 hours after Mike Brown's killing in Ferguson, all information about Mike Brown was coming from Twitter. When journalists first started covering it, for the first couple of days, the majority of their content was sourced from Twitter. What this meant was that users—in this case largely black users and activists—were able to control the narrative about Mike Brown, about Ferguson. Think about how odd—but amazing—it was that from the beginning, mainstream media—and even ideologically driven media on the right—framed Mike Brown as an "Unarmed, Black Teenager." This sympathetic framing is almost never afforded black, 17-year-old men in the context of media reporting or their adjudication by the criminal justice system. That narrative took hold from the beginning because the community—not journalists—did the framing.

Twitter introduced hashtags to contemporary social media, a text tool that allowed people to follow or contribute to a group or discussion. McIlwain explains that the hashtag has a unique quality to it in that it allows activists to "hail" one another. The hashtag, he points out, "says to allied individuals and the general public, 'Hey, look over here. Here we are. Here are your people. Here are the people fighting for what you believe in.'" He adds that five years after the police shooting of Michael Brown in Ferguson, Missouri, "people took to the streets and their rallying cry was and continues to be #BlackLivesMatter."

McIwain attributes Twitter's effectiveness in advancing the cause of Black Lives Matter activists to the "knowledge, ingenuity, skill and expertise with which Black folks manipulated the medium for their purposes." Nevertheless, it has limitations. McIlwain describes one important limitation to the medium: its capacity to sustain attention is dependent upon provocative visual content. "We hear more about BLM when someone has been brutalized by police. Thus, the attention is good. It is necessary. It is effective. But it is also premised on the fact of, and the circulation of images and messages about something that is guaranteed to persist—the taking of black lives by law enforcement and the criminal justice system."

Exercise: Evaluating Adaptation to Advocacy Settings

Identify an instance of public policy advocacy. This may be a speech, a letter to the editor, a blog post, or a demonstration, for example. Evaluate how well the message you've chosen fits the setting using the principles discussed in this chapter. First, identify the message that you've chosen to analyze. Second, provide an overall evaluation, stating whether you believe the message was or was not well-adapted to the advocacy setting. Include in your evaluation the medium used for delivery (public address, YouTube video, letter to the editor, blog post, etc.). As best you can, define the exigency that the message addresses. Is the message well-adapted to the medium? If relevant, does the physical setting play an important role in the advocacy setting? If so, in what way(s)?

Notes

1 Lloyd F. Bitzer, "The Rhetorical Situation," *Philosophy & Rhetoric*, 1 no. 1 (January 1968): 1–14.

2 Ibid., 1.

3 Ibid., 6.

4 Ibid., 2.

5 For details regarding the bullhorn speech, see Bob Woodward, *Bush at War* (New York: Simon & Schuster, 2002), 69–70; and David Frum, *The Right Man: The Surprise Presidency of George W. Bush* (New York: Random House, 2003), 139–140. The bullhorn speech was actually one of three unscripted addresses Bush made in the immediate aftermath of the attacks (his first unscripted remarks were made before boarding Airforce One immediately after the attacks, his second were delivered from the Cabinet Room on September 12, and the third was the bullhorn speech on September 13). There were also formal addresses, an Oval Office speech on the night of September 11, a speech at the National Cathedral on September 13, and a speech before a Joint Session of Congress on September 20. "Fitting response[s]" is Bitzer's terminology (one "characteristic of the rhetorical situation is that it invites a fitting response, a response that fits the situation" [*Rhetorical Situation*, 10]).

6 Bitzer, *Rhetorical Situation*, 8.

7 Ibid., 8 (italics added).

8 Ibid., 8.

9 Martha Cooper, *Analyzing Public Discourse* (Long Grove, IL: Waveland Press, 1989), 22 (italics in original).

10 Woodward's account (*Bush at War*) is perhaps the best non-partisan record that highlights key moments of decision concerning how to describe the crisis. Rhetorical scholarship on the manner in which Bush framed the enemy and purpose of the war on terror includes, to name only a few: Robert L. Ivie, "Evil Enemy Versus Agonistic Other: Rhetorical Constructions of Terrorism," *Review of Education, Pedagogy, and Cultural Studies* 25, no. 3 (2003): 181–200; Denise M. Bostdorff, "George W. Bush's Post-September 11 Rhetoric of Covenant Renewal: Upholding the Faith of the Greatest Generation," *Quarterly Journal of Speech* 89, no. 4 (2003): 293–319; John M. Murphy, "'Our Mission and Our Moment': George W. Bush and September 11th," *Rhetoric and Public Affairs* 6, no. 4 (2003): 607–632; Debra Merskin, "The Construction of Arabs as Enemies: Post-September 11 Discourse of George W. Bush," *Mass Communication and Society* 7, no. 2 (2004): 157–175; Joshua Gunn, "The Rhetoric of Exorcism: George W. Bush and the Return of Political Demonology," *Western Journal of Communication* 68, no. 1 (Winter 2004): 1–23. See also: Robert L. Ivie, *Democracy and America's War on Terror* (Tuscaloosa: University of Alabama Press, 2006); and Carol K. Winkler, *In the Name of Terrorism: Presidents on Political Violence in the Post-World War II Era* (Albany: State University of New York Press, 2006), 155–187.

11 Richard E. Vatz, "The Myth of the Rhetorical Situation," *Philosophy & Rhetoric* 6, no. 3 (1973): 154–161.

12 Ibid., 159.

13 Ibid., 157.

14 Ibid., 158 (italics in original).

15 Nancy Fraser, "Rethinking the Public Sphere: A Contribution to the Critique of Actually Existing Democracy," in *Habermas and the Public Sphere*, Craig Calhoun, ed. (Cambridge, MA: MIT Press, 1992), 116.

16 Thomas B. Farrell, *Norms of Rhetorical Culture* (New Haven, CT: Yale University Press, 1995), 282.

17 Ibid., 288.

18 *Merriam-Webster*, s.v., "norm," https://www.merriam-webster.com/dictionary/norm.

19 Amy Louise Wood, *Lynching and Spectacle: Witnessing Racial Violence in America: 1890–1940* (Chapel Hill, NC: University of North Carolina Press, 2009).

20 Woodward, *Bush at War*, 70.

21 "2016 Campaign: Strong Interest, Widespread Dissatisfaction," Pew Research Center, July 7, 2016, https://www.pewresearch.org/politics/2016/07/07/4-top-voting-issues-in-2016-election/.

22 "Here's Donald Trump's Presidential Announcement Speech," *Time Magazine*, June 16, 2015, https://time.com/3923128/donald-trump-announcement-speech/.

23 Jim Norman, "Solid Majority Still Opposes New Construction on Border Wall," *Gallup*, February 4, 2019, https://news.gallup.com/poll/246455/solid-majority-opposes-new-construction-border-wall.aspx.

24 Raul Reyes, "How Sean Spicer uses Rape Case to Scapegoat Immigrants," CNN, March 27, 2017, https://www.cnn.com/2017/03/27/opinions/scapegoat-reyes/index.html.

25 Elise Foley, "Trump Goes After Asylum-Seekers in Latest Pre-Election Anti-Immigrant Push," *Huffington Post*, November 1, 2018, https://www.huffpost.com/entry/trump-border-asylum_n_5bd85d85e4b017e5bfd5ef71?ygc=.

26 Debbie Lord, "Trump Border Wall Speech: Read the Full Transcript," *Atlanta Journal Constitution*, January 26, 2019, https://www.ajc.com/news/national/trump-border-wall-speech-read-the-full-transcript/Zm6DfoKTbOb6mOvzxOBLwI/.

27 Julia Edwards Ainsley, "Exclusive – Trump Border 'Wall' To Cost $21.6 Billion, Take 3.5 Years to Build: Internal Report," *Reuters*, February 10, 2017, https://www.reuters.com/article/us-usa-trump-immigration-wall-exclusive/exclusive-trump-border-wall-to-cost-21-6-billion-take-3-5-years-to-build-internal-report-idUSKBN15O2ZN.

28 "Remarks by President Trump During Visit to Border Wall | San Diego, CA," WhiteHouse.Gov September 18, 2019, https://www.whitehouse.gov/briefings-statements/remarks-president-trump-visit-border-wall-san-diego-ca/.

29 Norman, "Solid Majority Still Opposes New Construction on Border Wall."

30 See Amy Howe, "Justices Take Immigration Cases Off February Calendar, *Scotusblog*, Feb 3, 2021, https://www.scotusblog.com/2021/02/justices-take-immigration-cases-off-february-calendar/; and Ilya Somin, "Supreme Court Removes Border Wall Case From its Oral Argument Calendar," *The Volokh Conspiracy*, *Reason*, February 4, 2021, https://reason.com/volokh/2021/02/04/supreme-court-removes-border-wall-case-from-its-oral-argument-calendar/.

31 We appreciate the fact that not all persons with communicative disorders can overcome them with practice and determination. We merely wish to encourage all individuals with disabilities to engage in advocacy to the greatest extent possible, regardless of the social norms and conventions of public address.

32 John Hendrickson, "What Joe Biden Can't Bring Himself to Say," *The Atlantic*, January/
    February 2020, https://www.theatlantic.com/magazine/archive/2020/01/joe-biden-stutter-
    profile/602401/; and Tim Elfrink and Teo Armus, "'Pure, Unvarnished, Courage': A
    13-year-old 'Regular Kid' with a Stutter Gave a Must-Watch Democratic Convention
    Speech," *Washington Post*, August 21, 2020, https://www.washingtonpost.com/nation/2020/
    08/21/brayden-harrington-joe-biden-dnc/.

33 Mitch McConnell (@senatemajldr), Twitter, June 29, 2020, https://twitter.com/sen-
    atemajldr/status/1277688154053644295?lang=en.

34 "Top News Websites," *EBizMBA*, July 2020, https://sites.google.com/site/mostpopularweb-
    sitessergio/home/top-news-websites.

35 Sheera Frenkel, Ben Decker, and Davey Alba, "How the 'Plandemic' Movie and its
    Falsehoods Spread Widely Online," *New York Times*, May 21, 2020, https://www.nytimes.
    com/2020/05/20/technology/plandemic-movie-youtube-facebook-coronavirus.html.

36 Em Steck and Andrew Kaczynski, "Trump Said Obama Administration Was Handling
    Early Days of Swine Flu Outbreak 'Fine,' Cautioned Not to Overreact," CNN, May 20,
    2020, https://www.cnn.com/2020/05/20/politics/obama-trump-swine-flu/index.html.

37 Edward Tufte, *Beautiful Evidence* (Cheshire, CT: Graphics Press, 2006), 9.

38 We cite some of McIlwain's research in Chapter One; see Deen Freelon, Charlton
    D. McIlwain, and Meredith D. Clark, "Beyond the Hashtags: #Ferguson, #Blacklivesmatter,
    and the Online Struggle for Offline Justice," a report of the Center for Media & Social
    Impact (American University's School of Communication, February 29, 2016), https://
    cmsimpact.org/wp-content/uploads/2016/03/beyond_the_hashtags_2016.pdf.   See   also
    Charlton D. McIlwain, *Black Software: The Internet & Racial Justice, from the AfroNet to
    Black Lives Matter* (New York: Oxford University Press, 2019).

39 This information and subsequent quotes are from email correspondence between Philip
    Dalton and Charlton McIlwain on August 7, 2019.

APPENDIX

Critical Questions

Critical Questions for Evaluating Causal Reasoning

(1) Is the identified cause significant enough to produce the problem?
(2) Are there other probable causes that might reasonably produce the problem?
(3) Will the proposed solution solve the problem?
(4) Is there something about the status quo that will prevent the proposed solution from working?
(5) Will the proposed solution cause additional problems or disadvantages not already occurring in the status quo?
(6) Is an identified disadvantage the likely result of the proposed solution, or might it be caused by other factors?

Critical Questions for Evaluating Deductive Reasoning

Categorical Reasoning

(1) Does the specific case or instance under consideration belong to the general category or rule?
(2) Is the specific case or instance under consideration accurate?
(3) Are the terms used throughout the argument consistent?

Disjunctive Reasoning

(1) Is the advocate considering all reasonable options?
(2) Is the advocate offering good reasons for rejecting options?
(3) Are combinations of considered options or other options more reasonable?

Critical Questions for Evaluating Inductive Reasoning

(1) Are the instances cited real occurrences as far as can be determined through reliable evidence?
(2) Are the instances representative of the practices, behaviors, activities, or phenomena under consideration?
(3) Is a single or limited occurrence compelling enough to indicate a problem?

Critical Questions for Evaluating Reasoning by Analogy

Literal Analogy

(1) Are the practices, behaviors, activities, or phenomena being compared similar enough to warrant the policy position being advocated?
(2) Can the comparison be characterized as fundamentally flawed or socially offensive?

Figurative Analogy

(1) Is the comparison offered likely to assist the advocate in his or her effort to gain the support of the audience?
(2) Can the comparison be characterized as fundamentally flawed or socially offensive?

Critical Questions for Evaluating Evidence from Authorities

(1) Is the authority known?
(2) Does the information offered by the authority support the claim?
(3) Is the authority capable of observing the phenomenon they claim to understand?
(4) Is the information offered by the authority likely to be affected by bias?
(5) Is the information offered by the authority accurate?

Critical Questions for Evaluating Statistics[1]

(1) Who wants to prove what?
(2) What do the figures really represent?
(3) What conclusions do the figures support?

Note

1 Robert P. Newman and Dale R. Newman, *Evidence* (Boston: Houghton Mifflin Co., 1969), 206.

INDEX